THE POLITICAL ECONOMY
OF GLOBAL RESTRUCTURING

VOLUME II

New Dimensions in Political Economy
*General Editor: Ingrid H. Rima, Professor of Economics, Temple University,
US*

This ambitious new series is designed to bridge the gap between received
economic theory and the real world that it seeks to explain. The dramatic
events in Eastern Europe, the resurgence of an invigorated market capitalism
and the prospects of integrated trading and financial communities have created
new interest in the term political economy, which will be a dominant theme
of titles included in this series.

The Political Economy of Global Restructuring

Volume II   Trade and Finance

Edited by

Ingrid H. Rima

Professor of Economics
Temple University, US

Edward Elgar

Published by
Edward Elgar Publishing Limited
Gower House
Croft Road
Aldershot
Hants GU11 3HR
England

Edward Elgar Publishing Company
Old Post Road
Brookfield
Vermont 05036
USA

A CIP catalogue record for this book is available from the British Library

ISBN 1 85278 638 8 (Volume I)
     1 85278 808 9 (Volume II)
     1 85278 817 8 (2-volume set)

Printed and bound in Great Britain
by Hartnolls Ltd, Bodmin, Cornwall

For Adolph Lowe as a tribute to his pioneering and inspirational intellectual leadership in understanding political economy.

Contents

List of figures   ix
List of tables   xi
List of contributors   xiii
Preface   xv

    An introduction to a political economy perspective of trade and
    finance   1
    Ingrid H. Rima

1   Full circle on business cycles: lessons from the 1920s and 1930s   13
    Warren Young

2   Neomercantilism: what does it tell us about the political
    economy of international trade?   27
    Ingrid H. Rima

3   A theory of mercantilism   41
    John S. Chipman

4   The international trade system, trade blocs and US trade policies   77
    Dominick Salvatore

5   The macroeconomic effects of exchange rate instability   91
    Steven Pressman

6   Real exchange rates and patterns of international specialization   104
    Fabrizio Onida

7   Italian joint ventures abroad: country-, industry- and firm-
    specific requirements   120
    Francesca Sanna-Randaccio

8   The impact on Spanish industry of accession with the European
    Economic Community   136
    Susan Wolcott

9   Globalization and new forms of industrial organization   159
     Klaus Weiermair

10   Globalization and the international debt trap   173
     Omar F. Hamouda

11   Structural changes in financial markets and financial flows to
     developing countries   183
     J.A. Kregel

12   Some scenarios for money and banking in the EC and their
     regional implications   190
     Victoria Chick

13   A post-Keynesian perspective of European integration   201
     Philip Arestis

14   Monetary economics after financial restructuring   220
     John Smithin

Index   231

Figures

3.1 Davenant's measure of the gains from trade 53
3.2 Gains from trade measured by Hicksian variations 59
3.3 Gains from trade measured by trade variations 61
6.1 Effects of a revaluation on export and import 114
6.2 Effects of a revaluation on export given different price elasticities 115
6.3 Effects of a revaluation on export under oligopoly with barriers to entry 116
6.4 Effects of a revaluation on imports given different price elasticities 117
8.1 Spain's share of total EC9 imports 147
10.1 Percentage of countries having external debt, 1970–90 (US dollars) 174

Tables

4.1	Estimates of the effects of 1992 on the EEC and on the US	85
4.2	Estimates of the effects of EEC protectionism on the US	87
5.1	Exchange rate variability for the G-7 countries	94
5.2	Economic growth and the growth of international trade for the G-7 countries	96
5.3	Productivity growth and real compensation growth in manufacturing for the G-7 countries	98
5.4	Decline in productivity growth by country	99
5.5	Decline in labour's share of additional manufacturing output by country	100
7.1	Determinants of the probability that a subsidiary is a joint venture	129
8.1	The five most important Spanish exporting and importing industries by value of the trade flow, 1980, 1985 and 1988	138
8.2	Community and Spanish trade barriers	140
8.3	Growth of Spanish exports to the EC9 since accession	142
8.4	Growth of EC9 exports to Spain since accession	144
8.5	Value share of the five largest SITC groups contained in selected ISIC groups in 1985 and 1988	148
8.6	Authorized foreign direct investment in Spain by industrial sector	153
8.7	Authorized foreign direct investment in Spain by national origin	153
12.1	Some present monetary systems and their possible futures	193
13.1	Range of GDP per capita in EC countries	210
13.2	Unemployment rate 1987	211
13.3	Growth differential rates for convergence	214

Contributors

Philip Arestis	University of East London, London, U.K.
Victoria Chick	University College London, London, U.K.
John S. Chipman	University of Minnesota, Minneapolis, Minnesota, USA
Omar F. Hamouda	Glendon College of York University, Toronto, Canada
J. A. Kregel	University of Bologna, Italy
Fabrizio Onida	Bocconi University of Milan, Milan, Italy
Steven Pressman	Monmouth College, Monmouth, New Jersey, USA
Francesca Sanna-Randaccio	University of Rome 'LaSapienza', Rome, Italy
Ingrid H. Rima	Temple University, Philadelphia, Pennsylvania, USA
Dominick Salvatore	Fordham University, Bronx, New York, USA
John Smithin	York University, Toronto, Canada
Susan Wolcott	Temple University, Philadelphia, Pennsylvania, USA
Klaus Weiermair	York University, Toronto, Canada
Warren Young	Deakin University, Victoria, Australia

Preface

The concept for this volume of collected papers and its companion volume, *Economic Organization and Production*, and the idea of offering them to the community of scholars worldwide who are concerned with the political economy of global restructuring, was developed in tandem with the idea for an international Workshop to be sponsored jointly by 'La Sapienza', the University of Rome, Italy, and Temple University in Philadelphia, Pennsylvania, US. In the division of labour agreed upon, Giancarlo Gandolfo and Ferruccio Marzano planned the local arrangements and secured the financing necessary to host forty scholars at a Workshop convened at the Hotel Jolly in Rome 29–30 May 1991. Ingrid Rima undertook the responsibility for editing those papers that were made available for publication, joining them with others that were commissioned for inclusion in these volumes, though their authors were not able to participate in the Workshop.

Special thanks are due to Ernesto Chiacchierini, Dean of the Faculty of Economics and Commerce, University of Rome, 'La Sapienza' and the members of his distinguished faculty, and to Banca Nazionale del Lavoro, which provided generous financial support.

Ingrid H. Rima
Philadelphia, Pennsylvania

An introduction to a political economy perspective of trade and finance

Ingrid H. Rima

While the transition towards privatization and market-driven economies to replace the command economies of Central and Eastern Europe is the most dramatic example of global restructuring (and, perhaps, most forcefully challenges economists to develop political economy as a science), the chief problem in the West is the restoration of growth in economies whose structural changes have caused them to diverge from their expected growth paths. For those who are concerned with these problems, the task of political economy is to examine the circumstances of these divergences, and to identify the conditions for growth and the policies needed to restore particular economies to their respective growth paths.

It is clear that there is no guarantee that the traumas of the Great Depression may not be repeated in the market economies of the West and the US, especially since the notion of government spending to maintain levels of aggregate effective demand no longer has the popular or legislative support it once enjoyed. With the absence of strong investment and/or export trade sectors, and in the face of mounting government deficits and high interest rates, the market economies of the West are encountering their own challenges. No less than the formerly planned economies, they are concerned about their progress (or lack thereof) towards opulence. In the US the divisive debate over international trade is one manifestation of this concern. The persuasiveness of its free trade ideology has been substantially compromised by the profound structural changes in the global economy that have put it under pressure to maintain production and employment in its once strong heavy industries by whatever protectionist measures are necessary to this end. Thus the free trade principle and the codes developed under the General Agreement on Tariffs and Trade (1947) (GATT) and the many rounds of tariff negotiations that followed it, have been compromised by internal political forces that resist the shift of labour and capital out of declining sectors.

The European Community, on the other hand, has taken steps to eliminate fully impediments to trade among its member states. The seemingly natural tendency which nations have towards mercantilistic restrictions on imports, quite clearly can be curbed only to the extent that many nations work

1

towards joint removal. A consensus also appears to have emerged among EC members that a monetary and political union is an essential complement to their trading community. Twelve nations of the European Community signed the Maastricht Treaty (February 1992) which commits all members except Britain to introduce a common currency and establish a European Central Bank before 1999. This development would transfer monetary policy, which is traditionally a crucial tool of governmental economic control, to a transnational board.

Several additional countries have expressed their wish for eventual admission to the Community. Though Denmark voted 'no' in the first public referendum of the Treaty, Finland, Russia, Poland, Hungary, Austria, Czechoslovakia, Sweden and Switzerland have expressed their interest in joining. Thus, the Maastricht Treaty poses a conflict between the objective of deepening the ties between the 12 present member states and the possible 'widening' of the Community to include as many as 12 additional members. Thorny problems are on the horizon even without the possible enlargement of the Community. In particular, the French are fearful about surrendering authority over domestic monetary affairs to a European Central Bank, while the Germans are equally reluctant to give up the Deutschmark. The site of the new Central Bank, whether it is to be London, Frankfurt, Barcelona, Amsterdam or elsewhere is, of course, also a matter of contention.

Nevertheless, the emergence of the European Economic Community (and its likely Pan American and Pacific Rim counterparts), and the G-7 expression of willingness to provide financial support to assist the Community of Independent States (the former Soviet Union) towards a free market, may portend increased international support for the production of public goods. If so, a fertile new area for research in political economy may emerge which has much to learn from classical political economy. Understood as 'a branch of the science of the statesman or legislator', it is among the tasks of political economy 'to supply the state or commonwealth with a revenue sufficient for public services' (Smith, 1776, p. 397). When judged by modern standards, the scope for public sector activity is extremely circumscribed in Smith's famous Book V, yet a consensus toward international economic support for providing public goods such as the International Monetary Fund, the World Bank and the European Central Bank (if and when it becomes a reality) is a reasonable extension of Smith's vision of the scope of political economy.

The world-wide depression of the 1930s was a financial débâcle that might have been avoided had there been a nation or group of nations able to assume a leadership role. The critical need was for a lender of last resort after the 1931 failure of the *Kreditanstalt* to halt the destructive 'beggar thy neighbour' policies that led to competitive exchange rate devaluations. Britain was no longer able to exercise her historical leadership role that neither France nor Germany were able to assume in her stead. As for the United States, it was still too immature in its political leadership potential to serve as the hegemon it became after World War II. Today there appears to be agreement among nations that 'international linkage' problems require co-operative efforts to prevent crises like the 1929 crash.

There is also a greater prospect for international financial co-operation because improvements in opulence have never been more fully realized than in post-war Germany, Japan and the United States. The rich countries of the world increasingly appear to be willing to 'tax' themselves to support inter-nationalizing certain controls. As technological progress frees humankind from the constraints of nature that dominated the dismal perspective of the 19th century, the less relevant the Malthus–Ricardo vision of a zero-sum game environment will become. Their world view was predicated on a finite land supply and diminishing returns, whereas contemporary political econo-mists are thinking in terms of models in which the economy expands in historical time. As the 21st century approaches, the struggle by humankind will be seen less in terms of an intractable nature, and more in terms of an enlarged surplus and a greater prospect for accumulation and growth. Thus, the pessimistic prognosis of classical political economy may not be as near to hand as might have been thought when the stagnation theses of the 1930s gained serious attention. The economic reasons for 'beggar thy neighbour' policies may thus become less compelling, so that nations may become more favourably disposed towards free trade and the provision of international public goods, especially if their increasing opulence improves the affordability of the 'price tag' (Kindleberger, 1986). Nevertheless, the quest among na-tions to improve their relative positions, though it be at the expense of their neighbours, is an historical reality and remains a source of international conflict.

The happy prospect of easing resource constraints through science and technology will, of course, help. Yet these gains are likely to be offset by the limits to growth from another direction; that is, population explosion. The limited capacity of spaceship earth (to use Kenneth Boulding's descriptive metaphor) to absorb additional waste, the gradual exhaustion of essential natural resources and the progressive deterioration of the environment pose problems whose complexities are almost beyond comprehension. It is im-possible here for reasons of space to do more than record our acknowledge-ment of their magnitude and urgency. The scope of the papers in this volume has been limited strictly to examining the trade and financial aspects that relate to the emergence of a new global order. Several are necessarily his-torical in perspective, for most of the problems and vexations of the present are best understood in terms of the proverbial 'long view'. These are followed by papers that are forward-looking in the sense of undertaking to sketch out, either explicitly or implicitly, by the use of instrumental analysis, some possible policy agendas that appear to be compatible with the emerging global order. They are thus firmly in the Smithian tradition, and are a step in the direction of establishing political economy as a purposive discipline.

Chapter 1, '*Full Circle on Business Cycles: Lessons from the 1920s and 1930s*' by Warren Young, sets the stage with a comprehensive retrospective about alternative theoretical approaches to the trade cycles that flourished in the 1920s and 1930s. Their link to political economy is inherent both in their policy implications and the economic institutions through which (or on which) policies were made operative. Central banks were accorded a stellar role until their failure as managers of countercyclical policy became the turning point, both in terms of economic analysis and policy, which marks the beginning of the Keynesian Revolution. Thus, Young reflects on the revived dominance of central bank policy in the 1970s and 1980s in order to derive lessons for the 1990s about the prospective place of the central banks as the dominant institutions for determining economic policy. The critical question, he suggests, turns on the role of central banks as 'rational institutions' in the economic sense. That is, does a central bank, such as the Federal Reserve, exhibit 'rational behaviour', or is its behaviour 'non-rational' in the sense of not having learned how to avoid systematic mistakes? Harking back to Hawtrey's observations and applying them to evaluating Federal Reserve policy in the 1970s and 1980s, Young argues that the United States' banking and credit system is characterized by institutional defects which may well dispose it to failure. The potential that the 1979 deflationary policy had for setting off world-wide recession (which was avoided by its reversal in 1982), and the more recent saving and loan crisis are, in Young's view, a disturbing parallel to the lessons of the 1930s. The lesson is *not* that the economy should be left to run itself even if it runs itself aground, for that is to deny the essential role of political economy as a science that envisions a positive role for policy.

The management of international trade and its associated financial flows has been a much relied on technique for achieving national economic objectives from the 17th century onwards. The pursuit of the macroeconomic goals of increasing an economy's per capita GNP and political power *vis-à-vis* other nations, along with providing higher employment and domestic absorption levels for its citizens, is by no means characteristic only of the present phase of modern capitalism. The quest by nations and their citizens has always been to mount the kind of trade policy which extracts real or financial resources from its trading partners. Ingrid Rima's paper, 'Neomercantilism: What Does It Tell Us About the Political Economy of International Trade?' (Chapter 2), argues that the free trade policy derived from Ricardo's principle of comparative advantage was intended to maintain or raise profit rates by tapping into the cheap food supply available to England from its trading partners. Its effect in terms of gaining access to real resources from its trading partners is thus analogous to the effect which mercantilists sought from inflows of gold (that is financial resources) which were expected to lower interest rates. Ricardo's support for free trade in corn was appropriate to the stage of England's economic development in the 19th century, just as the mercantilist quest for gold was consistent with her goals in the 17th and early 18th centuries.

Rima argues that since the collapse of the Bretton Woods system there have been numerous examples of national behaviour to use an economy's foreign trade sector as an instrument to achieve national economic objectives. The dollar shortage of the 1950s and 1960s reflected the desire of West European countries and the UK to increase their standard of living beyond their ability to finance fully their purchases by exports. The technique of using trade as a macromanagement vehicle has now become globalized. It is manifested, for example, in the import surpluses of the United States and England, offset in such recently developed economies as Japan and Taiwan by high savings rates and export surpluses. The latter's objective is unabashedly to increase the absorption potential and standard of living of later generations, even though in the US their trade policies are viewed as reflecting, on the one hand, 'unfair trade practices' and, on the other, a loss of American competitiveness.

The perspective of a trade deficit versus a trade surplus as a vehicle for attaining a desired standard of living is the basis for John S. Chipman's historical re-examination of trade theory and policy. His paper, 'A Theory of Mercantilism' (Chapter 3), pursues the notion that a dual approach to a country's maximization problem is necessary to evaluate whether an improvement in a country's welfare requires a trade surplus or deficit. He utilizes Hicks's notion of 'compensating variation' as a basis for drawing a series of elegant trade indifference maps to illustrate that improvement in a country's standard of living is consistent with varying combinations of trade deficits (surpluses) and compensating price changes. He also shows that the principle of compensating variation can be transformed to measure a country's balance of trade and its gain from trade. Mercantilist thinkers were concerned, he maintains, with the *relative* prosperity and power of their country, rather than its absolute level. The concept of relative prosperity is extended to examine the effect of a factor-augmenting improvement on the welfare of trading partners by evaluating their reciprocal net demands for one another's exports. It is possible for a technical improvement to be consistent with improving a country's relative prosperity, even though it may deteriorate its terms of trade.

Adverse changes in a country's terms of trade frequently induce countervailing restrictive measures such as tariffs, quotas and exchange controls. Non-tariff trade barriers have become an increasingly common form of trade obstruction. Voluntary export restraints are used by most industrial nations to limit exports of textiles, apparel, steel, automobiles, consumer electronics and other products, especially from Japan and the newly industrializing countries. In his paper 'The International Trade System, Trade Blocs and US Trade Policies' (Chapter 4), Dominick Salvatore extends the theory of trade protectionism with voluntary export restraints to examine the reason for the increased popularity of this form of trade restraint. Arguing that voluntary export restraints can also be viewed as alternatives to industrial subsidies to domestic industries that might not be able to survive international competition, he notes that the former are more common in the United States while the latter are somewhat more common in Europe.

The second part of his paper develops, estimates and validates a simultaneous equations model for analysing the causes and effects of escape clause protectionism in the United States. Two important conclusions follow from the estimation of the model. The first is that the demand for escape clause protection is cyclical in nature, rising when the level of domestic economic activity is low and falling when domestic economic activity is high. The second is a confirmation of the harassment thesis. That is, the possibility of filing an escape clause complaint is effective in reducing import penetration, and independent of success in actually obtaining a favourable ruling.

Low levels of domestic activity have also caused nations to rely on exchange rate alterations as policy instruments to control their trade balances in order to 'export' their unemployment to other economies. The feature which the gold standard, the Bretton Woods Agreement and the European Monetary System have in common is that they stipulated relatively fixed exchange rates. It is in the light of controversy about the gains (or losses) that are attributed to volatile versus fixed exchange rates that Steven Pressman undertakes an empirical evaluation of the effects of exchange rate volatility in his paper, 'The Macroeconomic Effects of Exchange Rate Instability' (Chapter 5). Using data for all the G-7 countries for the period 1961-1987, during which rates were quite volatile, his finding is that countries which had the *least* stable rates, Italy and Japan among them, enjoyed the greatest growth in exports relative to GDP. By contrast, Canada, which enjoyed a relatively stable exchange rate, experienced relatively poor export growth. Pressman's study established that, overall, there is no reliable relationship between the exchange rate stability of pairs of G-7 countries and growth in their bilateral trade. Indeed, bilateral trade between Canada and the UK as a fraction of their joint GDP fell between the 1960s and the end of the 1980s. While the number of available data points may be too small to establish this finding conclusively, a reliable relationship between exchange rate stability and economic growth at the aggregate level appears to exist. The greater exchange rate volatility that developed after 1971 increased the variability of economic growth among G-7 nations and was associated in some cases with economic decline and changes in the distribution of income in favour of capital.

In a paper that is complementary to Pressman's, Fabrizio Onida focuses on the effect which a deviation from a given initial level in a country's real exchange rate has on the patterns of its industrial specialization and trade. His paper, 'Real Exchange Rates and Patterns of International Specialization' (Chapter 6), argues that, initially at least, the most likely impact of a persistent real appreciation in an economy's exchange rate is that it will assist in consolidating its inherited sectoral comparative advantages. This tends to encourage an upgrading of products and processes instead of encouraging a country to acquire new comparative advantages at the industry level. It is also his expectation that multi-plant enterprises are likely to be encouraged by Europe's economic and monetary union because intra-area mergers and acquisitions favour both horizontal and vertical product differentiation.

Francesca Sanna-Randaccio notes that because virtually all countries limit the outright ownership of local firms by foreign nationals, joint ventures are the preferred ownership pattern. Her paper 'Italian Joint Ventures Abroad: Country-, Industry- and Firm-Specific Requirements' (Chapter 7), defines a joint venture as a subsidiary in which the parent company owns less than 95 per cent of the outstanding equity of the company. Her study is of particular interest because it utilizes firm level data instead of industry proxies, which offers greater insight into the reasons why profit-maximizing firms seek out joint ventures. She finds that small and medium sized firms in such fast-growing fields as robotics, biotechnology and solar energy are especially likely to be attracted to joint ventures. Foreign participation is also likely to be attractive in mature industries that are ripe for restructuring. Sanna-Randaccio's database relating to Italian multinationals for the period 1974–86 established that Italian multinationals prefer to share ownership with local producers in order to obtain access to technical resources. This is particularly the case for smaller firms. The probability of shared ownership is also greater when the 'cultural differences' between the host country and the prospective investor are substantial. On the other hand, a joint venture is less likely to be formed when the parent company has adopted a policy of global co-ordination.

While the advent of multinational firms during the 1950s and 1960s represented a change in business relationships in a world used to thinking in terms of national firms, the global trading network envisioned by the European Economic Community is a genuine restructuring of economic and political institutions. Greece, Portugal and Spain are among the developing nations that have sought to advance their economic futures by joining the EC. This has required them to reduce or eliminate their trade barriers with the nine more industrialized members. Other developing countries, among them Turkey and the newly democratic Central and Eastern European countries, are likely to petition for entry some time in the future. The recent experience of Spain, which joined the EC in 1986, is therefore of critical interest. Susan Wolcott's study, 'The Impact on Spanish Industry of Accession with the European Economic Community', presented as Chapter 8, establishes some surprising findings. Accession led to a sharp decrease in Spain's overall bilateral trade balance. The balance went from a surplus in excess of one million US dollars to a deficit in excess of ten billion US dollars. Moreover, the trade balance deteriorated for every major Spanish export industry. Accession has thus *slowed* Spain's progress in becoming a supplier of industrial goods to the EC countries. Simultaneously, exports from the EC industries to Spain have increased above trend for all but the relatively insignificant industries.

The substantial importance of Spain's assembly trade may well blunt the pessimistic implication of these findings. What appears as inter-industry trade in Spain's trade statistics may mask imports from EC countries that are inputs into finished products that are re-exported. This is particularly the case in automobile manufacturing, the production of which relies heavily on imported parts. It is also possible that Spain's import surge reflects an ongoing capital build-up that may implement an export expansion in the future. There has been a substantial surge in investment in Spain by multinationals. Tight monetary policy has encouraged the inflow of foreign capital while keeping the peseta expensive, thereby reducing the competitiveness of Spanish goods. Thus it will be necessary for Spanish firms to improve the quality of their products. The Spanish experience strongly suggests that a nation's potential for gaining from liberalizing her trade policies is only likely if it is possible to set in motion the kinds of improvement in production practices that will gain the home country a substantial competitive edge.

This point is reinforced and elaborated by Klaus Weiermair who argues in his paper, 'Globalization and new forms of industrial organization' (Chapter 9), that international success and competitiveness reflect the way in which industry- and firm-specific skills are created through specialized schooling and training. This has been very much in evidence in Italy's success in the textile and clothing industry, which is *not* attributable to low wages or big economies of scale or cheaper technologies. Rather, it is attributable to the technical and organizational 'know-how' that has been developed within specific firms. Much the same kind of specific expertise accounts for Denmark's success in enzyme and furniture production. Similarly, Germany's widely renowned apprenticeship system has given her a leading edge in such fields as automobile assembly, printing and tool making, as has the international competitiveness of the Japanese in robotics production. Thus, the shifting competitive advantages of firms and nations are interrelated through the interpenetration of the socio-economic and technical systems of production and distribution. These include national systems of learning and schooling, of industrial relations and the system of government and business relations. Thus, a systems view is needed to help us understand technological trajectories and evaluate competitive advantages. These were initially predicated on the Ford–Taylor model of production and management which encouraged multidivisional large scale industrial structures and multinational business activities.

The extraordinary success of Ford–Taylor managerial capitalism, especially in the United States, Weiermair notes, has become compromised by the productivity failures that manifested themselves even before the first (1973) oil shock, despite increases in the capital/labour ratio. The several serious recessions that followed have served to highlight that the mass production system is inherently too rigid to address unexpected variations in demand. New models of management, work organization and relationships are evolving in which there is co-operative networking among company-, government- and university-owned organizations. The outcome may be a reconceptualization which can help revive and reverse mature industries through new technologies and organizational innovation. Weiermair expects these developments to nurture the J-form of organization and management in much the same way as Ford–Taylor principles were dominant 60 years ago.

The counterpart of the restrictive trade policies of the industrialized economies of the world is that the less developed economies have been unable to penetrate foreign markets to earn the hard currency they need to finance imports of capital and competitive technology. In consequence they have strangled themselves with international debt. Omar F. Hamouda's paper, 'Globalization and the International Debt Trap' (Chapter 10), argues that as long as restrictive trade policies remain in place, the LDC debt problem is quite certain to persist. He urges the necessity for seeking solutions within the context of globalization as well as international macroeconomic polarization. What is needed, Hamouda maintains, is an overall increase in world wide demand; in the absence of such an expansion, the LDCs confront a growth rate which is incompatible with the growth rate of 8 to 10 per cent per annum which is needed for a population that is growing at the rate of 3 to 4 per cent per annum. International fiscal control may be necessary to protect against capital inflows that take advantage of the weakness of the LDCs.

Indeed, it may be appropriate for LDCs to form their own federation as they confront the trading blocs of the European Community, North America and the Pacific Rim.

Since the 1980s the US has become a capital importer, competing with the developing countries in international capital markets. This reflects a basic change in the historical tradition in which the flow of capital internationally has been towards underdeveloped economies. Jan Kregel's paper, 'Structural Changes in Financial Markets and Financial Flows to Developing Countries' (Chapter 11), argues that the reversal of tradition is substantially attributable to the altered structure of the US financial system that has taken place since the 1960s. Regulations have operated to drive US commercial banks to engage in foreign branch banking and to develop such new financial instruments as variable rate loans. The increasing variability of interest rates (also the result of the deregulation that allowed banks to compete for funds with other financial institutions) correspondingly increased the variability of asset prices and exchange rates. Short-term rates in the US are both absolutely and relatively higher than in other financial markets; this directs capital to the US and away from developing countries. Prospectively this reallocation will include the newly developing economies of East and Central Europe, even though this reallocation is not matched by greater productivity in the US. Thus Kregel views the changes that have taken place in the American financial system as impinging adversely on the process of economic development elsewhere. Development is likely to become increasingly dependent on the economic integration of trading areas such as the EC and the North American Free Trade Association.

Yet considerable debate surrounds the monetary arrangements that are evolving within the framework of the EC. As Victoria Chick points out in her paper, 'Some Scenarios for Money and Banking in the EC and Their Regional Implications' (Chapter 12), the restructuring of Europe as a unified trading area makes questions that relate to a common currency and a unified banking system unavoidable. Her insight into the historical development of the banking systems of the US, the UK, Germany and Italy leads to the inference that member countries are unlikely to benefit equally either from a common currency or a unified banking system. Despite the conventional wisdom of the neoclassical view that intercountry income and growth rates will tend towards convergence, she argues that investment funds that are drained away from peripheral regions to financial centres are unlikely to return from whence they came as new investments. The regional disparities and imbalances that now exist are likely to persist and become even more pronounced as some national centres become downgraded as banking decisions become centralized. Countries in the periphery are thus likely to be better served by separate national banks and/or currencies.

While Chick's currency and monetary policy scenarios reflect her reserva-tions about neoclassical regional economics, the paper 'A Post-Keynesian Perspective of European Integration' by Philip Arestis (Chapter 13), inter-prets disparate growth rates as a reflection of the power relationships that characterize the capitalist mode of production. At the present stage of its development the megacorp is the most representative form of enterprise. Given the mark-up pricing behaviour of the megacorp, Arestis identifies the rate of profit as the key determinant of investment behaviour. He envisions that a European Central Bank, should it come into existence, will exert control over the EC via their discount rates and, through them, their exchange rates. He recognizes, of course, that a central bank's degree of control may well be 'compromised' by the tendency of market forces to exacerbate regional disparities and imbalances, be they of the north/south, centre/pe-riphery or Fordist/post-Fordist variety. During the 1980s these disparities worsened both within regions and countries. There is little to indicate that disparities will shrink in an integrated Europe or that there will be shared views about the appropriateness of policy *vis-à-vis* the power of market forces to achieve convergence of the economies within the EC. Arestis thus urges the need for both a strong regional policy and an industrial policy in which the state promotes development opportunities, in particular at the regional level. It should also allow for the active role of trade unions and give special attention to removing obstacles to full employment. For Arestis, achievement of these objectives is likely to be more difficult when there is a unified market such as the EC than it is in national economies. His paper, like Chick's, serves to alert economists and policy-makers to the greater sensitivity of member states (such as those of the EC) to regional disparities and imbalances and also to the exacerbated cumulative disturbances that characterize free market systems left to themselves. This feature of the capitalistic system has long been recognized as attributable chiefly to the behaviour of private investment in response to volatile expectations and business confidence. Thus it will be the responsibility of the European Central Bank to create financial stability through its control over interest and exchange rates.

These insights put us in mind of the trade cycle analyses of the 1920s and 1930s which Warren Young's paper set forth in Chapter 1. The inherent instability of money and credit is a key contributor to disturbance, whatever the *causa causans* of economic crisis. The lessons of the 1920s and 1930s relate equally to an economically integrated Europe in which there is a central bank issuing a single currency, conducting monetary policy and harmonizing it with the monetary and fiscal policies of the member states. This is a task of the highest order for political economists. The critical need is not only for value judgements (*à la* Robbins, 1981) but also for an approach that identifies the optimal adjustment path from among a set of possible paths in order to design public controls and institutions to encourage business and household and government behaviours at the national level that are consistent with a desired global outcome.

The complexities of instrumentalism at this level clearly exclude specifics about either institutional changes or policies. Nevertheless, there is a fundamental specific which can and must be injected even at this early stage in the resurgence of political economy. The changes that have already taken place in monetary and financial systems, and which are expected as part of global economic and political restructuring, imply the necessity for re-examining the basic principles of monetary theory. Despite the vitality of mainstream macromodels which abstract money except as a convenience, their Walrasian microfoundations render them irrelevant to the real world. The credit money economies that are evolving, even more than those of the present, cannot realistically be modelled 'as if' they were commodity money economies. The fact that we live in a monetary economy will in no way be compromised if and when a Central Bank of Europe becomes a reality. This fact, John Smithin argues in his paper, 'Monetary Economics After Financial Restructuring' (Chapter 14), behooves economists to theorize in terms of monetary flow macromodels in which the rate of interest charged by the central institution is the ultimate monetary control variable. From the standpoint of the nature of monetary theory, the unequivocal implication is that the body of analysis known as 'new classical monetarist economics' is without relevance for the real world and the task of instrumental analysis, which is 'to search for the economic means suitable for the attainment of any stipulated end' (Lowe, 1976, pp. 11–12). From this perspective, a thorough rethinking of monetary theory is thus an essential first step though, as the other papers in this volume make clear, not the only one needed to proceed in the direction of developing political economy as a science for providing informed guidance for designing policy.

Bibliography

Hansen, Alvin H. (1938), 'Full Recovery or Stagnation?', New York: W.W. Norton and Co.

Heilbroner, Robert (1990), 'Analysis and Vision in the History of Modern Economic Thought', *Journal of Economic Literature*, **XXVIII**, (3), September, 1097–1114.

Kindleberger, Charles P. (1986), 'International Public Goods Without International Government', *American Economic Review*, **76**, March, 1–13.

Lowe, Adolph (1976), *On Economic Knowledge Toward a Science of Political Economics*, Armonk, N.Y.: M.E. Sharpe Inc.

Robbins, Lionel (1932), *The Nature and Significance of Economic Science*, reprinted 1981, London: Macmillan.

Robbins, Lionel (1981), 'Economics and Political Economy', Papers and Proceedings of the American Economic Association, **71**, (2), May, 1–10.

Smith, Adam (1776), *The Wealth of Nations*, Books III, IV and V, Modern Library edition, New York: Basic Books.

1 Full circle on business cycles: lessons from the 1920s and 1930s

Warren Young

Introduction: semantic form and substance, stylized facts and Swedish flags

The years 1936–37 are usually recognized as a turning point in economic thought and analysis because of the publication of Keynes's *General Theory* and its initial variant interpretations (Young, 1987; Patinkin, 1990). But other significant events occurred and works were published in these years which, as will be seen below, mark them as a watershed for economic inquiry overall and for trade cycle analysis in particular. To paraphrase Hicks (1960), it is not my intention in this paper to act either as 'tool-maker' (theorist) or 'explainer' (historian) with regard to the global trade cycles of the 1920s and 1930s or the 1970s and 1980s. Rather, the insights from the 1920s and 1930s that I would like to convey here emanate from those 'tool-makers' who analysed the global trade cycle and the institutions that tried to control it during that period and how such 'tools' link-up with those of the 'tool-makers' and institutions that have dealt with the global trade cycle of the 1970s and 1980s.

Before proceeding, however, a semantic 'benchmark' is necessary. There has been a recent revival in the use of the term 'political economy' by those who are, in fact, neoclassical in their economic 'world view'. This started with the analysis of 'rent-seeking' and 'DUP activities' in the guise of 'neoclassical political economy' (for example Colander (ed.) 1984), and has progressed to the 'new political economy' and 'constitutional political economy', which is related, for the most part, to issues of 'public choice' (Mitchell, 1988; Yandle, 1990; Wiseman, 1990; Buchanan, 1990). There has also been a recent revival of the linkage between the terms 'political' and 'cycle' in the economic context; that is, in the notion of the 'political business cycle' in its original (Nordhaus, 1975) and augmented 'rational' form (Cukierman and Meltzer, 1986; Rogoff and Sibert, 1989).

Political economy in the context of this paper – and its relation to the global trade cycle – is 'concerned with the assumption of policy and the results flowing from it', that is, it 'involves all the modes of analysis and explicit or implicit judgements of value which are usually involved when economists discuss assessments of benefits and the reverse or recommendations for policy' (Robbins, 1981, p. 7). As Robbins advocated a decade ago in his Ely lecture entitled, 'Economics and Political Economy', the use of the term, 'should be revived as now covering that part of our sphere of interest which involves judgements of value', rather than shunning 'judgements of value of which we do not wish to be accused' (Robbins, 1981, pp. 6–7). Indeed, it was this approach which Robbins took on his own account in 1937 (Robbins, 1937a; 1981, p. 8), although he later came to change his mind regarding the fundamental nature of the trade cycle of the period (see Robbins, 1934; 1971, p. 153; Haberler, 1976, pp. 24, 26, note 50).

Some 'tool-makers', such as Harrod and Robertson, came to recognize that the political economy of the trade cycle of the 1920s and 1930s was fundamentally different from the earlier pattern of periodic 'ups and downs in trade' (Young, 1989, pp. 30–38; Robertson, 1934, 1937; Hawtrey, 1928). Influential 'tool-makers', such as Hayek, Hicks and Robbins himself, tried to analyse the trade cycle of the period by recourse to the method of 'equilibrium analysis', inventing 'tools' which came back into fashion – or were actually 'reinvented' in the 1970s and 1980s (Hayek, 1928, 1933; Hicks, 1933; Robbins, 1934, 1937b). The views of other prominent trade cycle analysts of the 1920s and 1930s, such as Hawtrey and Haberler were, on the other hand, put aside; (although Haberler still continued in the 1970s in his attempt to change the 'conventional wisdom' regarding the period 1919–39 (Haberler, 1976)). But all of these 'tool-makers', including Robbins himself, had one thing in common: their respective approaches to trade cycle analysis clearly followed from explicit or implicit judgements of value they made with regard to their analyses *per se*, and their explicit or implicit policy recommendations. It is not surprising, therefore, that critics of the approaches of Hayek and Hicks such as Morgenstern and Hawtrey, took issue with their underlying analytical framework, even before going on to criticize their policy recommendations – or rather the lack of them (Morgenstern, 1935, 1941; Hawtrey, 1939; Young, 1991). It is only recently that some 'mainstream' economists have come to grips with the methodological problems that can be dealt with by the type of approach Robbins advocated in 1981 (Greenwald and Stiglitz, 1987, pp. 119, 131).

At this point, some 'stylized facts' regarding the 1920s and 1930s should be recalled. As Peter Temin recently put it in his 1989 Robbins Lecture entitled 'Lessons from the Great Depression', paraphrasing Churchill, the 1914–45 period can be characterized as the 'second 30 years war', with World War I and the conflict and tension of the 1920s being the shocks leading up to the depression of the 1930s. Moreover, Temin asserted that rather than any abnormal instability which may have characterized the international economy of the late 1920s, it was actually the deflationary policies of the period that constituted the major contractionary shock. These policies were pursued even after the downturn due, as Temin maintained, to the international adherence to the rules of classical economy (Temin, 1989).

It is the role of the 'explainer' to agree or take issue with Temin's stylized facts – as his view is indeed contrary to that held by other economists and economic historians. The descriptive–analytic tool used by Temin (that is, the impulse–propagation distinction) however, is still very relevant for describing and classifying categories of the trade cycle analysis of both the 1920s and 1930s and the 1970s and 1980s (Frisch, 1933). Indeed, Leijonhufvud used this distinction along with his 'Swedish flag device', in a 1987 lecture entitled 'Is There a Future for Keynesian Economics?' to enable him to classify 'business cycle theories according to the hypotheses that they make about the typical impulse and the typical propagation mechanism', with categories of 'nominal', 'mixed' and 'real' (intertemporal)' respectively (Leijonhufvud, 1987, pp. 3–4). He used his framework for classifying what are usually considered 'modern approaches to the "business cycle"', such as those of Kydland and Prescott, Phelps, Lucas, Friedman, Brunner and Meltzer, as against those of his own 'economics of Keynes', on the one hand, and what he called the 'standard textbook' version of Keynesian economics on the other (1987, pp. 4–9). In his discussion of the relationship between monetarism, the 'new classicals' and the Keynesian approaches (both his own and the 'old Keynesian aggregate demand' approach), Leijonhufvud also noted 'the conceptual tension between value and allocation theory and monetary and cycle theory ... in the decade or so before the *General Theory*' (1987, p. 11).

However, conceptual tension during this period was not limited to what Leijonhufvud mentioned, but also related to the very basis of the integrative syntheses represented, for example, by Hicks's *Value and Capital* (1939) (Young, 1991). The impulse–propagation distinction used by Temin and Leijonhufvud can also be used to classify approaches to the trade cycle put forward by the 'tool-makers' of the 1920s and 1930s, thereby enabling us to compare some 'modern' theories and tool-makers with their 'ancient' predecessors and counterparts. It is to this that I now turn.

Complementary approaches to the trade cycle: some 'ancients' and 'moderns'

Briefly put, what Leijonhufvud meant by a purely nominal impulse is 'a disturbance such that the equilibration of the economy requires only a scaling up or down of money values, leaving real magnitudes unaffected', while a real impulse means 'a parametric change' which requires resource reallocation 'between sectors or occupations' and thus a 'corresponding change in relative prices'. According to Leijonhufvud, 'purely real impulses should not require any adjustment in the general price level', so that 'the relevant real

impulses are intertemporal'. As Leijonhufvud put it, 'the typical real disturbance is then either a change in Keynes's marginal efficiency of capital or a
change in the productivity of labour *à la* Kydland, Prescott *et al.*'
(Leijonhufvud, 1987, p. 4). In his 1987 paper, which used a 'Swedish flag'
scheme, Leijonhufvud applied this to categorize the relationship between
monetarist, variants of 'new classical' ['Lucasian' and 'Real Business Cycle'],
and variants of 'Keynesian' approaches he delineated; that is, the 'economics of Keynes' and 'Keynesian economics'.

Inserting 'ancients' into Leijonhufvud's device instead of 'moderns' (to
borrow a phrase from Hicks) facilitates a nominal/real framework for cat-
egorization which is described below in terms of: (1) purely monetary; (2)
monetary overinvestment and maladjustment; (3) non-monetary overinvestment; and (4) derived demand based on overinvestment theories of the
trade and business cycle.

It is not my intention here to stress what may differentiate the alternate
theories of the trade cycle, but to focus on those characteristics which are
complementary to show how the theories of 'moderns' relate to those of
'ancients' in similar categories of Leijonhufvud's device and the tools they
use to analyse the trade cycle. Particular interest attaches to their notions of
equilibrium and disequilibrium and, especially, the role of expectations and
institutions. To do this, however, a brief outline of the theories of some of
the 'ancients' is needed, and this is given below.

Some 'ancient' theories of the trade cycle: Hawtrey's 'purely monetary'
theory
In a series of publications over the period 1913–33, Hawtrey set out his
approach to the trade cycle, which he maintained was 'a purely monetary
phenomenon' since, in his view, changes in the flow of money were the only
cause of fluctuations or, as he put it, of 'good and bad trade' in the sense of
Haberler's notion of prosperity and depression (Hawtrey, 1913, 1919, 1923,
1926, 1927 (p. 141), 1928a (p. 331), 1931,1933; Haberler, 1936, p. 14).
Hawtrey's basic position is as follows. When the money demand for goods
(that is, what he calls 'the flow of money') increases, trade, production and
prices all increase and, when money demand falls, they fall concomitantly
(Hawtrey, 1927, pp. 141–2). The money demand for goods, Hawtrey's 'flow
of money' and its 'rhythmic' or 'regular' swings result, then, from the
inherent instability of money and credit (Hawtrey, 1928a, pp. 344, 347) as it
affects what Hawtrey calls 'consumer's outlay'. The latter is expenditure out
of income on consumption of goods *and* new investment, which is that part
of income that is both saved and invested, so that changes in 'consumer's
outlay' are due mostly to changes in the quantity of money and credit.
Swings of expansion and contraction resulted from an inherent instability of

credit, that is, a credit cycle which, in turn, brought on the trade cycle in the modern economic system. These cycles could be self-sustaining and cumulative, with equilibrium like a razor's edge. Thus, in his view, central banks could alleviate this via measures such as international co-ordination of credit via discount rate policy and open-market operations, and a specific monetary rule of keeping 'consumer's outlay' constant so as to stabilize the price level of factors of production (Hawtrey, 1927a, 1928, pp. 344–9; Haberler, 1936, pp. 22–5).

Four decades after publishing his own monumental work, *Prosperity and Depression* (1936), Haberler noted (1976, p. 14) the similarities between the approaches of Friedman on the one hand and Hawtrey on the other, both as regards their notions of a 'monetary rule' and the need for fiscal measures – such as tax cuts or expenditure increases – to ensure a quick recovery from a depression due to the inability of monetary measures to accomplish this (Hawtrey, 1933, pp. 146–7, 159–60, 1937; Young, 1987, p. 131).

Monetary overinvestment and maladjustment theories: Hayek, Robbins and Hicks
In what Haberler (1976, p. 24) has also called the 'neo-Austrian theory' of the trade cycle, Hayek argued that the monetary explanation should not be treated as merely depending on the general price level – the upswing going with rising prices and vice versa – but that it should be analysed via its effects on the structure of production, saving and investment, and business motives and expectations (Hayek, 1933, pp. 116, 123–4). Briefly put, Hayek found the 'power unit' – the self-generating force of the 'pendulum' – that is, the *impulse*, to be in the monetary system. But the swings take place in the *real* system, and are accentuated by monetary conditions of investment, business motives, forecasts and expectations. Thus, in Hayek's view, any complete explanation of the actual cycle must also incorporate these other forces which intensify booms and depressions once credit elasticity has set the swing moving. In other words, credit elasticity, a nominal phenomenon, is the impulse that sets off the system, and the propagation works through investment (Hayek, 1931, 1933 (pp. 82–4, 132–5); 1934, 1939, pp. 354–9, 364–5; Haberler, 1936, pp. 47–9). Robbins (1934, pp. 48–53) took a similar position at the time to that of Hayek; but perhaps the most significant and long-lasting theoretical contribution to the Hayekian position was that of Hicks (1933), who concluded that:

> The Trade Cycle is a purely monetary phenomenon in one sense only: that every large change in economic data affects risk and hence affects the velocity of circulation of money. It has additional real effects through its monetary repercussions. Whatever the *causa causans* of an economic crisis, it is bound to have

a monetary aspect...cyclical fluctuations have nothing necessarily to do with monopolistic or political interference, though they may be aggravated by such interference. Even a system of pure *laissez-faire* would be subject to monetary disturbances...(1933[1980], p. 529).

The Lucasian position (for example, Lucas 1987) for its part, is based on the premise that the trade cycle is simply a rational response – to nominal exogenous shocks. Thus, as Hayek and Hicks asserted over 50 years earlier, no policy intervention is required since the system is self-equilibrating; such interference can even aggravate systemic fluctuations, at least in their view.

Non-monetary overinvestment theories: Wicksell, Cassel, Schumpeter and Spiethoff

As Haberler noted, 'the theory of the writers of this group does not run in monetary terms; they mention monetary forces, but relegate them to a relatively subordinate role...monetary factors are for them passive conditions which can be taken for granted rather than impelling forces' (1936, p. 69). For example, Wicksell's *Lectures on Political Economy* (1934, trans. by Classen, pp. 209 ff), ascribed the trade cycle:

> ... to *real* [Wicksell's emphasis] causes independent of movements in commodity price, so that the latter become of only secondary importance...The principal and sufficient cause of cyclical fluctuations should be sought in the fact that in its very nature technical or commercial advance cannot maintain the same even progress as does, in our days, the increase in needs...but is sometimes precipitate, sometimes delayed.

Not only did Wicksell adopt Spiethoff's explanation of the cycle (Haberler, 1936, pp. 68–76), but there is a substantial similarity between Spiethoff (1925) and Cassel (1918, 1923, 1932). Schumpeter (1934), for his part, offered a variant of Spiethoff's theory, at least in Haberler's view (1936, p. 78). Briefly put, however, all the non-monetary versions of the overinvestment theory had one thing in common. While the monetary versions started from the gap between 'natural' and 'money' interest rates, and held monetary factors as the reason for recurrent overinvestment and maladjustment, the non-monetary versions emphasize non-monetary factors such as technological change, innovation, discovery and shifts in the pattern of investment resulting from reductions in the prices of factors of production, the opening up of new markets, and the adoption of new methods of production. It is this, rather than increased demand for consumption goods, that is critical (Haberler, 1936, pp. 76–80).

Derived demand-based overinvestment theories: J.M. Clark and Harrod

Among the many insights in Haberler's *Prosperity and Depression* (1936), we may note his observation that while 'the explanations which are built on the acceleration principle are not as a rule classified as overinvestment theories, [they]...can easily be combined with the overinvestment explanation. The acceleration principle and the overinvestment theory...are in reality not alternative but complementary explanations' (1936, p. 81). The initial impulse brings the accelerator principle into play along with factors that propagate its effects. He also explained the cumulative process involved, and the possibility, on the one hand, of capital shortage or, on the other, a shortfall in consumer's demand (1936, pp. 92–8). The nature and length of the production process, the durability of capital, and the anticipated increases in demand are all factors that affect the outcome of the acceleration principle and cumulative process of the trade cycle (1936, pp. 93–7). It is relevant that Leijonhufvud (1987, p. 7) similarly noted that 'real business cycle theorists have used the durability of capital or its gestation period ('time-to-build') to spread out the effects of productivity shocks through time' (Kydland and Prescott, 1982).

According to some of the approaches outlined above, investment will be undertaken when there is optimism and business confidence, and there will be a lack of investment in conditions of uncertainty and pessimism. Alternatively, other approaches cited, as Harrod put it (Harrod, 1936, p. 75): 'miscalculations, errors of judgement, or inflation (deflation) on the part of the banks' and so on. In Harrod's view, however, none of these factors was enough to explain the trade cycle (1936, pp. 75, 98). Rather, he presented his 'dynamic determinants' (the multiplier–accelerator interaction and the 'cumulative process' it brought about) as being a viable explanation of the trade cycle (Young, 1989). While he did not explicitly introduce the role of expectations in his 1936 book, what he did do was to focus on the role of the long term interest rate as reflecting expectations of the future, while short term interest rates are not a reflection of future expectations *per se*. As Harrod put it (1936, p. 180):

> That the banks can operate very effectively on short-term rates need not be disputed. But it is a matter of legitimate doubt whether the stimulus to net investment due to a fall of short-term rates is of appreciable importance. Long-term rates depend primarily on the prevailing view as to what the future has in store.

Moreover, in his 1936 book, Harrod took issue with Keynes's *General Theory* approach to monetary policy and presented his own version of the 'liquidity trap' that would greatly limit the effectiveness of central bank policies in the depression phase of the trade cycle (Harrod, 1936, pp. 124–5, 180–1).

Equilibrium, theoretical shifts and controversy

The 'purely monetary' approach, as expressed by Hawtrey, starts from a situation which can be called unstable equilibrium that is disturbed by exogenous factors (Hawtrey, 1927, pp. 140–49; Haberler, 1936, pp. 22–3). The 'monetary overinvestment' approach, on the other hand, takes a diametrically opposite view in starting from the norm of a static system in equilibrium that is also self-equilibrating. In this context, Hayek saw the fundamental trade cycle problem in terms of the question: 'Why do the forces [price system] which would appear to be sufficient to restore equilibrium once it has been disturbed become temporarily ineffective and why do they only come into action again when it is too late?' (Hayek, 1933, p. 65). Hayek implied, in effect, that in an economy in which money prices exactly reflect the relative forces of supply and demand with perfect markets, there is no reason for a trade cycle to develop during which goods are under- or over-produced. In other words, in his static self-equilibrating economic system there need not be any fluctuation at all. But, Hayek noted, if money or credit is spontaneously created or expanded the problem begins, since, as Haberler put it 'the authors of the monetary overinvestment school conclude that every credit expansion must lead to overinvestment and to a breakdown' (Haberler, 1936, p. 48).

The 'non-monetary overinvestment' position is also apparent in Cassel (1918, 1923, 1932), who asserted that if no stimuli such as invention or discovery were forthcoming, cyclical activity would gradually decline; however, this would also bring with it a 'steady state' or even a declining system. Schumpeter (1934) proposed that entrepreneurs would preclude the system settling into an equilibrium position during any time period.

Finally, the 'derived demand'-based overinvestment approach to equilibrium is evident in Harrod's 1936 book, *The Trade Cycle*, which talks about the 'inevitability of the cycle' in the cases where there is either a drop in the 'rate of advance', or an 'advance' that would *not* be greater than that warranted (1936, p. 105); or, in other words, a divergence from a 'steady advance' that *is* warranted (1936, pp .104–6).

In his 1987 paper, Leijonhufvud noted that shifts in theories based on the Keynesian perspective had occurred from his 'real/real' to 'real/nominal' categories, so that the 'monetarist controversy' was between 'nominal/nominal' and 'real/nominal' categories. In the late 1970s, on the other hand, the controversy between aggregate demand-based Keynesianism and the new classical macroeconomics of the Lucasians was between the 'real/nominal' and 'nominal/real' categories respectively. However, while the new classical monetarist (NCM) approach has shifted position from being originally at 'nominal/nominal' to the 'nominal/real' category of the Lucasians, Leijonhufvud also noted that what he called 'the contemporary vanguard in economic theory' that is the 'real business cycle' (RBC) theorists, had come around to the 'real/real' category of his 'Swedish flag device', which 'is where we started with Keynes 50 years ago' (1987, pp. 6–8).

In all of the above-mentioned approaches, however, the role of institutions and institutional change is crucial, and it is to this – in both 'ancient' and 'modern' contexts – that I now turn.

Institutions, institutional change and the trade cycle: 'personalization' and 'globalization'

An institution can be defined as a 'structure in which powerful people are committed to some value or interest' (Stinchcombe, 1968, p. 107). Keynes noted the considerable influence of the ideas of economists and political philosophers upon society as a whole and decided that, in general, they and 'not vested interests' – such as institutions – were 'dangerous for good or evil'. Indeed, the same may be said for the influence of economists and their ideas on central banks, institutions which, as seen above, were considered by trade cycle theorists to be *primus inter pares* with regard to economic policy matters for 'good or evil'.

Moreover, the role of specific central bankers and the influence of certain economists on the making of economic policy (or the lack of it), that is, the 'personalization' of policy-making, was, and still is, characteristic of central banks, with both negative and positive outcomes. Further, the 'globalization', that is, the world-wide influence of these personalities and their policy recommendations and policies was, and still is, characteristic of a world economic system quite sensitive to central bank intervention or the absence of it.

Galbraith noted that economic institutions – such as the large corporations – undergo rapid change (Galbraith, 1973, p. viii). In the case of central banks, on the other hand, the old adage regarding 'change', or rather the lack of it, would seem to hold. What *have* changed are the objectives of central bank policies (or lack of them), not the policy instruments or the means by which they are implemented. For example, while money supply or interest rate may have occupied important places in the central bank policy 'toolkit' in the 1970s and 1980s, they were used to combat inflation rather than as countercyclical tools

In fact, the role of central banks in both domestic and international economic policy has been completely revived in the 1970s and 1980s, having diminished as a result of failures in countercyclical policy-making. In the 1930s (especially in 1937) the central bank failed miserably, after which the role of the Federal Reserve declined for almost the next two decades as a key institution in policy-making (see, for example, Chandler, 1970; Galbraith, 1975; Haberler, 1976, p. 32; Friedman and Schwartz, 1963). On the other hand, the role of the central banker in the United States has undergone considerable revival under Paul Volcker and Alan Greenspan, and also in Germany under Manuel Johnson and Karl Otto Pohl, whose personalities are reminiscent of Strong, Eccles, Currie and Norman. For example, during the 1987 'crash', Greenspan was able to stabilize the stock and money markets around the world by abandoning his 'neo-Wicksellian' world view (*Economist*, 28 April 1990, pp. 102–4) and promising 'as much liquidity as necessary' to ensure the operation of financial markets (what could be considered a triumph for the 'LM' curve). Only recently Greenspan has again promised to provide as much liquidity as necessary to overcome the 'credit crunch' in the US (*Economist*, 24 May 1991).

To derive lessons from the 1920s and 1930s for the 1990s for a central bank as the dominant institution in determining economic policy, a question must first be posed: is a central bank such as the Federal Reserve a 'rational institution', in the economic sense of a 'rational agent' exhibiting 'rational behaviour'; or, alternatively, does it operate along the lines of 'non-rational' behaviour in the sense of Keynes? (I leave the category of 'irrationality' for those who would deal with the psychology of economic policy-making.) According to Leijonhufvud, if a central bank such as the Federal Reserve operated as a 'rational agent' on the basis of 'rational behaviour' (that is, along Hayekian–Lucasian lines), then it 'will have learned not to make systematic mistakes but will know the structure of the economy (at least one step ahead of economists)' and it 'will not leave any gains from trade unexploited' (Leijonhufvud, 1987, p. 9).

But as early as 1926–8, Hawtrey complained that the banks in the Federal Reserve system had been watching the wrong indicator, that is 'reserve proportions', since they 'gave too tardy a warning of credit expansion, and credit expansion was allowed to gather impetus for years before the banks took effective steps to stop it' (Hawtrey, 1928a, p. 349; Haberler, 1936, p. 24). This is hardly characteristic of a 'rational agent' exhibiting 'rational behaviour'. Whether the Federal Reserve had exhibited 'rational behaviour' over the 1970s and 1980s is readily seen by reference to the deflationary policies initiated in 1979 by Volcker and only reversed in mid-1982. These policies, at least according to Temin (1989), could have brought about a severe world-wide recession had they not been reversed. More crucial, perhaps, is the fragility of the present United States banking and credit system itself, which, having failed once due to its institutional defects, can fail again. As Viner noted in March 1936 – only a month after the publication of Keynes's *General Theory* and over half a century prior to the most recent systemic collapse in the United States system (the 'savings and loan' collapse):

> The depression...was more severe in the United States than in most other countries...the weakness of the banks must be held largely responsible for this...What are the causes of this particular weakness of the American banking system? The explanation, I am convinced, lies in the fact that of all the modern national banking systems it alone has adhered predominately to the eighteenth-century mode of individual small-scale banking institutions with many branches (Viner, 1936, pp. 106–107).

The parallels of the late 1980s and early 1990s to the 1930s, as the *Economist* put it (5 January 1991), 'are all too easy to find'. First, despite automatic stabilizers, de-synchronization of cyclical movements in the G-7 countries, and the globalization of economic weight, as the *Economist* put it: 'parallels with the 1930s are far more compelling now than they were in 1987' (5 January 1991, p. 17).

The parallels are indeed disturbing. Have the lessons of the 1930s been learnt by central banks and central bankers such as at the Federal Reserve? Lessons such as not listening to the 'contemporary vanguard in economic theory' or 'academic scribblers' whose ideas may in fact prove 'dangerous', and implicitly call into question the necessity for the 'vested interests' such as central banks. The political implications and the institutional dilemma confronting the 'contemporary vanguard', that is, the New Classical Monetarists and Rational Expectation Theorists, are as clear today as they were to the Hayekians (neo-Austrians) of the 1930s. Given independent central banks, they may implement policies that will not be to the liking of those who advocate letting the economic system equilibrate itself. If central banks are, on the other hand, subject to government directives, and if the government decides on 'intervention', they will implement such policies. It would be better, in the view of the New Classical Monetarist and Real Business Cycle theorists to remove such a possibility by trying to show that any economic policy intervention to ameliorate or eliminate the trade cycle is simply counter-productive.

But, as Harrod noted in his 1933 essay on the 'political economy of the trade cycle', written at the height of the Great Depression, the 'new economic problem' then also had its political corollaries, with potentially severe implications such as political reaction and war. He was indeed proven correct, and tragically so. At the time, Harrod said that 'politicians should take cognisance of the new economic problem and devise a suitable plan of action. The problem of securing full employment then becomes merged into the more general one of preventing industrial recession and eliminating the trade cycle' (Young, 1989, pp. 36–8).

The political implications of what the NCM–RBC theorists advocate is, then, that elected political leaders, government and central banks and bankers should leave the economy to 'run by itself', even if it runs itself aground, or worse still 'into the ground'. In other words, they advocate taking the 'political' out of economic policy-making, or rather, making or implementing no economic policy at all. In this context, then, perhaps the political leadership of the G-7 countries should take Harrod's advice and remember the adage that says, in effect, that economics is 'too serious a business' to be left in the hands of the NCM–RBC theorists and those central bankers who *may* adhere to some of their views.

It is relevant that Lionel Robbins, author of *The Nature and Significance of Economic Science* (1932) and a leading early proponent of the Hayekian position at the beginning of his career, should have come full circle and, as he put it in 1981 'at the approaching end' of his career, not only 'make peace' with some of his critics but also say that:

> In the application of Economic Science to problems of policy, I urge that we must acknowledge the introduction of assumptions of value essentially incapable of scientific proof…Instead I recommend what I call Political Economy which, at each relevant point, declares all relevant non-scientific assumptions (1981, p. 9).

It would seem to be the task then of Robbins's suggested political economy to deal with problems of policy such as those of the global trade cycle. Some progress has been made, for example, by Alesina (1989) who, in his seminal article entitled 'Politics and Business Cycles in Industrial Democracies', stated that 'a better understanding of the political economy of macroeconomic policy is a crucial prerequisite for the design of efficient institutions', and then went on to discuss in detail the 'normative issues' involved (Alesina, 1989, pp. 82–7). This view offers a stark contrast to the approach of NCM–RBC theorists such as Kydland and Prescott (1977), and Barro and Gordon (1983), who would assert that all such issues are simply 'out of bounds'.

Bibliography
Alesina, A. (1989), 'Politics and Business Cycles in Industrial Democracies', *Economic Policy*, **8**, April, 55–90.
Barro, R. and Gordon, D. (1983), 'Rules, Discretion and Reputation in a Model of Monetary Policy', *Journal of Monetary Economics*, **19**, 101–21.
Buchanan, J. (1990) 'Editorial Statement', *Constitutional Political Economy,* cited in Yandle (1990).
Cassel, G. (1918), *Theoretische Sozialokonomie*, Leipzig: C.F. Winter. See Cassel (1923) for English translation.
Cassel, G. (1923), *The Theory of Social Economy*, London: T. Fisher Unwin, trans. by J. McCabe.
Cassel, G. (1932), *The Theory of Social Economy*, New York: Harcourt Brace, trans. by S. Barron.

Chandler, L. (1970), *America's Greatest Depression 1929–1941*, New York: Harper and Row.
Clark, J.M. (1917), 'Business Acceleration and the Law of Demand', *Journal of Political Economy*, **25**, March, 217–35.
Clark, J.M. (1932), 'Capital Production and Consumer Taking: A Further Word', *Journal of Political Economy*, **40**, October, 691–3.
Clark, J.M. (1934), *Strategic Factors in Business Cycles*, New York: Columbia University Press.
Colander, D. (ed.) (1984), *Neoclassical Political Economy: The Analysis of Rent-Seeking and DUP Activities*, Cambridge, Mass.: Ballinger.
Cukierman, A. and Meltzer, A. (1986), 'A Positive Theory of Discretionary Policy, the Cost of a Democratic Government and the Benefits of a Constitution', *Economic Inquiry*, **24**, 367–88.
Economist (London), issues as cited in text.
Friedman, M. and Schwartz, A. (1963), *The Monetary History of the United States 1867–1960*, Princeton: Princeton University Press for NBER.
Frisch, R. (1931), 'The Inter-Relation Between Capital Production and Consumer Taking', *Journal of Political Economy*, **39**, October, pp. 646–54.
Frisch, R. (1933), 'Propagation and Impulse Problems', in *Economic Essays in Honour of Gustav Cassel*, London: Routledge.
Galbraith, J. (1973), *Economics and the Public Purpose*, Boston: Houghton-Miflin.
Galbraith, J. (1975), *Money*, Boston: Houghton-Miflin.
Greenwald, B. and Stiglitz, J. (1987), 'Keynesian, New Keynesian and New Classical Economics', *Oxford Economic Papers*, **39**, 119–32.
Haberler, G. (1936), *Prosperity and Depression*, Geneva: League of Nations.
Haberler, G. (1976), *The World Economy, Money, and the Great Depression 1919–39*, Washington: American Enterprise Institute.
Harrod, R. (1933), 'The Political Economy of the Trade Cycle', cited in Young (1989).
Harrod, R. (1936), *The Trade Cycle: An Essay*, Oxford: Clarendon.
Hawtrey, R. (1913), *Good and Bad Trade*, London: Constable.
Hawtrey, R. (1919), *Currency and Credit*, London: Longmans.
Hawtrey, R. (1923), *Monetary Reconstruction*, London: Longmans.
Hawtrey, R. (1926), 'The Trade Cycle', *The Economist*, reprinted in Hawtrey (1928b).
Hawtrey, R. (1927), 'The Monetary Theory of the Trade Cycle and its Statistical Test', *Quarterly Journal of Economics*, **41**, 471–86.
Hawtrey, R. (1928a), *Trade and Credit*, London: Longmans, Chapter 5.
Hawtrey, R. (1928b), 'The Trade Cycle', reprinted in AEA *Readings in Business Cycle Theory* (1944), Philadelphia: Blakiston, 330–49.
Hawtrey, R. (1931), *Trade Depression and the Way Out*, London: Longmans.
Hawtrey, R. (1932), *The Art of Central Banking*, London: Longmans.
Hawtrey, R. (1933), *Trade Depression and the Way Out*, 2nd edn, London: Longmans.
Hawtrey, R. (1937), *Capital and Employment*, London: Longmans.
Hawtrey, R. (1939), 'Review of Hicks' *Value and Capital*', *Journal of Royal Stat. Soc.*, 102, pt. II.
Hayek, F. (1931), *Prices and Production*, London: Routledge.
Hayek, F. (1933), *Monetary Theory and the Trade Cycle*, London: Cape, trans. by Kaldor and Croome.
Hayek, F. (1934), *Prices and Production* (2nd edn), London: Macmillan.
Hayek, F. (1937), 'Economics and Knowledge', *Economica*, February.
Hayek, F. (1939), 'Price Expectations, Monetary Disturbances and Malinvestments', in *Profits, Interest and Investment*, London: Routledge, reprinted in AEA *Readings in Business Cycle Theory* (1944) cited above.
Hicks, J. (1933), 'Gleichgewicht und Konjunktur', *Zeitschrift für Nationalökonomie*, **4**, June, trans. and reprinted as Hicks (1980), 'Equilibrium and the Trade Cycle', *Economic Inquiry*, **18**, October, 523–34.
Hicks, J. (1960), 'Thoughts on the Theory of Capital', *Oxford Economic Papers*, (n.s.) **12**, June, 123–32.

Keynes, J.M. (1936), *The General Theory of Employment, Interest and Money*, London: Macmillan.

Kydland, F. and Prescott, E. (1977), 'Rules Rather than Discretion: The Inconsistency of Optimal Plans', *Journal of Political Economy*, **85**, 473–92.

Kydland, F. and Prescott, E. (1982), 'Time to Build and Aggregate Fluctuations', *Econometrica*, **50**, 1345–70.

Leijonhufvud, A. (1968), *On Keynesian Economics and the Economics of Keynes*, Oxford: Oxford University Press.

Leijonhufvud, A. (1987), 'Is There a Future for Keynesian Economics?', invited guest lecture, Western Economic Association annual meetings, 7–10 July, 1987.

Lucas, R. (1987), *Models of Business Cycles*, Oxford: Blackwell.

Mitchell, W. (1988), 'Virginia, Rochester, and Bloomington: Twenty Five Years of Public Choice and Political Science', *Public Choice*, **56**, 101–19.

Morgenstern, O. (1935), 'Perfect Foresight and Economic Equilibrium', *Zeits. für Nat.*, **5**, trans. by Morgenstern and later circulated as Princeton Econometric Research Memorandum Number 55, April 1963.

Morgenstern, O. (1941), 'Professor Hicks on "Value and Capital"', *Journal of Political Economy*, **49**, June.

Nordhaus, W. (1975), 'The Political Business Cycle', *Review of Economic Studies*, 169–90.

Patinkin, D. (1990), 'On Different Interpretations of "The General Theory"', *Journal of Monetary Economics*, **26**, 205–43.

Robbins, L. (1932), *The Nature and Significance of Economic Science*, London.

Robbins, L. (1934), *The Great Depression*, London.

Robbins, L. (1937a), *Economic Planning and International Order*, cited in Robbins (1981).

Robbins, L. (1937b), 'Economic Commentary', in *Lloyd's Bank Rev.*, May.

Robbins, L. (1971), *Autobiography of an Economist*, London.

Robbins, L. (1976), *Political Economy: Past and Present*, London.

Robbins, L. (1981), 'Economics and Political Economy', *American Economic Review*, papers and proceedings, 71 (Ely Lecture).

Robertson, D.H. (1934), 'Industrial Fluctuation and the Natural Rate of Interest', *Economic Journal*, **44**, December.

Robertson, D.H. (1937), 'The Trade Cycle – An Academic View', *Lloyd's Bank Review*, September.

Rogoff, K. (1987), 'Equilibrium Political Budget Cycles', NBER Working Paper No. 2428 cited in Alesina (1989).

Schumpeter, J. (1934), *The Theory of Economic Development*, Cambridge, Mass.: Harvard University Press.

Spiethoff, A. (1925), 'Krisen', in *Handworterbuch der Staatswissenschaften*, **6**, Jena.

Stinchcombe, A. (1968), *Constructing Social Theories*, New York: Harcourt, Brace and World.

Temin, P. (1989), *Lessons from the Great Depression*, Cambridge, Mass.: MIT Press.

Viner, J. (1936), 'Recent Legislation and the Banking System', *American Economic Review*, supplement, **26**, March.

Wicksell, K. (1934), *Lectures on Political Economy*, vol. II, trans. by Classen, London.

Wiseman, J. (1990), 'Principles of Political Economy: An Outline Proposal, Illustrated by Application to Fiscal Federalism', *Constitutional Political Economy*, **1**, 101–24.

Yandle, B. (1990), 'The Decline and Rise of Political Economy', *European Journal of Political Economy*, **6**, (2), 165–79.

Young, W. (1987), *Interpreting Mr Keynes*, Oxford: Polity Press.

Young, W. (1989), *Harrod and His Trade Cycle Group*, London: Macmillan.

Young, W. (1991), 'The Early Reactions to "Value and Capital": Critics and Critiques and Correspondence in Comparative Perspective', *Review of Political Economy*, **3**, (3), 1991 (special issue on Sir John Hicks).

2 Neomercantilism: what does it tell us about the political economy of international trade?

Ingrid H. Rima

Introduction

With the demise of the Bretton Woods system in 1973 and the subsequent erosion of the General Agreement on Tariffs and Trade (GATT), the world has slipped into what is substantially a 'non-system' in which no country is required to agree to any 'substantial curtailment of their freedom of action' (Williamson, 1987, p. 18). Thus, the emergence of the European Economic Community (and its American counterpart in the making), along with the efforts to rebuild the international financial order that ended in March 1973 with the adoption of generalized floating exchange rates, marks a new attempt to re-establish an international economic order.

Two major (and ongoing problems) have already presented themselves. The first is the reluctance of EC members (Britain in particular, but also Germany) to relinquish the autonomy over monetary policy that is inherent in the establishment of a single currency. The second is widespread reluctance to give up neomercantilist trade policy. The politics of trade policy are frequently, if not typically, at odds with the dicta of received economic theory, which regards protectionism and other techniques for 'beggaring one's neighbour' by cultivating an export surplus, and also policies that fail to curb import surpluses, as irrational. Export surpluses are condemned as being inconsistent with raising living standards by importing products (or services) from countries that enjoy a comparative advantage in their production. Import surpluses are equally condemned as reflecting a country's penchant for 'living beyond its means'. Thus, the so called 'dollar shortage' of the 1950s was interpreted as signifying that the world was short of dollars because the demand for US goods and services exceeded their capability of generating exports to pay for them. Analogously, the US is now equally remiss in running an import surplus which reflects its loss of international competitiveness and, thus, export markets. In short, the conventional wisdom is equally critical of policies that produce either an export or import imbalance as being indicative of what in the days of the Bretton Woods system would have been termed 'a fundamental disequilibrium', that is, an inability to achieve a balance of trade at the current exchange rate.

27

J.M. Keynes offered a well-known rebuttal to the export surplus argument with his counterargument that in a world of chronic demand deficiency, which he had come to regard as the norm, mercantilist policy to encourage an export surplus is entirely rational when viewed from a national perspective (Keynes, Collected Writings, 1923, VII, pp. 348–9). May an import surplus be equally rational? This paper will argue that when trade policy is dictated by national objectives, which is typically the case, international trade serves a country as a vehicle for achieving a unilateral transfer of real and/or financial resources from its trading partners. Whether its national interests are better served by an export or import surplus depends chiefly on its stage of economic development. Despite the familiarity of the open economy perspective, contemporary discussions of trade issues typically abstract from the role of trade as a vehicle for increasing domestic absorption.[1]

In the absence of data suitable for empirical evaluation, Part 1 of this paper undertakes an historical interpretation of trade theory and policy to support the view that the economic objective of trade has always been to achieve a unilateral transfer of real and/or financial resources to the home country. What emerges is an essential similarity between the objectives of classical and mercantilist prescriptions for trade policies, which is quite contrary to the conventional wisdom that nations trade to exploit differences in comparative cost. This change in the conventional interpretation of the role of trade offers a logical basis for understanding and assessing contemporary practices in a world in which trading partners are not only at different stages in their economic development, but are at stages that are not as naturally complementary as they were in the 19th and early 20th centuries.

The profit rate as a framework for historical comparison
Few excerpts in the history of economics are as familiar as Thomas Mun's posthumously rendered policy recommendation:

> The ordinary means, therefore, to increase our wealth and treasure is by Foreign Trade wherein we must ever observe this rule; to sell more to strangers yearly than we consume of theirs in value...by this order duly kept in our trading, we may rest assured that the Kingdom shall be enriched yearly...because that part of stock which is not returned to us in wares must necessarily be brought home in treasure....(Mun, 1630, pp. 125–6).

A century and a half later David Ricardo offered a 'rule' that has survived as the basis for classical trade theory and policy. Specifically:

> cloth cannot be imported into Portugal, unless it sells there for more gold than it cost in the country from which it was imported; and wine cannot be imported into England unless it sells for more there than it cost in Portugal. If the trade

were purely a trade of barter, it could only continue whilst England could make cloth so cheap as to obtain a greater quantity of wine with a given quantity of labour, by manufacturing cloth than by growing vines; and also whilst the industry of Portugal were attended by the reverse effects (Collected Works, 1951, p. 137).

Both rules conceived of foreign trade as a vehicle for achieving a rate of profit that is higher because some component of production cost is, in effect, financed by their trading partners. The mechanism each envisions is tantamount to a transfer of either real or financial resources. Mercantilists sought 'wealth', principally in the form of gold, by 'trading with money'; inflows of gold would raise profit rates through their effect on interest rates. Ricardo's rule sought to raise (or maintain) the profit rate by substituting lower cost imports, chiefly food, for domestic production. The feature which they have in common is that both sought to use trade as a vehicle for raising the economy's profit rate.

While it is more usual to stress the differences between mercantilist and classical thinkers, for the latter are generally credited with being more sophisticated theoretically as well as more enlightened with respect to policy, the perspective of trade as a mechanism for raising (or maintaining) the rate of profit reveals unexpected similarities in their underlying goals for England, despite the difference in their *modus operandi*. It also provides a basis for recognizing that the choice to run an import surplus to raise a country's level of absorption may also be defensible from an economic standpoint, and that autarchy has at times been, and is likely to continue to be, a perfectly rational economic policy.

Mercantilism
In the 16th–18th centuries an excess of exports over imports served as a major tool of wealth acquisition for national governments, for a favourable trade balance was expected to be paid in gold or silver. Leaving aside the political aspects of statecraft, mercantilist writers, many of whom were businessmen, were constantly preoccupied with the problem of a shortage of money.[2] Initially, this dictated the prohibition of bullion exports, and later the enactment of measures to regulate the flow of precious metals by identifying the economic causes for their flow. However, the critical objective of an ongoing export balance was to provide for a continuing accumulation of bullion as wealth, in addition to enhancing and preserving England's national power. Its economic goal was unequivocably a unilateral transfer of financial resources. What one nation acquires, the rest of the world must lose.

The conventional 'two gap' model that derives from the ISLM simplification offers a convenient paradigm for representing the role of trade as a vehicle for the transfer of resources. Conceptually, the problem is to show that aggregate supply and demand can be brought into equilibrium in an open economy that functions according to the mercantilist model.

The equilibrium condition in the absence of government is satisfied if:

$$C + S = I + X - M \text{ or}$$
$$S - I = X - M$$

when C = Consumption
$\quad\quad S$ = Savings
$\quad\quad I$ = Investment
$\quad\quad X$ = Exports
$\quad\quad M$ = Imports

New capital formation is compatible with either domestic saving from the savings–investment gap or foreign capital formation from the export–import gap. Mun's argument was that policy should be directed towards an enhanced export–import gap. Mun's anti-bullionist argument was that by trading with money a favourable balance, that is an enhanced export–import gap, will generate larger gold flows (that is, transfer financial resources) from other nations into England. He viewed this policy as a more effective way of enhancing England's treasure than simply to restrict the outward flow of specie. The latter would merely affect the investment–savings gap but not transfer treasure as would his recommended policy of trading with money.

Whereas the conventional interpretation of mercantilism looks to gold inflows to close the export–import gap, the Grampp (1952)–Keynes (1936) interpretations envision the policy of cultivating an export trade balance and a net specie inflow as a strategy for stimulating the domestic economy. The stimulative effect of a net specie inflow derives from an expanded money supply operating on aggregate demand and employment and hence, on income and savings. Their interpretation of mercantilist policy thus envisions the closing of the investment–savings gap, but doing so at a higher level of employment that is financed by one's trading partners.

The notion of trading to encourage 'foreign paid incomes' is an analogous example of mercantilistic reasoning which appeared in successive issues of the *British Merchant* (Johnson, 1937, Chapter 15). The essentials of the foreign paid incomes argument are that the export of goods abroad is, in effect, equivalent to having foreigners pay the wages of workers employed in the making of goods for export. Conversely, consumption of imports involves like payments to foreign workers by English households. In terms of the taxonomy outlined above, the requisite resource transfer is achieved via a current account change that is the equivalent of an income transfer.

While it is not always clear that the mercantilists understood the difference between real and financial resources, it is to them that we owe the idea that export trade serves as a vehicle for accomplishing the transfer, and that such infusions of wealth are the basis for national prosperity because they serve the interests of the businessman, that is they raise profits. J.M. Keynes recognized the soundness of their argument in his famous 'Notes on Mercantilism' (1936, Chapter 13, pp. 333–71). It is also on this principle that later writers, in particular Gerard de Malynes and Josiah Tucker, were able to accord the merchant, who is clearly the intellectual antecedent of the 19th century 'economic man', such a central role in promoting 'public benefits' though they pursued 'private vices'.[3]

Classical theory: comparative cost as the basis for trade

The classical theory of international trade was formulated primarily with a view to addressing questions of national policy that arose in the context of the issues of restoring the Corn Laws. The free trade doctrine that is the kernel of classical theory derives from the 18th century recognition that there is an advantage to a country in importing those commodities which either cannot be produced at home at all or can be produced only at a cost absolutely greater than that at which they could be acquired in exchange for native products. Smith's case for free trade did not advance beyond this.

Ricardo incorporated Smith's argument into his trade theory and his campaign against the Corn Laws. The profit rate connection and the notion of trade as a vehicle for transferring resources were critical to both. In Ricardo's day, favourable terms of trade in the importation of wage goods was the mechanism that was to transfer real resources into England. Ricardo wanted to abolish the Corn Laws to lower the cost of the chief staple of wage-earner consumption in order to raise the rate of profit. Though 'comparative advantage' is what has been transmitted as Ricardo's chief contribution, the main point of his stance on the Corn Laws was that England's absolute disadvantage in corn production, coupled with her absolute advantage in manufacturing, was the rationale for abolishing the Corn Laws in favour of free trade. Ricardo argued as follows:

> In rich countries, on the contrary, where food is dear, capital will naturally flow, when trade is free, into those occupations wherein the least quantity of labour is required to be maintained at home: such as the carrying trade, the distant foreign trade, and trades where expensive machinery is required; to trades where profits are in proportion to the capital, and not in proportion to the quantity of labour employed. (Collected Works, 1951, p. 211)

Ricardo's criticism of Smith's doctrine is implicit in his campaign against the Corn Laws. His Corn Law stance can be interpreted as a proposal to facilitate the emergence of industrial capitalism by enhancing the process of accumulation and productive investment by means of policies favourable to capitalist profits. In terms of the contemporary macromodel, Ricardo envisioned that the savings–investment gap could be closed by the importation of a cheap food supply. This would keep the profit rate higher than it would be if the supply of corn were chiefly produced at home. It would provide more funding for capital expansion and economic growth financed, at least in part, by England's trading partners.

There is thus an essential similarity in the role of trade in the classical and mercantilistic systems. Both cultivated international trade with a view to achieving a higher profit rate by either financial or real resource transfers from abroad. Mercantilists expected the export–import gap to serve as a conduit for gold inflows; classical economists similarly sought to enhance profit margins by means of cheap food imports to check the rise in wage costs. The special context of Ricardo's argument and its critical connection to the profit rate is thus missed by most contemporary discussions (see Steedman, 1979).

The terms of trade and specie movements

The essential similarity between mercantilist policy objectives and those of Ricardo and other anti-Corn Law proponents seems to have been obscured by later neoclassical expositions which focus almost entirely on the gains from trade that can be achieved by *all* trading partners. Their concerns seem to have overshadowed that aspect of the classical theory and trade policy that envisioned the gains to England, given her small amount of land, from concentrating her labour and capital on industries enjoying increasing returns in order to buy the products of 'increasing cost' industries abroad. Thomas Malthus was particularly appreciative of this point and how it relates to a country's stage of economic development. He emphasized that the gains from trade do not simply derive from the possibility of obtaining cheaper commodities.[4]

The classicists' concern with promoting real resource transfers via trade is also implicit in their preoccupation with what is now referred to as the 'terms of trade'. While they were familiar with what modern economists call 'the commodity terms of trade' (what Taussig called the 'net barter terms of trade'), they also thought in terms of the ratio of the quantities of the productive factors necessary to produce quantities of outputs of equal value in foreign trade. This latter concept is now known as the 'double factoral terms of trade'; it is the basis for the classical conclusion that in the absence of transportation costs, commodities will be exported or imported according to their domestic supply prices when compared with the domestic supply prices in foreign countries.

While the classicals disdained the mercantilist preoccupation with gold as treasure, their concern with the relevance of financial resources to the profit rate is evident in their concern that their trading partners supply the imports they wanted by absorbing English exports of merchandise and services rather than by receipts of English gold. It is useful to identify the question to which they addressed themselves, for it was not to explore why the terms of trade for particular countries (for example, the ratio between English cloth and Portuguese wine) behaved as they did. Rather, their concern was to examine what is the mechanism of international adjustment to an increase (or decrease) in capital exports in the form of bullion, and to identify what part in that mechanism was played by changes in the terms of trade. Their specific concern was provoked by the effects of a series of bad harvests and the issues of the bullion controversy – in particular, the renewed controversy concerning the high price of gold bullion. The bullionist position (which Ricardo articulated in his first published work, the essay *The High Price of Bullion*), was that the decline in the rate of sterling exchange and the increase in the price of bullion and its exodus from England was due to excessive note issue by the Bank of England which could not have taken place under convertibility.

The anti-bullionist position was that the decline in the sterling exchange was due to the pressures associated with the extraordinary wartime remittances of foreign exchange and was unrelated to the Bank's domestic policy. Indeed, it is relevant that Napoleon allowed grain shipments through the blockade, opting to wreck the British balance of payments as a more devastating weapon than exacerbating her food shortages. In modern terminology, Napoleon created a 'transfer' problem.[5] England's reliance on food imports coupled with the loss of bullion to pay for it impeded the transfer of real resources from her trading partners by deteriorating the terms of trade. Movements of bullion, instead of being the mechanism for bringing about mutually beneficial trade patterns, were seen not only as a reflection of a depreciated English pound and England's deteriorated terms of trade, but also as evidence that trade was no longer effecting a transfer of real resources into England. Indeed, John Stuart Mill argued that England was at risk of experiencing a 'double burden'. Specifically:

...the imposition of a tribute is a double burden to the country paying it, [in consequence of a bad harvest or a subsidy to a foreign power] and a double gain to that which receives it. The tributary country pays to the other, first, the tax, whatever be its amount, and next, something more, which the one country loses in the increased cost of its imports, the other gains in the diminished cost of its own (Mill, 1844, p. 43).

Thus there were English complaints against the trade restrictions in place elsewhere in Europe, even though the Corn Laws remained in place until 1846 (Clapham, 1926, p. 476).

The terms of trade under free trade

After Britain adopted free trade and tariffs were generally lowered over a large part of Europe in the third quarter of the 19th century, the most rapidly growing sector of world trade was that which proceeded among the industrialized countries. Britain's increasing industrial development went hand in hand with a rapid expansion of trade, as well as international investment and finance. By the beginning of the 20th century Britain's trade rivals, Germany and the US, were beginning to surpass her in exports of basic iron- and steel-dependent heavy industries and also goods produced by new industries dependent on applied scientific skills, among them chemicals, electrical supplies and machines. Not only was England ceasing to be the workshop of the world, but also her agricultural prosperity was substantially at an end. By the 1870s a prolonged agricultural depression in England led her to abandon her earlier efforts to compete domestically in the production of grain. Before long other Commonwealth countries and Argentina were exporting not only foodstuffs, but also agricultural raw materials, into England.

This kind of British import reliance had little in common with that of the 18th and early 19th centuries. The products of the highly developed rural economies of the US, the Commonwealth countries and even Argentina were produced by large-scale cost-reducing production units which were structured essentially like British manufacturing industries. Thus by 1923 J.M. Keynes and Sir William Beveridge were debating the nature of the change in Britain's foreign terms of trade since 1900.

Keynes's conclusion, based on Professor Bowley's study of the quantity of exports given for a uniform quantity of imports, is that while there were uninterrupted improvements in the terms of trade from 1881 to 1900, 'We are no longer able to sell a growing volume of manufactured goods (or a volume increasing in proportion to population) at a better real price in terms of food' (Collected Writings, 1923, IX, p. 482). Both Beveridge and Keynes recognized that the worsening in the terms of trade (that is, relative to the price of exports) represented a decrease in income per unit of employment for the country as a whole. In the short run at least, a worsening in the terms of trade for a major trading country is likely to produce a neomercantilistic reaction in the form of 'beggar thy neighbour' remedies, either via exchange depreciation, wage reductions, export subsidies and/or restrictions of imports by means of tariffs and quotas. The object of these expedients, each of which has important effects on the distribution of employment and income between industries in the home country, is to improve the balance of trade.

This increases employment and income in the export industries, but it also raises the home price of export goods that rival imports. Although such policies have the effect of reducing average real wages, they are nevertheless viewed as beneficial when circumstances dictate that the game of 'beggar thy neighbour' is appropriate policy.[6]

Shortly afterwards, Frank Taussig extended the Bowley–Keynes computations to distinguish between the gross and net barter terms of trade, noting that the period between 1900 and 1915 was not only a period during which the barter terms of trade moved against England, but that it was also a period characterized by an increased export of capital accompanied by a lowering of both money incomes (wages included) and domestic prices (Taussig, 1924, p. 10). That is, a worsening in the terms of trade (relative to the price of exports) represents a decrease in income per unit of employment for the country as a whole. The adverse implications for the volume of trade worldwide were later pointed out by Joan Robinson:

As soon as one [nation] succeeds in increasing its trade balance at the expense of the rest, others retaliate, and the volume of international trade sinks continuously, relatively to the total volume of world activity. Political, strategic and sentimental considerations add fuel to the fire and the flames of economic nationalism blaze ever higher and higher (1947, Part III, Chapter 2).

In sum, a significant worsening in the terms of trade for a major trading country will produce, in the short run at least, a neomercantilistic reaction in the form of 'beggar my neighbour' remedies, either via exchange depreciation, wage reductions, export subsidies and/or restriction of imports by means of tariff and quotas.[7]

An important passage in Keynes's *General Theory* similarly recognized that in conditions of chronic demand deficiency mercantilist policies are perfectly rational:

For an economy subject to many contracts and customs more or less fixed over an appreciable period of time, while the quantity of the domestic circulation and the domestic rate of interest are primarily determined by the balance of payments... there is no orthodox means open to the authorities for countering unemployment at home except by struggling for an export surplus and an import of the monetary metals at the expense of their neighbours. Never in history was there a method devised of such efficiency for setting each country's advantage at variance with its neighbour's as the international gold (or formerly, silver) standard. For it made domestic prosperity directly dependent on a competitive pursue of market and a competitive appetite for precious metals (1936, pp. 348–9).

Thus, the inter-war period taught by painful experience a lesson that was already apparent to Thomas Mun and other mercantilists, but also to the classicists. The lesson is that the presence of the foreign sector confers a degree of latitude for increasing domestic absorption that is not available to a closed economy, but that its pursuit is likely to be confrontational *vis-à-vis* its trading partners. This confrontation is clearly at the heart of the substantial collapse of the Bretton Woods system, the so-called dollar shortage of the 1950s and 1960s and the 'loss of competitiveness' that is currently being invoked to explain US (and British) import surpluses. These are but recent manifestations implying that the role of trade is chiefly to provide a vehicle for international resource transfer, not only for increasing domestic absorption but to accomplish this goal without compromising the profit rate (or the wage–profit share relationship) of the economy.

The dollar shortage and the yen shortage

The dollar shortage derived from 'the fact that the rest of the world feels the need of American products in greater value amounts than the United States requires foreign commodities' (Kindleberger, 1943, p. 375). 'The basis for the chronic world shortage of dollars is to be found in the technical superiority of the United States in the production of many goods necessary to a modern standard of living and to the natural desire in other countries to raise real income faster than the basic condition of their economic productivity justify' (ibid. p. 379). Williams (1952, p. 12) made essentially the same point when he attributed the episode of the dollar shortage to the increasing reliance of the rest of the world on the USA in consequence of 'its high productivity and rapid technical progress…'. The problem was that, 'if they [Western Europe] had to live within their present means, on their current output, they would have to undergo a considerable reduction in their standard of living' (Haberler, 1948, p. 435). Richard Kahn (1950) went so far as to suggest that the consequence of discontinued Marshall plan aid to European countries would be to deteriorate their terms of trade to such a degree that they would be justified in imposing tariffs or other restrictions on their imports (p. 96). What he was emphasizing was that it is quite appropriate to 'beggar thy neighbour' to achieve a targeted rate of increase in living standards.

Today, in the closing decades of the 20th century, the objective of using trade to increase the nation's absorption rate has become a globalized objective. It has been argued that the basic reason for the high Japanese savings rate and her high growth rate is that her people 'desire to accumulate wealth in order for their children to live as well as Americans do' (Hayashi, 1986, p. 199). Had Japan followed the conventional wisdom, she would have adopted free trade and would have specialized in industries of the labour-intensive variety. Instead, the Ministry of International Trade and Industry (MITI) established industries predicated on intense employment of capital and modern technology. This policy choice, which also severely limited Japanese imports, was absolutely irrational within the context of traditional theory. But over the longer period, the industries which MITI promoted were ones in which labour productivity rises fast.

These policies are analogous in their outcome to the increasing return industries which England chose to support when she abolished the Corn Laws to pursue free trade in primary commodities. For 19th century England, import substitution of cheap food raised the profit rate which facilitated industrialization and provided access to world markets. In the case of contemporary Japan, the lateness of her industrialization was thought by her policy-makers to be compatible only with a protected domestic market, whose high savings rate and rapid growth became the basis for her world export market. The international economic order has thus come full circle in terms of policy. This point of fact supports the inference that the *raison d'être* of international trade has historically been to effect a real resource transfer from one's trading partners.

Concluding comments
The history of international trade policy, from 17th century mercantilism to classical free trade and 20th century neomercantilism, makes it clear that the objective of trade has always been to effect a transfer of real and/or financial resources from one's trading partners. It was precisely the goal of the mercantilists to achieve this objective; it was similarly the goal of those who opposed the Corn Laws in the name of the principle of comparative advantage to fashion policy measures to effect the transfer of resources from England's trading partners. Because of the respective stages of their development, free trade supported the capital accumulation and growth which the British empire enjoyed up to 1900. During the relatively brief economic order characterized by free trade, a convertible gold standard and a world capital market centred in London, there appeared to be a global consistency compatible with international order. Two World Wars and the devastating depression of the 1930s destroyed the old order and paved the way for a post-war economic order of which Keynes was the principal architect. Its key feature became the fashioning of international organizations intended to liberalize trade and develop new mechanisms to facilitate resource transfers in ways the free market failed to do.

In recent years the case for free trade has been reasserted with new vigour (Bhagwati, 1989). Free trade is supposed to maximize the potential of all nations to benefit from the cost advantages of buying goods from their trading partners. How then is the accumulation of reserves and foreign assets instead of taking goods by some to be explained? The answer lies in large part in the fact that they cannot simulate the 19th century English experience to raise their profit rate because their trading partners are also industrialized.

History verifies that Ricardo's Corn Law position related to a particular period in England's economic development, and that the conventional wisdom about the universal gain from free trade is predicated on trading among partners whose economies are at different stages of economic development. The historical record also substantiates the fact that the role of trade has always been – and is today – a vehicle for achieving resource transfers from one's trading partners to satisfy: (1) the frequently conflicting objectives of businesses to maintain or increase the rate of profit and of consumers to increase domestic absorption; and (2) the invariably conflicting goals of nations – developed and developing – to gain access to the world's income and wealth. That is what contemporary neomercantilism tells us about the political economy of international trade.

Notes

1. Rudiger Dornbush (1980) notes that 'unlike the pure theory of trade, open economy macroeconomics has become an applied and policy-oriented area of study'. Historians of thought are tempted to note that for the classicists and their precursors, it was ever thus.
2. 'Memorandum on the Reasons Moving Queen Elizabeth to Reform the Coinage', 1559, in R.H. Tawney and E. Power, Tudor Economic Documents, II, 194–5.
3. Schumpeter also credits Malynes who 'saw nearly the whole of the automatic mechanism' (1954, p. 365).
4. Thomas Malthus was particularly appreciative of this point and how it relates to a country's stage of economic development, for he emphasized that the gains from trade do not simply derive from the possibility of obtaining cheaper commodities. 'If we do not import from foreign countries our silk, cotton and indigo...[and] many other articles peculiar to foreign climates, it is quite certain that we should not have them at all. To estimate the advantage derived from their importation by their cheapness, compared with the quantity of labour and capital which they would have cost if we had attempted to raise them at home, would be perfectly preposterous. In reality no such attempt would have been thought of. If we could by possibility have made fine claret at ten pounds a bottle, few or none would have drunk it: and the actual quantity of labour and capital employed in obtaining these foreign commodities is at present beyond comparison greater than it would have been if we had not imported them.' Foreign trade 'by giving us commodities much better suited to our wants and tastes than those which had been sent away [that is, exported] had decidedly increased the exchangeable value of our possessions, our means of employment, and our wealth' (Malthus, 1820, p. 462).
5. Henry Thornton was a key contributor to the analysis of the transfer problem. He also had a particular interest in the depreciation of the Irish pound and its relation to remittances of rent to absentee landlords from their tenants. Not only Thornton, but also Malthus and J.S. Mill treated the loss of bullion as being akin to granting a subsidy to a foreign power (Malthus, 1811a, pp. 344–5) or suffering the imposition of a tribute (Mill, 1844, p. 42; 1848, Book III Chap XXI, 4, pp. 166–7).
6. Even an orthodox thinker like A.C. Pigou recognized that a tariff can produce an increase in employment in the short run (Pigou, 1947, p. 224).
7. Joan Robinson examines the different impacts of each of these policies in detail in 'The Foreign Exchanges', in *Essays in the Theory of Employment*, 2nd edn, Part III, Chapter 1.

Bibliography

Bhagwati, Jagdish (1989), *Protectionism*, Cambridge, MA.: MIT Press.

Clapham, F.G.H. (1926), *An Economic History of Modern Britain*, Vol. I, Cambridge: Cambridge University Press.

Condliffe, J.B. (1950), *The Commerce of Nations*, New York: W.W. Norton.

Dornbush, Rudiger (1980), *Open Economy Macroeconomics*, New York: Basic Books.

Grampp, William (1952), 'Liberal Elements in English Mercantilism', *Quarterly Journal of Economics*, **46**, November.

Haberler, Gottfried (1948), 'Dollar Shortage?', in Seymour Harris (ed.), *Foreign Economic Policy for the United States*, Cambridge, MA.: Harvard University Press, 426–45.

Hayashi, Fumio, (1986), 'Why Is Japan's Savings Rate So Apparently High?', in S. Fischer (ed.), *NBER Macroeconomic Annual*, Cambridge, MA.: MIT Press, 147–210.

Heckscher, Ely (1931), *Mercantilism*, 2 volumes, Allen and Unwin, 1934.

Hollander, Samuel (1979), *The Economics of David Ricardo*, Toronto: University of Toronto Press.

Irwin, Douglas (1988), 'Welfare Effects of British Free Trade: Debate and Evidence for the 1840s', *Journal of Political Economy*, **96**, (6), December, 1142–64.

Johnson, E.A. (1937), *Predecessors of Adam Smith*, New York: Prentice Hall, Chapter 15.

Kahn, R.F. (1950), 'The Dollar Shortage Devaluation', *Economia Internationale*, **3**, February, 89–113.

Keynes, J.M. (1923), 'A Tract on Monetary Reform', in *The Collected Writings of John Maynard Keynes*, London: Macmillan, for the Royal Economics Society.

Keynes, J.M. (1929), 'The German Transfer Problem', *Economic Journal*, **39**, March, 1–7. 'A Rejoiner', ibid., June 179–82. 'A Reply', September, 404–8.

Keynes, J.M. (1936), *The General Theory of Employment, Money and Interest*, New York: Harcourt Brace and Co.

Keynes, J.M. (1946), 'The Balance of Payments of the United States', *Economic Journal*, **56**, June, 404–8.

Kindleberger, Charles P. (1943), 'International Monetary Stabilization', in Seymour E. Harris (ed.), *Postwar Economic Problems*, New York: McGraw-Hill, 375–95.

Kindleberger, Charles P. (1950), *The Dollar Shortage*, Cambridge, MA: The Technology Press of MIT and New York: John Wiley & Sons, Inc.

Kindleberger, Charles P. (1966), *Europe and the Dollar*, Cambridge, MA.: MIT Press.

Krugman, P. and Taylor, L. (1978), 'Contractional Effects of Devaluation', *Journal of International Economics*, **8**, (3), August, 445–56.

Malthus, Thomas (1811), 'Depreciation of Paper Currency', *Edinburgh Review*, **17**, February, 340–72.

Malthus, Thomas (1815), *Inquiry into the Nature and Progress of Rent*, London: John Murray.

Malthus, Thomas (1820), *Principles of Political Economy*, Reprints of Economic Classics, New York: Augustus Kelley, 1964.

Mill, John Stuart (1844), *Essays On Some Unsettled Questions of Political Economy*, London: London School of Economics (1948 edn).

Mill, John Stuart (1848), *Principles of Political Economy*, London: Longmans Green.

Morley, Richard (1988), *The Macroeconomics of Open Economies*, Aldershot, Hants: Edward Elgar.

Mun, Thomas (1630), *England's Treasure by foreign trade*, reprinted in J.R. McCulloch (ed.), *Early English Tracts on Commerce*, Cambridge: Cambridge University Press, 1952.

O'Brien, D.P. (1981), 'Ricardian Economics and the Economics of David Ricardo', *Oxford Economics Papers*, **33**, (3), November, 352–86.

Pigou, A.C. (1947), *A Study in Public Finance*, 3rd edn, London: Macmillan.

Ricardo, David (1815), *The High Price of Bullion, Collected Works of David Ricardo*, McCulloch edition, London, 1886.

Ricardo, David (1951), *Principles of Political Economy and Taxation, Collected Works*, edited by J.R. McCulloch, London: John Murray, 1886.

Robinson, Joan (1947), 'Beggar My Neighbour Remedies', *Essays in the Theory of Employment*, 2nd edn, Oxford: Basil Blackwell.

Robinson, Joan (1947), 'The Foreign Exchanges', *Essays in the Theory of Employment*, 2nd edn, Oxford: Basil Blackwell.

Schumpeter, J.A. (1954), *A History of Economic Analysis*, New York: Oxford University Press.

Steedman, Ian (1979), *Fundamental Issues in Trade Theory*, New York: St Martin's Press.

Taussig, F.W. (1924), 'The Change in Great Britain's Terms of Trade', *The Economic Journal*, March, 1–10.

Thornton, Henry (1802), *An Inquiry into the Nature and Effect of the Paper Credit of Great Britain*, reprinted London: Frank Cass and Company, New York: Augustus Kelly, 1962.

Williams, J.H. (1952), 'The Theory of International Trade Reconsidered', *The Economic Journal*, **XXXIX**, 195–209.

Williams, J.H. (1953), *Trade Not Aid: A Program for World Stability*, Cambridge, MA.: Harvard University Press.

Williamson, John (1985), 'The Theorists and the Real World', in L. Tsoukalis (ed.), *The Political Economy of International Money. In Search of a New Order*, London: Sage Publications for the Royal Institute of International Affairs, reprinted in Chris Milner (ed.), *Political Economy and International Money: Selected Essays of John Williamson*, New York: New York University Press, 1987.

Viner, Jacob (1937), *Studies in the Theory of International Trade*, New York: Harper and Brothers.

3 A theory of mercantilism

John S. Chipman*

Introduction

Recent concern with the so-called 'declining international competitiveness' of the United States has drawn attention to some striking parallels with mercantilist concepts, and led many to wonder whether we are entering a new mercantile era. I have in Chipman (1994) analysed the concept of international competitiveness at length; in the present paper I examine closely the doctrines of what seem to me the ablest English mercantilist writers, and try to develop a logical theory that captures the essential features of their doctrines. My aim is neither to attack nor to defend these doctrines; rather, simply to understand them. My hope is that if we can better sort out the extent to which differences between mercantilist and classical points of view are differences in methods of analysis and differences in value judgments, and if we can develop a common framework and vocabulary which can encompass both approaches, more rational discussion of policy proposals will be possible.

The term 'mercantile system' was introduced by Adam Smith (1776, Book IV, Ch. I) to describe the body of thought typified by Mun (1664) according to which a country's prosperity would best be achieved by policies to ensure a 'favourable' balance of trade, and thus an inflow of precious metals. According to Viner (1930, p. 252), the term 'mercantilism' was introduced 'with the aid of the Germans'; but no references were given. The first use of the term that I have found is that of Roscher (1851, p. 123) who has this to say: 'The usual classification of economic literature into mercantilism, physiocracy, and the industrial system is convenient enough, to be sure, but in reality is without adequate basis'. The term has been used by Heckscher (1955) to describe the practice of economic policy in Western Europe in the 16th and 17th centuries, which emphasized the management of trade by national governments.

To try to formulate a single theory to embrace a set of often inconsistent policies as well as a variety of disparate and conflicting views of many writers would be a futile task. Instead, I will try to formulate a theory that is internally consistent and also consistent with a reasonable interpretation of the main arguments of the most able mercantilist writers, and consistent as well with most of the types of economic policies that one associates with mercantilism.[1]

In the next section I analyse the reasons invariably given in mercantilist writings for the emphasis on the balance of trade, which is the analogy with the excess of income over expenditure of a family. Owing to insufficiently developed principles of national accounting, they overlooked the fact that the balance of trade corresponds not to saving but to the excess of saving over investment. However, there is little textual evidence to justify Viner's view that they advocated indefinite accumulation of precious metals, and indeed Mun strongly advocated that the trade surplus be reinvested in more roundabout trades – certainly a form of investment.

In the third section I show that the mercantilists recognized that there were mutual gains from trade starting from autarky, but that they were principally concerned with obtaining greater gains starting from free trade which, of course, could only be at the expense of other countries. The question arises whether the balance of trade can correctly measure these gains from trade. I argue that what the mercantilists were groping for was a money measure of the gains from trade. I point out that Davenant used a measure of the balance of trade in which the old imports and exports were multiplied by the new prices, so that his measure corresponds to what I call the Paasche trade-variation, which in a special case coincides with the compensating trade-variation. I also point out that Pollexfen's objective was to maximize the balance of trade subject to a standard-of-living constraint, which is simply the dual of the problem of maximizing a country's standard of living subject to a balance-of-trade constraint. If a country follows such a policy, any deterioration in its terms of trade will lead to a trade deficit, and any improvement in its terms of trade to a trade surplus – an extreme form of the Laursen–Metzler effect. Under such conditions, a country's balance of trade would correctly indicate its gains from trade. A discussion of various money measures of gains from trade is given in the fourth section.

Finally it is argued that, given the mercantilists' formulation of a country's objectives, often what matters most is not a country's absolute welfare, but its welfare relative to that of the rest of the world – what Hume called the 'jealousy of trade'. In the last section I show that while stringent conditions are needed to produce the result that technical change in one country will worsen the terms of trade (and thus the standard of living) of another, if a cardinal measure of welfare is adopted (and the Hicksian equivalent variation is recommended), much weaker conditions are needed to produce the result that a technical change in one country will improve its standard of living more than those of other countries: briefly, that the share of the expanding country's exports in its national income be 'small', by which is meant less than half of the sum of the countries' elasticities of demand for imports less one.

The balance of trade as the excess of income over expenditure
Throughout the mercantilist literature one finds at the very basis of their reasoning, the analogy between a country and a family. A family grows rich if it saves, that is, spends less than it earns, and grows poor if it dissaves. Likewise, a country grows rich if it maintains a positive balance of trade, and grows poor if it maintains a negative one. This analogy (or parable), may be found in one of the earliest mercantilist tracts, written in 1549 and first published in 1581, and recently attributed to Sir Thomas Smith (1969, p. 63):

> For we must always take heed that we buy no more of strangers than we do sell them; for so we should impoverish ourselves and enrich them. For he were no good husband, that had no other yearly revenues but of his husbandry to live on, that would buy more in the market than he sells again.

The first sentence of this passage was quoted by Viner (1930, p. 256) (who attributed the authorship to John Hales) to support his contention that 'the mercantilists wanted an export surplus primarily because they wanted more bullion and because they saw that for a country without gold or silver mines a favourable balance of trade was the only means available to procure bullion' (p. 264). However, he omitted the explanation provided in the second sentence.

Mun (1621) opened his *Discourse of Trade* with a passage that provided a similar explanation of the desirability of a positive balance of trade (pp. 1–2):

> The trade of Merchandize, is not onely that laudable practize whereby the entercourse of Nations is so worthily performed, but also (as I may terme it) the verie *Touchstone* of a kingdomes prosperitie, when therein some certain rules shall be diligently obserued. For, as in the estates of priuate persons, wee may accompt that man to prosper and growe rich, who being possessed of reuenues more or lesse, doth accordingly proportion his expences; whereby he may yearelie aduance some maintenance for his posteritie. So doth it come to passe in those Kingdomes, which with great care and warinesse doe euer vent out more of their home commodities, then they import and vse of forren wares; for so vndoubtedly the remainder must returne to them in treasure. But where a contrarie course is taken, through wantonnesse and riot; to ouerwaste both foreign and domestike wares; there must the money of necessitie be exported, as the meanes to helpe to furnish such excesse, and so by the corruption of mens conditions and manners, manie rich countries are made exceeding poore, whilest the people thereof, too much affecting their owne enormities, doe lay the fault in something else.

A similar, expanded, account was given in Mun's posthumous work (1664, pp. 7–8), including an entire paragraph expanding on the analogy between a country and 'the estate of a private man'.

Misselden, who first coined the expression 'balance of trade' in the published literature, returned many times to the analogy among a merchant, a
family and a country. In one interesting passage he used accounting concepts
(1623, p. 130):

> A *Merchant* when hee will informe himselfe how his Estate standeth, is said to
> take a *Ballance* of his Estate: wherein he collecteth and considereth all his *Wares,*
> and *Monyes,* and *Debts,* as if hee would cast euery thing into the *Scale* to bee tried
> by waight: Which is therefore in *Merchants* and *Accomptants* termes, so called a
> *Ballance* of Accompt, or a *Ballance of Trade.* ...
> A *Father* or *Master of a Family,* doth also consider his Estate, by comparing
> his *Expence* with his *Reuenue:* and if he finde, that his *Expence* exceedeth his
> *Reuenue;* either he must *Lessen his charge,* or els *Consume his Estate.*

The analogy between a country and an individual economic unit was also
stressed by Locke (1696). According to him (p. 27): 'A Kingdom grows
Rich, or Poor just as a Farmer doth, and no otherwise'. He goes on to
illustrate how a farmer and his heirs could grow in wealth if they saved, or
become poor if they dissaved. Again (p. 118): 'Tis with a *Kingdom* as with a
Family. Spending less than our own Commodities will pay for, is the sure
and only way for the Nation to grow Rich'. Pollexfen (1697a, p. 81) stated:
'That undeniable Maxim, *That the way to be Rich is to be careful in Saving,
as well as industrious in Getting,* hath the same reference to Nations as to
particular Persons, or Families'.

What these passages make extremely clear is that the mercantilists considered a country's balance of trade to be equal to the excess of its income over
its expenditures – an insight that was considered novel and important when
rediscovered by Alexander (1952).

There is, however, an important difference between the concept as they
conceived it and as it is defined today. In the case of an individual or family,
the surplus referred to by the mercantilists was clearly an excess of income
over *consumption* expenditures, that is, *saving*; whereas under contemporary
balance-of-payments accounting, a country's balance of payments on goods
and services is equal to the excess of saving over investment. Since the
mercantilists invented the concept of the balance of trade, they should presumably be entitled to their own definition of it. Logically, then, it should
exclude imports and exports of capital goods; thus, a country that exported
only consumer goods and imported both consumer and capital goods should
be considered to have a favourable balance of trade.[2] Indeed, Petty (1691a,
pp. 18–19, 35–6) came very close to such a concept in including imported
durable goods as well as gold and silver in the capital balance; however, he
esteemed them more as a store of value than as instrumental goods. Pollexfen
(1697b, pp. 7, 40, 49) even judged the worth of a trade by the balance of

exports over imports of 'perishable Commodities, and Materials to supply Luxury' (p. 40), as well as manufactures (p. 47). This idea would, if carried out explicity, include non-perishable necessities in the capital balance – presumably to help maintain human capital.

There will, of course, be objections that mercantilists included only gold and silver in the capital balance, and that they therefore confused money with capital goods (compare with Viner, 1930, p. 266), as might be suggested by Mun's statement – that has so misled historians of economic thought – that the trade surplus 'must return in treasure'[3]. Mun, who was a very successful merchant, surely could not be supposed to believe that individuals saving to build up the wealth of their families and heirs would simply accumulate gold and not invest it.[4] And, indeed, he argued that the 'treasure' accumulated from a trade surplus should be reinvested abroad (Mun, 1621, pp. 21–2): 'whatsoeuer Summes of forren readie monyes are yearly sent from hence ... shall yearely bring in as much siluer, as they send forth; which hath beene always truly performed, with an ouerplus, to the increase of this Kingdomes treasure'.

This argument, which was further elaborated in Mun (1664, Ch. IV), was ridiculed by Adam Smith (1776), but deserves to be interpreted more carefully. Mun argued specifically against 'the keeping of our mony in the Kingdom' (p. 23), since this would reduce trade and cause inflation at home, hence it should be employed in more roundabout trade, that is, 'to enlarge our trade by enabling us to bring in more forraign wares, which being sent out again will in due time much encrease our treasure' (p. 20). He explained that importation of goods from the East-Indies for re-export to Europe would require investment in shipping and other expenses that would tie money up for a considerable time, but ultimately bring a good return (pp. 22–3):

> For it is in the stock of the Kingdom as in the estates of private men, who having store of wares, doe not therefore say that they will not venture out or trade with their mony (for this were ridiculous) but do also turn that into wares, whereby they multiply their Mony, and so by a continual and orderly change of one into the other grow rich, and when they please turn all their estates into Treasure; for they that have Wares cannot want money.

From the point of view of Austrian capital theory, the adoption of more roundabout methods of production such as the re-export trade discussed by Mun is certainly a form of investment; but unfortunately there is no way to identify such investment activities in statistics of merchandise trade.[5] These would show a zero balance from the activities Mun describes; hence the confusion.[6] But, as is clear from the parable at the end of the chapter, investment is what Mun had in mind (1664, p. 27):

> For if we only behold the actions of the husbandman in the feed-time when he casteth away much good corn into the ground, we will rather accompt him a mad man than a husbandman: but when we consider his labours in the harvest which is the end of his endeavours, we find the worth and plentiful encrease of his actions.

The confusion over different concepts of the balance of trade is reminiscent of the confusion that followed the publication of Keynes's *General Theory* over the senses in which saving and investment were unequal or necessarily equal. This was resolved by the concepts of *ex ante* and *ex post* saving and investment. The first expresses a disequilibrium concept useful in theory, according to which an excess of desired saving over desired investment will lead to a fall in interest rates which in turn will choke off some of the saving and call forth the remaining investment, with the result that *ex post* saving and investment – which alone can be observed statistically – will be equated at a higher level. In similar fashion we may regard Mun's treasure as the excess of *ex ante* exports over *ex ante* imports, obtained from short-term trades, providing the cash-in-advance needed to finance the more roundabout trades, resulting in *ex post* exports and imports – again, which alone can be observed statistically – becoming equated at a higher level than previously.[7]

The question of exactly how accumulated gold and silver can be used to increase a country's wealth is admittedly not treated in a very satisfactory manner in many mercantilist writings. This is illustrated by the following curious passage from Pollexfen (1697a, pp. 7–8):

> Though it be granted that our *Gold* or *Silver* cannot afford us any increase while kept within the Kingdom, yet it being that in which the Riches of the Nation doth so much consist, and so necessary for the Payment of Fleets and Armies, and carrying on of Commerce, that we cannot be Safe, nor Rich, without it; this Nation being so well stored with Staple Commodities of our own growth, as well as others, from our Plantations, and other places for Exportation, it may be said, we rather want *Trade* than *Stock*. But if it should be thought we want *Stock,* it is more our Interest to apply our selves to increase our Products and Manufactories, and Consumption of them, and to retrieve our *Fishing Trade,* to add to our *Stock,* then to incourage the Exportation of *Bullion* ...

This could imply, for instance, that the precious metals are used in part to purchase ships from Sweden; although later (p. 91) Pollexfen suggests: 'Building more great Ships of our own' to retaliate for Sweden's high tariffs on English manufactures. But the passage shows that Pollexfen considered gold and silver useful for purposes other than mere hoarding; it also undoubtedly reflects his view that at the time he was writing, the existing stock was insufficient to satisfy the needs he enumerated (1697b, p. 8). In contrast to Mun, he was very guarded about reinvesting gold and silver in trade (pp. 8–9):

Before Countenance should be given to *Trades* carried on by the Exportation of *Gold* and *Silver,* an Exact Inquiry should be made, what Returns we shall have for it, or wherein it will be Advantageous to the Nation; and if it appear, that except for the Uses aforesaid, for Stores or Goods for a further Manufactory, no *Trade* carried on by the Exportation of *Bullion* can bring us in any Returns, but what must be consumed in Luxury, or Prodigality, or hinder the expence of our own Manufactures, we should make but a bad Exchange.

Unsatisfactory as these explanations may be, I do not see how they can support the thesis that the mercantilists advocated *indefinite accumulation* of bullion, as Viner (1930, p. 264) insisted.[8]

The mercantilists were more convincing when they discussed the causes and remedies of a deficit rather than a surplus in the balance of trade. This was attributed to an excess of consumption over production. Misselden spoke of the 'want of money' and explained (1622, p. 11):

The *general remote* cause of our want of money, is the *great excesse* of this *Kingdom,* in cōsuming the *Commodities* of *Foreign Countries,* which prove to *us discommodities,* in hindering us of so much *treasure,* which otherwise would bee brought in, in lieu of those *toyes.*

Misselden's antagonist, Malynes, though in complete agreement that the chief cause of 'the decay of trade in England' was the 'want of money' (Malynes, 1622, p. 104), attributed the problem to the exchange rate being below par (pp. 11–14).[9] The following year Misselden argued – somewhat more logically in not singling out foreign commodities (1623, p. 132):

But if all the *Causes* of our *Vnder-ballance of Trade,* might be contracted in two words, surely they might be represented, in two extremities of the Kingdome at this day: *Poverty* alas, and *Prodigality.* The *Poore* sterue in the streets for want of labour: The *Prodigall* excell in excesse, as if the world, as they doe, ran vpon wheels. The one drawe's on the *Over-ballance of Forraine Trade*: The other keepe's backe in *Vnder-ballance our Trade.*

Likewise, Pollexfen (1697a, p. 41) stated:

Those that are prodigal in the consumption of Foreign Commodities, do by that prodigality bring the Nation in Debt more than necessary, as much as they might have saved to themselves in their own Expences; and those that are prodigal in the expence of their own Products, do decrease the Exportation of so much as they might have saved.

and quite succinctly said (p. 51): 'it being not the way to grow Rich to have many Eaters, and few Workers'.

Mun (1664, pp. 37–8) expressed the matter in terms almost identical with those used in recent discussions:

> ...the Commonwealth shall decline and grow poor by a disorder in the people, when through Pride and other Excesses they do consume more forraign wares in value than the wealth of the Kingdom can satisfie and pay by the exportation of our own commodities, which is the very quality of an unthrift who spends beyond his means.

It is hard not to compare such a passage with similar ones that occurred in the 1940s when Misselden's 'want of money' was renamed 'dollar shortage' by Crowther (1941), Kindleberger (1943), Balogh (1946) and others, and in the 1980s when a similar concern arose over the growing lack of 'international competitiveness' of the United States. Harrod (1947, p. 43) said of the phrase 'dollar shortage' that 'it is no more than the young man going forward and living beyond his resources without leave'. Haberler (1948, p. 435), who could certainly not be accused of being a mercantilist, observed that: 'the dollar shortage is merely a consequence of the fact that many countries are unwilling or unable for one reason or another to live within their means'. Hatsopoulos, Krugman and Summers (1988, p. 299) noted that: 'the trade deficit represents, in essence, a US economy that has been living beyond its means'.

Misselden's proposed remedies consisted of the protection of manufactures to increase employment and production, and the prohibition of imports of luxuries to discourage consumption. It is interesting that Pollexfen advocated tackling the problem directly, and protective measures only as a last resort (1697b, p. 47):

> So long as the Nation keeps to Frugality and industry Laws may not be absolutely Necessary to Limit the Consumption of any Foreign Commodities, nor to increase or promote our own Manufactures: But if there be an appearance, that a Nation is running into a luxurious Prodigal Expence of Foreign Commodities, and to a neglect in Manufacturing and promoting their own, and to idleness, and spending of time in what is not profitable for the Nation, the usual Consequences of Luxury (which we fear is our Case at present) then Laws will be necessary to put a stop to it, that the Treasure of the Nation may not be Consumed thereby: For by the Course of Trade no stop can happen to any such Consumptions nor Idleness, till want of Money occasion it.

and again (p. 56):

> ...whether such Laws be good and necessary, or not, depends wholly upon the Genius and Inclination of the People. If Parsimonious and Industrious, then no need of such Laws; but if Luxurious and Idle, must be Ruin'd without them.

In the late mercantilist writings we even find an anticipation of a phenomenon perceived by Kindleberger (1950, p. 181) and which became Nurkse's

(1953) celebrated 'demonstration effect'. According to Steuart (1767, Book II, Ch. XXIX; 1805, II, p. 112):

> ...the young people of one country travel into the other, where the inhabitants stay at home: a circumstance which would prove very prejudicial to the country of the travellers, if a wise stateman did not, by reasonable prohibitions upon certain articles of foreign consumption, prevent the bad consequences of adopting a taste for what his subjects cannot produce.

The great void in mercantilist writings is the lack of any concept of capital as a produced good and productive factor. In the absence of capital accumulation, one can only explain imbalances of trade on the basis of saving in one country offset by dissaving in another, or, more generally, in differential propensities to save among countries. Pollexfen (1697a, p. 19) asserted that:

> ...no Reason can be given why *Bullion* or *Money,* should be Exported out of any Nation to a Foreign Country, to remain and continue there, but in order to pay, or contract some Debt; unless the Person that Exports it, intend to remove himself also, or to give it away.

In the absence of productive investment this would imply that a country with a surplus must be lending to a country that is living beyond its means (or at least saving at a lower rate), the first country merely acquiring property in the second – hardly a promising investment. The same reasoning would apply within a country: for every family that saves and becomes rich, there must be another that dissaves and becomes poor (or at least saves at a lower rate), the first ultimately purchasing its estate from the second. If it is true, as Pollexfen states (1697a, p. 134), that 'Gains should arise by what got from Foreigners, which can only inrich the Nation, and not so much out of our own people, which can only make Riches change hands', then the same reasoning would imply that the gains of one country can only come at the expense of another. It should not be concluded, however, that the problem of explaining capital movements among countries was resolved by the classical economists; Adam Smith rather avoided the question of foreign investment than resolved it.

The balance of trade as a measure of gains from trade
The balance of trade in mercantilist writings was an indicator not only of increased wealth resulting from saving, but also of the gains from trade.

That there was some mutual gain from trade was recognized already by Malynes (1601), but expressed in mystical terms and not brought to bear on the more practical aspects of the discussion (p. 6):

> God caused nature to distribute her benefits, or his blessings to seuerall climates, supplying the barennesse of some things in our countrey, with the fruitfulnesse and store of other countries, to the ende that enterchangeably one common-weale should liue with another.

This passage reappeared in Malynes (1622, pp. 58–9) where it was now clearly used as an argument against autarky. The argument was accepted by Malynes's antagonist, Misselden (1622, p. 25):

> And to the end there should be a *Commerce* amongst men, it hath pleased *God* to inuite as it were, one Countrey to traffique with another, by the variety of things which the one hath, and the other hath not: that so that which is wanting to the *one,* might be supplied by the *other,* that all might have sufficient.

On the face of it, this seems to conflict with Misselden's view that the balance of trade is a measure of a country's gains from trade (1623, p. 116):

> So is also this *Ballance of Trade,* an excellent and politique Inuention, to shew vs the difference of waight in the *Commerce* of one Kingdome with another.

However, this can be interpreted to mean either that: (l) starting from a position of free trade, any further gains one country makes from trade are necessarily at the expense of another country (which, of course, is simply a definition of the Pareto optimality of global free trade), and that such gains may be measured by the balance of trade; or that (2) what is important is not so much a country's *absolute* gains from trade as its gains *relative* to other countries.

In Pollexfen (1697a, p. 59), we find the mystical confronted with the practical:

> Most *Trades* are carried on between Nations by a permutation of Commodities, as a mutual conveniency, for the supplying each the other with what they want; Providence having so ordained that different Nations may abound with different Commodities, and to want others, which makes the Exchange commodious. Those that want least, and have most to Export (to which Industry added to Natural Advantages doth much contribute) generally have the advantage;... .

Again (p. 157):

> It is true, that the continuance of Trade depends much upon a mutual conveniency, but the advantage and increase of Riches, expected by trade, depends upon our Exporting more Goods than we Import;... .

This may be interpreted as affirming that there is a mutual gain from trade, when starting from autarky, which should be continued; but that starting from free trade one country can gain only at the expense of another.

What is understood today by gains from trade is essentially the improved terms of trade resulting from liberalization of trade, or from a country's exploiting its monopoly position in trade. Passages recognizing the benefits of improved terms of trade can be found in quite early mercantilist writings. An anonymous document, 'A Discourse of Corporations' dating from 1587–89 and reproduced in Tawney and Power (1924, III, p. 267) contains the passage:

> ...it is the best policie so to gouerne our owne comodities that our Cuntrey and soile yeldeth, that they may carrie estimacion and value in those partes whither we transporte them, and not be too deare at home; and that forrein Comodities be kept at lowe and base prices amonge us.
>
> And another is that the thinges which we carrie out do surmount in price the thinges which we bringe in; else shall we sone make a poore land and a poore people.

Viner (1930, p. 256), who quoted the second paragraph above, interpreted it to refer to the balance of trade. However, the word 'prices' seems certainly to refer to the terms of trade.[10]

Reference to the terms of trade may also be found in Mun (1621), who stressed the role of trade in providing abundant and cheap commodities for the population. For example (pp. 7–8):

> Now as touching the Trade of *Callicoes,* of many sortes, into which the *English* lately made an entrance; although it cannot be truely sayd, that this commoditie is proffitable, for the state of *Christendome* in generall (in respect they are the manifacture of Infidells, and in great part the weare of Christians) yet neuertheless, this commoditie, likewise is of singular vse, for this common wealth in particuler; not onelie therewith to increase the Trade into forren parts; but also thereby, greatly to abate the excessiue prices of Cambricks, Holland, and other sorts of Linnen-cloath; which daily are brought into this Kingdom for a verie great summe of mony.

Mun also observed that the gain from trade could be measured by the amount of imports a country could get for its exports – that is, the barter terms of trade (1621, p. 15):

> ...neither the *Venetians, French,* nor *Dutche,* doe vent so much of their owne Country commodities in those partes, as doe prouide their necessarie wants of the proper wares of *Turkes*... . Only the *English* haue more advantage then any other Nation in this kinde, for they vent so great a quantitie of broad-cloathes, tinne, and other *English* commodities, that the proceede thereof, doth not only prouide a sufficient quantitie of part of the sayd *Turkish* wares (which fit their vse), but also a proportion of about 300 great balles of *Persia* Raw-silke yearely.

A very succinct statement is found in Petty (1691b, p. 83):

> Why should we forbid the use of any Foreign Commodity, which our own Hands and Countrey cannot produce, when we can employ our spare Hands and Lands upon such exportable Commodities as will produce the same, and more[?]

Post-mercantilist statements of the nature of the gains from trade (prior to Samuelson (1939)), do not go much beyond these, or even as far.[11]

The most precise statement of the nature of the gains from trade in mercantilist writings is to be found in Davenant (1696). It seems worthwhile to quote and analyse *in extenso* the following passage, in which he explains the advantage to England of the East-India trade (pp. 30–31; 1771, I, pp. 102–3):

> If the people of *England* are willing, and pleased to wear *Indian* Silks and Stuffs, of which the Prime Cost in *India*, is not above a Fourth part of what their own Commodities would stand them in here; and if they are thereby thus enabled to Export so much of their own Product, whatever is so sav'd, is clear Gain to the Kingdom in general. But to set this Matter in a clearer Light.
>
> Suppose 200,000 *l. per Annum* of the Prime Sum sent to *India,* is return'd in Commodities for our own Consumption: And,
>
> Suppose half this Sum, *viz.* 100,000 *l.,* to be return'd in such Goods as are Worn here, in the stead and room of the Woollen Manufactures.
>
> From 100,000 *l.* Prime Cost to *India,* there may Reasonably be   *l.*
> expected Goods that sell here for   400,000
> So that by sending to *India*   100,000
> We gain for our own Consumption clear   300,000
>
> Now this must be Clear Profit to the Kingdom, Because this Sum would be other-wayes laid out and consum'd in our own Product; which Product we are by this Means enabled to Export. For when we come to Examine into the True Reason of the Great Wealth of *Holland,* we shall find it chiefly to arise from this Frugality of Consuming at Home what is Cheap, or comes Cheaply, and carrying Abroad what is Rich, and will yield most Money.

In Figure 3.1, excess demands (imports if positive, exports if negative) of commodities 1 and 2 are measured on the horizontal and vertical axes respectively, commodity 2 being clothing which is imported, and commodity 1 being a representative export good. To reproduce Davenant's example, kinked trade-indifference curves are drawn with kinks at z^0 and z^1, supported by budget lines through the origin corresponding to price vectors p^0 and p^1 at the initial and final equilibrium respectively. It is assumed that trade is balanced in both equilibria. At the initial equilibrium, an amount $-z_1^0$ of the export good is exchanged for z_2^0 units of clothing imported, say, from France; at the new equilibrium, an amount $-z_1^1$ of the export good – one-quarter of the previous amount – is exchanged for the same amount $z_2^1 = z_2^0$ of clothing

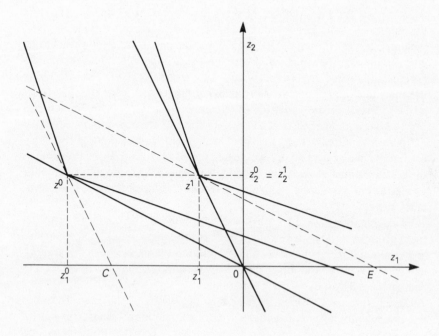

Figure 3.1:   Davenant's measure of the gains from trade

now imported from India. At the new prices, indicated by the line joining the origin and z^1, the minimum trade deficit (which, of course, is the negative of the maximum trade surplus) subject to the old trade-utility level is indicated by the dashed line through z^0. Measured in units of commodity 1, the gain from East India trade is measured by the distance OC, which is what in Chipman (1992) I called the compensating trade-variation, corresponding of course to Hicks's (1942) compensating variation. This, as in Davenant's example, is equal to three-quarters of the original outlay, Oz_1^0. Owing to the kinks in the trade-indifference curves, the compensating trade-variation also corresponds to what we may call, following Hicks, the Paasche trade-variation $p^1z^1 - p^1z^0 = -p^1z^0$ which is simply the old balance of trade denominated in the new prices. Intuitively, the gains from trade are measured by the maximum balance of trade the country would have to have – that is, the gold and silver it would have to acquire in exchange for consumable commodities at the new prices – in order for welfare to be reduced to the old level.

Figure 3.1 shows that a contra-mercantilist measure of gains from trade is equally possible. Starting from the original equilibrium, z^0, one can ask what the minimum trade deficit (the negative of the maximum trade surplus) would be at the original prices p^0 to make the country as well off as in the new situation, z^1. This is shown by the dashed line through z^1 intersecting the horizontal axis at E. Measured in units of commodity 1, the distance OE is the equivalent trade variation and, again because of the kinks, it is also equal to the Laspeyres trade variation. In money terms it is equal to $p^0z^1 - p^0z^0 = p^0z^1$, which is the negative of the new balance of trade denominated in the old prices. Intuitively, the gains from trade are now measured by the minimum trade deficit the country would need to have – or the amount by which the country would have to live beyond its means, or the amount of bullion it would have to give up in exchange for goods – at the old prices, in order to enjoy the new standard of living.

Of course, if we were to consider a worsening of the country's terms of trade given by a movement from z^1 to z^0, everything would be interchanged, and OE would measure the decline in welfare in terms of the compensating and Paasche trade variations, and OC the same decline in terms of the equivalent and Laspeyres trade variations.

Davenant did not assume fixed production, however, but recognized that the Indian imports would undersell domestic clothing manufactures. His suggestion – quite audacious for a mercantilist – was that these should be abandoned and the raw wool diverted to the production of textiles to be exported abroad (1696, pp. 32–3):

> That the *East-India* Goods do something interfere with the Woollen Manufacture, must undoubtedly be granted, but the Principal Matter to be Consider'd, is, Which way the Nation in General is more Cheaply supply'd.
>
> If 100,000 *l.* Prime Cost to *India*, brings Home so many Goods as stand in the stead, and supply the room of 400,000 *l.* of our own Manufactures, It must certainly be Adviseable not to Prohibit such a Trade, but rather to divert the Wooll used in these our Home Manufactures, and the Craft, Labour and Industry employ'd about 'em, to the Making Fine Broad Cloth, Course and Narrow Cloths, Stuffs and other Commodities, fit for Sale in Foreign Markets; since 'tis an undoubted Truth, that 400,000 *l.* worth of our Native Goods sold Abroad, does add more to the Nations General Stock and Wealth, than Four Millions worth of our Home Product Consum'd within the Kingdom.

This conclusion aroused the ire of Pollexfen (1697b), who devoted his pamphlet to attacking Davenant's position. The controversy is of great interest in bringing out the nature of the older hard-line mercantilist view of the nature of the gains from trade. It also sheds light on the role of bullion *vis-à-vis* other commodities.

Pollexfen opened his attack by spelling out his position on the latter question (1697b, pp. 66–7):

> ...what may properly be called the Riches or Treasure of a Nation? Or what may be esteemed the most Useful, after what is absoluely Necessary, to supply the Necessities of Nature? Some being of Opinion that nothing doth deserve that Name, or to be so esteemed, but Gold and Silver; because no other Metal is so lasting and durable, or so fit to receive the Royal Stamp, nor to be ascertained in Value, and divided into several Denominations, nor so convenient to pay Fleets and Armies; and because hath a general esteem in all parts of *Europe,* as fit for such uses, and to be the Standard for the carrying on of Commerce, and to be Barter'd off for all other Commodities.
>
> That Jewels, Lead, Tin or Iron, though durable, yet having not those other qualifications, do not so well deserve to be esteemed Treasure.
>
> That Silks, Woollen Goods, Wines, &c. may be esteemed Riches between Man and Man, because may be converted into Gold and Silver, yet do not deserve to be esteemed the Riches of the Nation, till by Exportation to Foreign Countries are converted into Gold and Silver, and that brought hither, because are subject to corruption, and in a short course of Years will consume to nothing, and then of no value.

It should be noted that the first paragraph states that gold and silver are valuable not in themselves, but because of their uses for the purposes enumerated, including that of being 'Barter'd off for all other Commodities'. The second states that this value is not absolute, but that other durable commodities have some, but not all, of these desirable properties and hence are not as useful for this purpose – hardly the position of someone suffering from the delusion of Midas. The third and most interesting paragraph singles out a class of goods – luxuries – that are of value to the nation (as opposed to individuals) only insofar as they can be converted into gold and silver by exportation. It has been asserted by Viner (1930, p. 269) that mercantilists: 'justify including other things than gold and silver as wealth only because gold and silver can be exchanged for them'. But Pollexfen's statement could be regarded simply as an early recognition that the value of a commodity is to be reckoned by its *marginal* utility, or 'value in exchange', rather than its total utility or 'value in use'. But what is especially noteworthy is that Pollexfen singled out luxuries in this way and distinguished value to the nation from value to individuals, that is, public from private interest. This is well brought out by the following passage (1697b, pp. 48–9):

> All Traders have Reason to make it their business to get Money by their Trades, by sending out and bringing Home such Commodities as are most vendible, and yield them most Profit. But whether send out Goods or Bullion, or

whether what bring back be necessary for the supply of our Necessities, or useful for a further Manufacture, or be spent in Prodigality, Luxury, or Debauchery, or to the hindrance of our Manufacture (so long as they get by it) they do not generally take it to be their Province to mind: But for the good of the whole, it may be presumed the State ought to mind it so far, as may be convenient to prevent the Exportation of our Treasure; if not, the Stock of Gold and Silver, which is absolutely necessary to Carry on trade, as well as for our Defence, will be Consumed; by which the Traders themselves as well as the generality will in time be involved in Misery.

Thus, the basic difference between Pollexfen and Davenant is one of value judgments. Davenant adhered to a principle of consumers' sovereignty, and in this completely anticipated Adam Smith. Pollexfen rejected this principle completely; for him, people should be supplied with the necessities of life, but no more. A policy of full employment should be pursued in order to maximize output, and to prevent people from becoming beggars and living on the welfare rolls and thus dissaving. For this purpose, protection of the labour-intensive industries was essential. Consumption of luxuries was to be discouraged by education, example, and, if necessary, by sumptuary laws and import restrictions. All the surplus productive power, which was to be maximized, was to go into building up the country's power.

One may not agree with these objectives, but they form a consistent set of principles of action. Formally, we may observe that just as, in contemporary demand theory, a position of maximum utility subject to a budget constraint (that expenditures equal income) is also a position of minimum expenditure subject to a utility constraint, the same duality theorem holds for trade-utility functions and the trade-demand functions that they generate. For a country, a position of maximum trade-utility subject to a balance-of-trade constraint (that the value of excess demand be equal to the deficit in the balance of trade) is also a position of minimum trade deficit, or maximum trade surplus, subject to a standard-of-living constraint. Davenant would wish to impose a constraint that the balance of trade be non-negative and, subject to this, maximize the country's standard of living. Pollexfen would wish to impose a constraint on the country's standard of living, that it be at the subsistence level and, subject to this constraint, maximize the country's balance of trade. The two principles agree completely except for the choice of the balance-of-trade level in the one case and the standard-of-living level in the other. One major difference, however, between Davenant and Pollexfen is that Davenant would accept individual preferences as social preferences, whereas Pollexfen would definitely not; he would impose his own social preferences and enforce them by various regulatory measures.

Another interesting feature of the debate between Davenant and Pollexfen is their position on the distribution of income or welfare within the country.

Davenant ignored any distributional effects of allowing imports from India, but Pollexfen emphasized them (1697b, pp. 17–18):

> If it be said, that this Trade hath a good foundation, because Materials are plenty, and Labour cheap in *India;* it being agreed that these Manufactured Goods are spent both Abroad and at Home, in the room of our own. This instead of being an Argument for recommending this Trade, will appear the most dangerous part of it: For unless our Wooll fall to nothing, and the wages of those that work it up to 2 *d. per* Day, and Raw Silk and Silk *Weavers* Labour proportionable, the *India* Goods will occasion a stop to the Consumption of them; because those from *India* must otherwise be Cheapest, and all People will go to the Cheapest Markets, which will affect the Rents of Land, and bring our Working People to Poverty, and force them either to fly to Foreign parts, or to be maintained by the Parishes: And therefore how the Landed men are concerned in the Contest about this Trade, they may do well to consider.

Not only would the import of silks from India bring down wages and cause unemployment, but it would benefit only the rich consumers (1697b, p. 16):

> ...it is plain, that the pretended Gains made by that Trade on the Goods sold here is not Gains to the Nation, but gotten out of our own Peoples Pockets, by the Sales of such Goods to the Gentlemen and Landed men, or others, who are the Consumers ... .

In his reply, Davenant made a headlong attack on the sanctity of gold and silver reserves (1698, II, p. 15; 1771, I, p. 345):

> Gold and Silver are indeed the Measure of Trade, but the Spring and Original of it, in all Nations, is the Natural, or Artificial Product of the Country, that is to say, what their Land, or what their Labour and Industry produces.
>
> And this is so true, that a Nation may be suppos'd, by some Accident, quite without the Species of Money, and yet, if the People are numerous, industrious, vers'd in Traffick, skill'd in Sea-Affairs, and if they have good Ports, and a Soil fertile in variety of Commodities, such a People will have Trade, and gather Wealth, and they shall quickly get among 'em, a plenty of Gold and Silver: So that the real and effective Riches of a Country, is its Native Product.

The latter paragraph foreshadows Hume (1752), as of course Locke (1696, p. 117) did also. Davenant continued, in answer to Pollexfen's statement, as follows (1698, II, p. 16;1771, I, p. 355):

> Gold and Silver are so far from being (as this author says) *the only Things that deserve the Name of Treasure, or the Riches of the Nation,* that in truth, Money is at Bottom no more than the Counters with which Men, in their dealings, have been accustom'd to reckon. ...
>
> When a Country begins to thrive by Trade, it must not be imagin'd that the Increase and Profit is presently converted into Coin or Bullion, and a great ready

> Cash is not the only Sign of a thriving People, but their growing wealthy is to be discern'd by other Symptoms.

Explaining what these symptoms consisted of, he went on (1698, II, pp. 209–10; 1771, II, p. 11):

> But here Mr. *P—n* will object, that there is no National Gain but where there is a return made in Gold and Silver, which he thinks is the only Balance, whereby we can guess at Loss and Profit. He insinuates that no Importation of Commodities for home Consumption, is to be esteemed a Gain, so that by his way of arguing, the Returns for what is Exported to Foreign Parts, is only to be call'd Profit, and that not unless it come in Bullion. ...
>
> We shall endeavour to show, that, generally speaking, by whatever the Returns are more worth than the Commodity exported, the Nation is by so much a Gainer, let the Goods imported be perishable or not.

He continued with a restatement of the same kind of analysis that he had used in his previous work, explaining that the returns consisted of the saving in the cost of imports that resulted from the improved terms of trade. He still used the balance of trade, however, as the criterion of gains from trade (1698, II, p. 217; 1771, II, p. 16):

> To come at the right Knowledge of what a People get by Trade, it must be examin'd, to what Value they can naturally export of their own Product, and to what Value they can carry to Market of the Product of other Parts: It must afterwards be computed what their own Consumption is of Foreign Materials, by balancing this together; if there be an Overplus, that Overplus a Nation may be said to get by Traffick.

The apparent contradiction may be resolved by noting that, in calculating the balance of trade, he multiplied the old imports and exports by the new prices, thus using the Paasche trade-variation as explained in Figure 3.1.

A money measure of the gains from trade

The analysis in the preceding section of Davenant's explanation of the nature of the gains from trade may, of course, be generalized. Figure 3.2 shows the diagram familiar to all students of international-trade theory – a diagram for which Viner (1937, p. 521) claimed priority. An equilibrium under autarky is shown at the point where the production vector y^0 is equal to the consumption vector x^0, where a community-indifference curve is tangential to the production-possibility frontier. When trade is opened up, a new equilibrium is established, where the new price line is tangential to the production-possibility frontier at y^1 and to a community-indifference curve at x^1. The price line has swung in a clockwise direction, indicating an im-

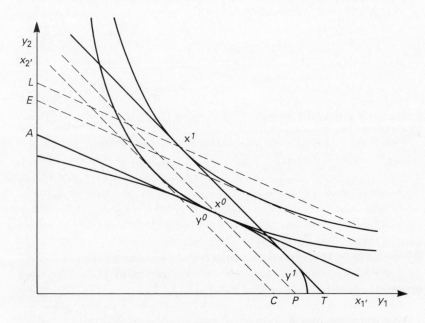

Figure 3.2:   Gains from trade measured by Hicksian variations

provement in the terms of trade. The community has moved to a higher indifference curve, indicating that potential welfare has increased. As we know, some groups will necessarily become worse off (a point that was stressed by Pollexfen), but the classic argument of the 'new welfare economics' is that all groups *could* become better off since, if necessary, the gainers could compensate the losers.

Several money measures of the gains from trade can be defined, following Hicks (1942). If, at the new terms of trade, we seek the minimum expenditure that will make the community just as well off as under autarky, this is shown by the dashed line that intersects the horizontal axis at the point *C*. The distance *CT* is the *compensating variation*, measured in units of commodity 1. We may consider this as the situation that would exist if, at the new prices, the country was required to make reparation payments to foreign countries at an amount that would bring its standard of living back to the autarky level. To do this, it would have to develop a surplus in its balance of trade. In nominal terms, therefore, this balance-of-trade surplus measures the gains from trade.

A problem with this measure is that it may be difficult to estimate statistically. If instead we draw a dashed line, parallel to the new price line, through the autarky equilibrium point $x^0 = y^0$, which intersects the horizontal axis at P, the distance PT measures Hicks's *Paasche variation*. In nominal terms (at the new prices) this measures the amount of money the country would have to give away (that is, the surplus it would have to develop in its balance of trade) so as to be able to afford only the bundle it consumed under autarky. (Of course, under these circumstances, it could, and would, do better by moving to a higher indifference curve.) The Paasche variation underestimates the accurate measure, the compensating variation.

The corresponding measures can be derived using the old (autarky) prices as a base instead of the new (free-trade) ones. The budget line through $x^0 = y^0$, corresponding to the autarky equilibrium, intersects the vertical axis at A. The minimum expenditure at autarky prices that leaves the country as well off as under free trade intersects the vertical axis at E. The distance AE is the *equivalent variation,* measured in units of commodity 2. It may be interpreted as the *deficit* in the country's balance of trade that would be necessary (say by means of foreign aid) at autarky prices to achieve the same level of welfare as under free trade. Again, this is not so easy to measure statistically, so instead we may draw a line parallel to the autarky price line going through x^1 and intersecting the vertical axis at L. The distance AL is the *Laspeyres variation,* measured in units of commodity 2. It overestimates the accurate measure, the equivalent variation.

Similar concepts may be applied to a country's trade-indifference map, as was done in Figure 3.1 for a special case of kinked trade-indifference curves. This is shown in Figure 3.3.

Three possible competitive equilibria are shown: an autarky equilibrium at the origin, 0, where prices are given by the components of the vector p^0, and two free-trade equilibria indicated by the bases z^1 and z^2 of the normals p^1 and p^2 respectively, where solid price lines are tangential to the corresponding trade-indifference curves. Dashed lines corresponding to prices p^2 are shown which, at those prices, minimize the country's trade deficit (that is, maximize its trade surplus) subject to the welfare levels prevailing in situations 0 and 1 respectively. The intersections of these lines with the horizontal axis define the compensating trade variations C^{02} and C^{12}, considered as distances from the origin, 0, measuring (in units of commodity 1) the improvement in welfare from situation 0 (autarky) to situation 2, and from situation 1 to situation 2 respectively, with situation 2's prices as a base. The dotted line whose slope is situation 2's price ratio, and which goes through the equilibrium point z^1 and intersects the horizontal axis at P^{12}, is the Paasche trade variation, considered as a distance from the origin 0 and measured in units of commodity 1. As before, this underestimates the corresponding compensating trade variation. It should be noted, however, that the corresponding Paasche trade variation P^{02} is zero – showing that this is an

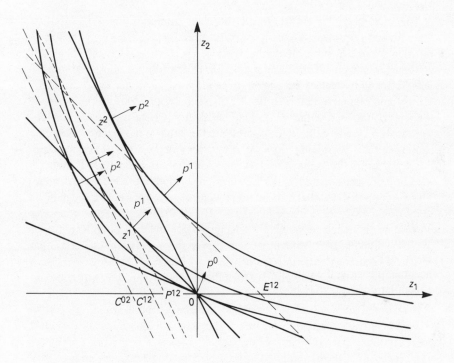

Figure 3.3:   Gains from trade measured by trade variations

unreliable indicator to use in the space of trades, as opposed to the space of quantities produced and consumed depicted in Figure 3.2.

Using situation 1 as a base, the equivalent trade-variation in going from situation 1 to situation 2 is measured by the distance from the origin to E^{12} in units of commodity 1. It measures the trade *deficit* the country would have to run if in situation 1 at prices p^1 it wanted to enjoy the standard of living that obtains in situation 2. In contrast, the distance from the origin to C^{12}, which is the compensating trade-variation with prices p^2 as a base, measures the same improvement in standard of living between situation 1 and situation 2 by the trade *surplus* the country would have to run if, in situation 2, it were to have its standard of living lowered to the level of situation 1.

So far, the trade surpluses and deficits we have defined in terms of Hicks's four welfare measures are purely hypothetical constructs, not corresponding to any actual surpluses or deficits that might be observed in a country's balance of trade. But for the mercantilist writers and their latter-day successors, these surpluses and deficits have always been something very real. How can we make the connection?

The answer is to be found in the dual approach to the country's maximization problem. Virtually every mercantilist, in theory as well as in practice (compare with Heckscher, 1955), has insisted that the means of subsistence and survival of the population be met; but no more. Of course, what is meant by 'subsistence level' depends very much on the culture of the society and objective realities. But if it is social policy that this subsistence level be maintained, whatever it may be, then any deterioration in a country's terms of trade will require a deficit in the balance of trade, whether this is financed by borrowing, foreign aid or loss of reserves. Likewise, any improvement in the terms of trade will provide some slack which, if mercantilist policies are adhered to, will result in a surplus in the balance of trade. The question arises, what will be done with this surplus? Perhaps it will be saved for a rainy day, or perhaps it will go to building up the country's power and influence by making loans and grants to other countries. Under this dual hypothesis, the hypothetical Hicksian measure of compensating variation becomes transformed into an actual observed measure of the country's balance of trade. The observed balance of trade is then a valid measure of the country's gains from trade.

A different mechanism may lead to the same result. Hicks (1953), in trying to find an explanation for the 'dollar shortage', assumed, as though it were obvious, that any external event that worsened a country's terms of trade (such as – in his analysis – import-competing technical change in a foreign country) would lead to a deficit in the country's balance of trade (or payments). None of the subsequent literature spawned by Hicks's paper questioned this cause-and-effect relationship (see, for example, Johnson, 1959). An explanation had been provided, however, by Laursen and Metzler (1950, p. 286). Their reasoning was that a worsening of the terms of trade would lead people to reduce their saving in order to partially preserve their previous standard of living, and conversely an improvement of the terms of trade would improve their standard of living and thus increase their propensity to save. Starting from balanced trade, the first would lead to a deficit, and the second to a surplus, in the balance of trade. As contemporary economists have pointed out (see, for example, Obstfeld, 1982; Svensson and Razin, 1983), and as Laursen and Metzler fully recognized, on the basis of pure intertemporal analysis the cause-and-effect relationship could just as well go the other way around (in which case a trade *deficit* would provide a better indicator of the gains from trade, in accordance with the above equivalent-variation criterion). The point is, however, that one can make a perfectly reasonable case for inferring gains from trade from empirical data showing a 'favourable' balance of trade. The dual criterion of maximizing the balance of trade subject to a standard-of-living constraint is simply an extreme form of the Laursen–Metzler effect.

It has been mentioned previously that a principal mercantilist objective has been promotion of a country's *relative* productive capacity, or *power*. Under the dual criterion of maximization of the balance of trade subject to a standard-of-living constraint, it is clear that only the relative position of a country matters. This relative position is exactly what Misselden meant by the *balance* of trade. Even if the objective includes not only power but also the achievement of higher absolute wealth, it is obvious that this will require only a high *relative* share of the world's purchasing power. Nowhere is this idea stated more pithily than in Locke (1696, p. 15):

> Riches do not consist in having more Gold and Silver, but in having more in proportion, than the rest of the World, or than our Neighbours, whereby we are enabled to procure to ourselves a greater Plenty of the Conveniencies of Life than comes within the reach of Neighbouring Kingdoms and States, who, sharing the Gold and Silver of the World in less proportion, want the means of Plenty and Power, and so are Poorer. Nor would they be one jot the Richer, if by discovery of new Mines the quantity of Gold and Silver in the World becoming twice as much as it is, their shares of them should be doubled.

In the discussions that took place in the 1940s concerning the so-called 'dollar shortage', the emphasis was on 'competitive power' and the world *distribution* of welfare (Balogh, 1946). Stolper (1950, p. 285), in trying to explain Balogh's thesis, suggested that, 'it may be that foreign countries, particularly those who have suffered from the war, wish to reach their pre-war standard of living. Or it may be that foreign countries wish (subconsciously or consciously) to maintain about the same ratio in their standard of living to that of the United States as existed before the war'. MacDougall (1957, pp. 71–2) suggested that, as a consequence of an increase in productivity in the United States, 'other countries will attempt in vain to emulate the higher standard of living in the United States that results from her higher productivity, and so tend constantly to live beyond their means'. In a similar vein, Hatsopoulos, Krugman and Summers (1988, p. 299) stated: 'We would not view the United States as competitive unless it is able in the long run to maintain a rate of growth in living standards that keeps pace with that of the rest of the industrial world'. Such hypotheses require one, of course, to adopt a cardinal measure of welfare; otherwise it would not be possible to compare the welfare of two countries. But a money measure of welfare such as the equivalent variation exactly fills the bill.

Following Hicks's (1953) seminal article, a flood of contributions appeared attempting to find conditions under which technical change in one country would lead to a deterioration in the terms of trade of another, and thus 'dollar shortage'. The conditions for this to take place turned out to be so narrow that atrocious terminology such as 'ultra-anti-trade-biased' (Johnson, 1959) had to be devised to describe them. However, if it is required only that a technical change in one country increase its welfare *relatively* to that of the foreign country, that is, that the foreign country's welfare decline *relatively* to but not necessarily absolutely to that of the progressive country, a considerably less stringent set of conditions is needed to produce the result. In the following and final section, the corresponding theoretical exercise is carried out.

The effect of technical change on countries' relative welfares

Let country k's demand function $h_j^k(p_1, p_2, Y^k)$ for commodity j – where p_i is the price of commodity i, assumed the same in both countries, and Y^k is country k's disposable income – be generated by a utility function $U^k(x_1^k, x_2^k)$ where x_j^k is the amount of commodity k consumed in country k. Let $\Pi^k(p_1, p_2, l_1^k, l_2^k)$ be country k's national-product function, which maximizes the value $p_1 y_1^k + p_2 y_2^k$ of country k's national product over the production-possibility set:

$$Y^k(l_1^k, l_2^k) = \{(y_1^k, y_2^k) \mid y_i^k = f_i^k(v_{1i}^k, v_{2i}^k) \ (j = 1, 2), \ v_{i1}^k + v_{i2}^k = l_i^k \ (i = 1, 2)\},$$

where f_j^k is the production function for commodity j in country k – assumed to be concave and homogeneous of first degree; v_{ij}^k is the amount of factor i allocated to industry j in country k; and l_i^k is country k's endowment in factor i. We may define country k's *indirect trade-utility function* by:

$$\hat{V}^k(p_1, p_2, D^k, l_1^k, l_2^k) = V^k(p_1, p_2, \Pi^k(p_1, p_2, l_1^k, l_2^k) + D^k) = \tag{1}$$
$$U^k(h_1^k(p_1, p_2, \Pi^k(p_1, p_2, l_1^k, l_2^k) + D^k), h_2^k(p_1, p_2, \Pi^k(p_1, p_2, l_1^k, l_2^k) + D^k)),$$

where $V^k(p_1, p_2, Y^k)$ is the consumers' aggregate indirect utility function and D^k is the deficit in country k's balance of trade.

We shall consider the factor endowments l_i^k to be measured in efficiency units, so that an increase in l_i^k is interpreted as a factor-augmenting improvement in the productive power of factor i in country k. Assuming trade to be balanced between the two countries under consideration, we may define the *potential-welfare function* for country k by:

$$W^k(l_1^1, l_2^1, l_1^2, l_2^2) = \hat{V}^k(\bar{p}_1, \bar{p}_2(l_1^1, l_2^1, l_1^2, l_2^2), 0; l_1^k, l_2^k), \tag{2}$$

where the price of commodity 1, p_1, is taken as numéraire and held constant ($= \bar{p}_1$), and the function $\bar{p}_2(\cdot)$ is defined implicitly by the condition for world equilibrium:

$$\hat{h}_2^1(\bar{p}_1, \bar{p}_2(\cdot), D^1; l_1^1, l_2^1) + \hat{h}_2^2(\bar{p}_1, \bar{p}_2(\cdot), D^1; l_1^2, l_2^2) = 0, \tag{3}$$

where $\hat{h}_j^k(\cdot)$ is country k's trade-demand function for commodity j, defined by:

$$\hat{h}_j^k(p_1, p_2, D^k; l_1^k, l_2^k) = h_j^k(p_1, p_2, \Pi^k(p_1, p_2, l_1^k, l_2^k)) - \hat{y}_j^k(p_1, p_2, l_1^k, l_2^k) \tag{4}$$

where $\hat{y}_j^k = \partial \Pi^k / \partial p_j$ is the Rybczynski (supply) function for commodity j.

Uniform technical progress in country 2
I consider first the case in which there is uniform factor-augmenting technical improvement in country 2, the effect of which on country k's potential welfare is measured by a scale parameter, λ, by which country 2's factor endowments are multiplied. I shall assume that preferences within each country are identical and homothetic; from this it follows that both commodities are superior goods. Later it will be assumed that preferences are also identical between countries. We define the respective countries' potential welfares and the world price of commodity 2 as functions of the two countries' factor endowments and this scale parameter:

$$\begin{aligned}
\breve{W}^k(l_1^1, l_2^1, l_1^2, l_2^2, \lambda) &= W^k(l_1^1, l_2^1, \lambda l_1^2, \lambda l_2^2) \quad (k = 1, 2), \\
\breve{p}_2(l_1^1, l_2^1, l_1^2, l_2^2, \lambda) &= \bar{p}_2(l_1^1, l_2^1, \lambda l_1^2, \lambda l_2^2).
\end{aligned} \tag{5}$$

From definitions (5) and (2) we obtain:

$$\begin{aligned}
\frac{\partial \breve{W}^1}{\partial \lambda} &= \frac{\partial \hat{V}^1}{\partial p_2} \frac{\partial \breve{p}_2}{\partial \lambda}, \\
\frac{\partial \breve{W}^2}{\partial \lambda} &= \frac{\partial \hat{V}^2}{\partial p_2} \frac{\partial \breve{p}_2}{\partial \lambda} + \frac{\partial \hat{V}^2}{\partial l_1^2} l_1^2 + \frac{\partial \hat{V}^2}{\partial l_2^2} l_2^2.
\end{aligned} \tag{6}$$

Now, from equation (3) (replacing $\bar{p}_2(\cdot)$ by $\breve{p}_2(\cdot)$) we find that:

$$\frac{\partial \breve{p}_2}{\partial \lambda} = - \frac{\dfrac{\partial \hat{h}_2^2}{\partial l_1^2} l_1^2 + \dfrac{\partial \hat{h}_2^2}{\partial l_2^2} l_2^2}{\dfrac{\partial \hat{h}_2^1}{\partial p_2} + \dfrac{\partial \hat{h}_2^2}{\partial p_2}} \tag{7}$$

To evaluate the numerator, we see from (4) that:

$$\frac{\partial \hat{h}_j^2}{\partial l_i^2} = \frac{\partial h_j^2}{\partial Y^2} w_i^2 - \frac{\partial \hat{y}_j^2}{\partial l_i^2},$$

(8)

where we use the fact that $\partial \Pi^2/\partial l_i^2 = w_i^2$, hence – using the property $\partial h_j^2/\partial Y^2 = x_j^2/Y^2$ from homotheticity of preferences, as well as the homogeneity of $\hat{y}_j^2$ of degree 1 in the factor endowments:

$$\sum_{i=1}^{2} \frac{\partial \hat{h}_j^2}{\partial l_i^2} l_i^2 = \frac{\partial h_j^2}{\partial Y^2} [w_1^2 l_1^2 + w_2^2 l_2^2] - \left[\frac{\partial \hat{y}_j^2}{\partial l_1^2} l_1^2 + \frac{\partial \hat{y}_j^2}{\partial l_2^2} l_2^2\right]$$

$$= \frac{\partial h_j^2}{\partial Y^2} Y^2 - y_j^2$$

$$= \frac{x_j^2}{Y^2} Y^2 - y_j^2 = x_j^2 - y_j^2 = z_j^2.$$

Accordingly, (7) becomes:

$$\frac{\partial \breve{p}_2}{\partial \lambda} = -\frac{z_2^2}{\dfrac{\partial \hat{h}_2^1}{\partial p_2} + \dfrac{\partial \hat{h}_2^2}{\partial p_2}} = \frac{p_2 z_2^2 / x_2^1}{\eta^1 + \eta^2 - 1},$$

(9)

where

$$\eta^k = -\frac{p_j}{\hat{h}_j^k} \frac{\partial \hat{h}_j^k}{\partial p_j} \, (j \neq k)$$

is country k's elasticity of demand for imports (see, for example, Chipman, 1987, p. 944). Since $\eta^1 + \eta^2 - 1 > 0$ is the well-known 'Marshall–Lerner condition' of dynamic stability, formula (9) confirms the well-known fact that a uniform technical improvement in country 2 will lower p_2, that is, worsen country 2's terms of trade.

Returning to (6) we see from (1) that:

$$\frac{\partial \hat{V}^k}{\partial l_i^k} = \frac{\partial V^k}{\partial Y^k} w_i^k$$

(10)

hence

$$\sum_{i=1}^{2} \frac{\partial \hat{V}^k}{\partial l_i^k} l_i^k = \frac{\partial V^k}{\partial Y^k} \sum_{i=1}^{2} w_i^k l_i^k = \frac{\partial V^k}{\partial Y^k} Y^k.$$

Using these relations as well as the Antonelli–Allen–Roy partial differential equation,

$$\frac{\partial \hat{V}^k}{\partial p_i} = -\frac{\partial \hat{V}^k}{\partial D^k} \hat{h}_j^k, \tag{11}$$

substitution of (9) in (6) gives:

$$\frac{\partial \breve{W}^1}{\partial \lambda} = -\frac{\partial \hat{V}^1}{\partial D^1} \frac{p_2 z_2^2}{\eta^1 + \eta^2 - 1}$$

$$\frac{\partial \breve{W}^2}{\partial \lambda} = \frac{\partial \hat{V}^2}{\partial D^2} \left[Y^2 + \frac{p_2 z_2^2}{\eta^1 + \eta^2 - 1} \right]. \tag{12}$$

Now from (1) we have:

$$\frac{\partial \hat{V}^k}{\partial D^k} = \frac{\partial V^k}{\partial Y^k}. \tag{13}$$

From the assumption that preferences in each country are homothetic and representable by a utility function that is homogeneous of degree 1, and that preferences as between the two countries are identical, we have:

$$V^k(p_1, p_2, Y^k) = Y^k V^k(p_1, p_2, 1) \equiv Y^k \mu(p_1, p_2),$$

where $1/\mu(p_1, p_2)$ may be interpreted as a cost-of-living index. Accordingly, we have:

$$\frac{\partial \hat{V}^k}{\partial D^k} = \frac{\partial V^k}{\partial Y^k} = \mu. \tag{14}$$

It follows that:

$$\frac{\partial \hat{W}^1}{\partial \lambda} = \mu \frac{-p_2 z_2^2}{\eta^1 + \eta^2 - 1}$$

$$\frac{\partial \hat{W}^2}{\partial \lambda} = \mu \left[Y^2 + \frac{p_2 z_2^2}{\eta^1 + \eta^2 - 1} \right],$$

(15)

and therefore:

$$\frac{\partial \hat{W}^2}{\partial \lambda} - \frac{\partial \hat{W}^1}{\partial \lambda} = \mu \left[Y^2 + 2\frac{p_2 z_2^2}{\eta^1 + \eta^2 - 1} \right].$$

(16)

From these results we may now draw the following conclusions:

Theorem 1.   *Let country 2 experience uniform technical improvement. Then country 1's potential welfare always increases. Furthermore:*
(a) Country 2's potential welfare increases if and only if:

$$\frac{p_2 \mid z_2^2 \mid}{Y^2} < \eta^1 + \eta^2 - 1;$$

in words: if and only if the share of exports in country 2's national income is less than the sum of the two countries' elasticities of demand for imports minus one. Thus, the condition:

$$\frac{p_2 \mid z_2^2 \mid}{Y^2} > \eta^1 + \eta^2 - 1,$$

is necessary and sufficient for country 2 to experience 'immiserizing growth' (compare with Bhagwati 1958).
(b) Country 2's potential welfare increases more than country 1's if and only if:

$$\frac{p_2 \mid z_2^2 \mid}{Y^2} < \frac{\eta^1 + \eta^2 - 1}{2}.$$

Thus, country 1's potential welfare increases more than country 2's if and only if:

$$\frac{p_2 \mid z_2^2 \mid}{Y^2} > \frac{\eta^1 + \eta^2 - 1}{2}.$$

Thus, for both countries to gain, and for country 1 to gain more than country 2, it is necessary and sufficient that:

$$\frac{\eta^1 + \eta^2 - 1}{2} < \frac{p_2 \, | \, z_2^2 \, |}{Y^2} < \eta^1 + \eta^2 - 1.$$

Factor-augmenting technical progress in country 2

I shall adopt the convention that labels of the commodities and factors are so chosen that industry 1 (country 2's import-competing industry) uses factor 1 relatively intensively, and industry 2 (country 2's export industry) uses factor 2 relatively intensively. From (2) and the definition of $\bar{p}_2(\cdot)$ in (3) we have:

$$
\begin{aligned}
\frac{\partial W^1}{\partial l_i^2} &= \frac{\partial \hat{V}^1}{\partial p_2} \frac{\partial \bar{p}_2}{\partial l_i^2} \\
\frac{\partial W^2}{\partial l_i^2} &= \frac{\partial \hat{V}^2}{\partial p_2} \frac{\partial \bar{p}_2}{\partial l_i^2} + \frac{\partial \hat{V}^2}{\partial l_i^2}.
\end{aligned}
\tag{17}
$$

From (3) we have:

$$
\frac{\partial \bar{p}_2}{\partial l_i^2} = - \frac{\dfrac{\partial \hat{h}_2^2}{\partial l_i^2}}{\dfrac{\partial \hat{h}_2^1}{\partial p_2} + \dfrac{\partial \hat{h}_2^2}{\partial p_2}},
\tag{18}
$$

and applying Samuelson's (1953) reciprocity theorem to (8) we have:

$$
\frac{\partial \hat{h}_2^2}{\partial l_i^2} = \frac{\partial h_2^2}{\partial Y^2} w_i^2 - \frac{\partial \hat{w}_i^2}{\partial p_2} = \frac{w_i^2}{p_2} \left[p_2 \frac{\partial h_2^2}{\partial Y^2} - \frac{p_2}{w_i^2} \frac{\partial \hat{w}_i^2}{\partial p_2} \right].
\tag{19}
$$

Accordingly, using (11), (17) and (18):

$$
\begin{aligned}
\frac{\partial W^1}{\partial l_i^2} &= \frac{\partial \hat{V}^1}{\partial D^1} w_i^2 \frac{\omega_{i2}^2 - m_2^2}{\eta^1 + \eta^2 - 1} \\
\frac{\partial W^2}{\partial l_i^2} &= \frac{\partial \hat{V}^1}{\partial D^2} w_i^2 \left[1 - \frac{\omega_{i2}^2 - m_2^2}{\eta^1 + \eta^2 - 1} \right],
\end{aligned}
\tag{20}
$$

where

$$\omega_{ij}^k = \frac{p_j}{w_i^2}\frac{\partial \hat{w}_i^k}{\partial p_i} \quad \text{and} \quad m_j^k = p_j\frac{\partial h_j^k}{\partial Y^k}$$

define the Stolper–Samuelson elasticity of country 2's ith factor rental with respect to its jth factor price, and country k's marginal propensity to consume commodity j. Applying (14) we then obtain:

$$\frac{\partial \hat{w}^2}{\partial l_i^2} = \frac{\partial \hat{w}^1}{\partial l_i^2}\mu w_i\left[1 - 2\frac{\omega_{i2}^2 - m_2^2}{\eta^1 + \eta^2 - 1}\right]. \tag{21}$$

If $i = 1$, that is, the factor-augmenting improvement occurs in country 2's import-competing industry, then $\omega_{i2}^2 < 0$ by the Stolper–Samuelson theorem, hence from (20) we have immediately that $\partial W^1/\partial l_1^2 < 0$ and $\partial W^2/\partial l_1^2 > 0$; that is, country 1 loses and country 2 gains, absolutely as well as relatively. To examine the subtleties of relative versus absolute gains, therefore, I will focus on the case $i = 2$, in which country 2's factor-augmenting improvement occurs in the factor used relatively intensively in its export industry. The following theorem may be stated as a consequence of the above analysis.

Theorem 2.   *Let country 2 experience a factor-augmenting improvement in the factor used relatively intensively in its export industry (industry 2). Then country 1's potential welfare always increases (since* $\omega_{22}^2 > 1 > m_2^2$ *by the Stolper–Samuelson theorem and the superiority of commodity 1).*

(a) Country 2's potential welfare increases if and only if:

$$\omega_{22}^2 - m_2^2 < \eta^1 + \eta^2 - 1;$$

in words: if and only if the excess in country 2 of the elasticity of the rental of factor 2 with respect to the price of commodity 2 over the marginal propensity to consume commodity 2 exceeds the sum of the two countries' elasticities of demand for imports minus one. Thus, the condition:

$$\omega_{22}^2 - m_2^2 > \eta^1 + \eta^2 - 1$$

is necessary and sufficient for country 2 to experience immiserizing growth.

(b) Country 2's potential welfare increases more than country 1's if and only if:

$$m_2^2 - \omega_{22}^2 < \frac{\eta^1 + \eta^2 - 1}{2}.$$

Thus, for country 1 to gain more than country 2, it is necessary and sufficient that:

$$\omega_{22}^2 - m_2^2 > \frac{\eta^1 + \eta^2 - 1}{2}.$$

Thus, for both countries to gain, and for country 1 to gain more than country 2, it is necessary and sufficient that:

$$\frac{\eta^1 + \eta^2 - 1}{2} < \omega_{22}^2 - m_2^2 < \eta^1 + \eta^2 - 1.$$

These conditions may be related to those of Theorem 1 in the following way. By the Rybczynski theorem:

$$\frac{l_2^2}{y_2^2} \frac{\partial \hat{y}_2^2}{\partial l_2^2} > 1,$$

hence, using Samuelson's reciprocity theorem and homotheticity of preferences:

$$\frac{p_2}{w_2^2} \frac{\partial \hat{w}_2^2}{\partial p_2} = \frac{p_2}{w_2^2} \frac{\partial \hat{y}_2^2}{\partial l_2^2} > \frac{p_2}{w_2^2} \frac{y_2^2}{l_2^2},$$

from which it follows that:

$$\omega_{22}^2 - m_2^2 = \frac{p_2}{w_2^2} \frac{\partial \hat{w}_2^2}{\partial p_2} - p_2 \frac{\partial h_2^2}{\partial Y^2} > \frac{p_2}{w_2^2} \frac{y_2^2}{l_2^2} - p_2 \frac{h_2^2}{Y^2} > \frac{p_2 y_2^2}{Y^2} - \frac{p_2 x_2^2}{Y^2} = \frac{p_2 |z_2^2|}{Y^2}.$$

From this we obtain the following:

Corollary to Theorem 2.   *Under the assumptions of Theorem 2:*
   (a) A necessary condition for country 2's potential welfare to increase is that:

$$\frac{p_2 |z_2^2|}{Y^2} < \eta^1 + \eta^2 - 1$$

A sufficient condition for its potential welfare to decrease (that is, for immiserizing growth to occur) is that:

$$\frac{p_2 \mid z_2^2 \mid}{Y^2} > \eta^1 + \eta^2 - 1.$$

(b) A necessary condition for country 2's potential welfare to increase more than country 1's is that:

$$\frac{p_2 \mid z_2^2 \mid}{Y^2} < \frac{\eta^1 + \eta^2 - 1}{2}.$$

A sufficient condition for country 1's potential welfare to increase more than country 2's is that:

$$\frac{p_2 \mid z_2^2 \mid}{Y^2} > \frac{\eta^1 + \eta^2 - 1}{2}.$$

Notes

* Work supported by NSF grant SES86-07652.
1. The main references on mercantilist theory that I have benefited from are Roscher (1851, 1878), Oncken (1902), Dubois (1903), Suviranta (1923), Viner (1930, 1937), and Schumpeter (1954). I have found the Suviranta monograph particularly helpful in its scholarly approach to the subject.
2. This would provide an answer to Viner's criticism of the 'modern apologists for mercantilism' (1930, p. 264n): 'How a favourable balance of trade can increase the total amount of capital or wealth *within* a country they do not explain'.
3. In discussing Viner's view that the mercantilists confused wealth with money, Schumpeter (1954, p. 362) states (referring to Seligman (1935, p. 60)): 'Yet turns of phrase like Wealth is Money do occur frequently. Sometimes they can easily be disposed of as *façons de parler.* Why, Milles even says that 'Though money were the beames and exchange the very light, yet bullion is the sonne' (quoted by Seligman in his article 'Bullionists'). Shall we infer that he thought bullion and the sun were the same thing?'.
4. The anonymous editor of the 1910 reprint of Mun (1664) states (p. v): 'Mun continued to enjoy great prosperity in his business undertakings, and was able to buy several estates in Kent, and thus lay the foundations of a county family'. Yet Viner (1930, p. 264) would have us believe that: 'The central problem in the interpretation of the mercantilist theories is the discovery of the grounds on which their belief in the desirability of an indefinite accumulation of the precious metals was based'.
5. If they were many, and staggered, they would not even show up in monthly statistics. Indeed, neither would adoption of more roundabout methods of production be included under investment in the national accounts.
6. Mun also gave an example of surplus money being invested in industry in the East Indies which led to the subsequent importation of English metals (p. 26).
7. This may be one of the reasons that led Child (1693, pp. 148–9) to depart from the mercantilist criterion of the gains from trade and replace it by the volume of trade (the value of exports *plus* – rather than *minus* – the value of imports).
8. Cannan (1894, p. 3) made the observation:

It would be ridiculous, indeed, to contend that a nation could be well fed and comfortably clothed and housed by gold alone; but there is no reason to suppose that the wildest mercantilist ever suffered from this delusion. The mere existence of the fable of Midas was a sufficient safeguard.

Viner retorted (1930, p. 265): 'But I have failed to find any references to the Midas fable in the mercantilist literature prior to 1760', as if this proved that the mercantilists *did* suffer from the delusion of Midas. In fact, in a work Viner cited only four pages earlier (p. 261n), Barbon (1696, p. 4) devoted an entire paragraph to a discussion of the Midas myth. Other references may be cited: Bellers (1699; 1987, p. 93); Gramont (1620, p. 12).

9. Compare with Suviranta (1923, p. 77), who seems to have the order of Malynes's and Misselden's tracts reversed. The controversy between Malynes and Misselden proceeded in the order: Malynes (1601), Misselden (1622), Malynes (1622), Misselden (1623) and Malynes (1623). Publication lags were not as long in those days as they have become in modern times!

10. A passage from Malynes (1601, p. 3), also cited by Viner and interpreted by him as revealing in the words 'by selling our home commodities too good cheape: or by buying the forreine commodities too deare' (see also Malynes, 1622, p. 77) a confusion between money and wealth, likewise may be interpreted as referring to the terms of trade. Of course, the terms of trade and balance of trade are not unconnected: a deterioration of the terms of trade may lead to a movement towards deficit in the balance of trade. On this see the next section.

11. Ricardo stated (1815, p. 25): 'There are two ways in which a country may be benefited by trade – one by increase of the general rate of profits ... the other by the abundance of commodities, in which the whole community participates'. Cairnes stated (1874, p. 418): 'the true criterion of the gain on foreign trade [is] the degree in which it cheapens commodities, and renders them more abundant'. And according to Viner (1937, p. 533): 'free trade ....makes *available* to the community *as a whole* a greater physical real income in the form of more of *all* commodities ...'.

Bibliography

Alexander, Sidney S. (1952), 'Effects of a Devaluation on a Trade Balance', International Monetary Fund *Staff Papers*, **2**, April, 263–78.

Balogh, Thomas (1946), 'The United States and the World Economy', *Bulletin of the Oxford University Institute of Statistics*, **8**, October, 309–23.

Barbon, Nicholas (1696), *A Discourse Concerning Coining the New Money Lighter*, London: printed for Richard Chiswell. Facsimile reprint, Farnborough, Hants: Gregg International Publishers Ltd, 1971.

Bellers, John (1699), *Essays About the Poor, Manufactures, Trade, Plantations and Immorality*, London: printed and sold by T. Sowle. Reprinted in George Clarke (ed.), *John Bellers: His Life, Times and Writings*, London: Routledge and Kegan Paul, 1987, 83–112.

Bhagwati, Jagdish N. (1958), 'Immiserizing Growth: A Geometrical Note', *Review of Economic Studies*, **25**, June, 201–205.

Cairnes, J. E. (1874), *Some Leading Principles of Political Economy Newly Expounded*, New York: Harper & Brothers.

Cannan, Edwin (1894), *A History of the Theories of Production and Distribution in English Political Economy from 1776 to 1848*, London: Rivington, Percival & Co.

Child, Sir Josiah (1693), A *New Discourse of Trade*, London: John Everingham. [Includes *Brief Observations Concerning Trade, and Interest of Money*, London: Elizabeth Calvert, 1668; and *A Discourse about Trade*, London: A. Sowle, 1690.] Facsimile reprint in *Sir Josiah Child, Selected Works 1668–1697*, Farnborough, Hants, England: Gregg Press Limited, 1968.

Chipman, John S. (1979), 'The Theory and Application of Trade Utility Functions', in Jerry

R. Green and José Alexandre Scheinkman (eds), *General Equilibrium, Growth and Trade,* New York: Academic Press, 277–96.

Chipman, John S. (1987), 'International Trade', in John Eatwell, Murray Milgate and Peter Newman (eds), *The New Palgrave: A Dictionary of Economics,* Vol. 2, New York: Stockton Press, 922–55.

Chipman, John S. (1992), 'Trade Restrictions Versus Foreign Aid as a Means of Improving a Country's Welfare', in Donald J. Savoie and Irving Brecher (eds), *Equity and Efficiency in Economic Development. Essays in Honour of Benjamin Higgins,* Montreal and Kingston: McGill-Queen's University Press, 315–40.

Chipman, John S. (1994), *On the Concept of International Competitiveness,* Essays in International Finance, Princeton, N.J.: International Finance Section, Department of Economics, Princeton University, forthcoming.

Chipman, John S. and Moore, James C. (1980), 'Compensating Variation, Consumer's Surplus, and Welfare', *American Economic Review,* **70**, December, 933–49.

Crowther, Geoffrey (1941), 'Anglo-American Pitfalls', *Foreign Affairs,* **20**, October, 1–17.

Davenant, Charles (1696), *An Essay on the East-India Trade,* London. Reprinted in Davenant (1698, II) and Davenant (1771), Vol. I, pp. 83–123.

Davenant, Charles (1698), *Discourses on the Publick Revenues, and on the Trade of England,* London: James Knapton. In two Parts: Part I reprinted in Davenant (1771), Vol. I, pp. 125–302; Part II reprinted in Davenant (1771), Vol. I, pp. 343–459 and Vol. II, pp. 1–162.

Davenant, Charles (1771), *The Political and Commercial Works,* London: R. Horstfield, T. Becket and P.A. DeHondt, and T. Cadell, edited and collected by Sir Charles Whitworth, in five volumes.

Dubois, A. (1903), *Précis de l'Histoire des Doctrines Économiques,* Paris: Arthur Rousseau, Editeur.

Gramont, Scipion de (1620), *Le dernier royal. Traicté curieux de l'or et de l'argent,* Paris: Chez Tovssainct dv Bray.

Haberler, Gottfried (1948), 'Dollar Shortage?', in Seymour E. Harris (ed.), *Foreign Economic Policy for the United States,* Cambridge, Mass.: Harvard University Press, 426–45.

Harrod, R. F. (1947), *Are These Hardships Necessary?,* London: Rupert Hart-Davis.

Hatsopoulos, George N., Krugman, Paul R. and Summers, Lawrence H. (1988), 'U.S. Competitiveness: Beyond the Trade Deficit', *Science,* **241**, 15 July, 299–307.

Heckscher, Eli F. (1955), *Mercantilism.* Revised 2nd edition, in two volumes, London: George Allen & Unwin, and New York: Macmillan, 1955.

Hicks, J. R. (1942), 'Consumers' Surplus and Index-Numbers', *Review of Economic Studies,* **9**, Summer, 126–37.

Hicks, J.R. (1953), 'The Long-Run Dollar Problem', *Oxford Economic Papers,* NS, **5**, June, 121–35.

Hume, David (1752), 'Of the Balance of Trade', in David Hume (ed.), *Political Discourses,* Edinburgh: A. Kinkaid and A. Donaldson, 79–100.

Johnson, Harry G. (1954), 'Optimum Tariffs and Retaliation', *Review of Economic Studies,* **21**, (2), 142–53.

Johnson, Harry G. (1959), 'Economic Development and International Trade', *Nationaløkonomisk Tidsskrift,* **97**, Hæfte 5-6, 253–72.

Kindleberger, Charles P. (1943), 'International Monetary Stabilization', in Seymour E. Harris (ed.), *Postwar Economic Problems,* New York: McGraw-Hill, 375–95.

Kindleberger, Charles P. (1950), *The Dollar Shortage,* Cambridge, Mass.: The Technology Press of MIT, and New York: Wiley.

Laursen, Svend and Metzler, Lloyd A. (1950), 'Flexible Exchange Rates and the Theory of Employment', *Review of Economics and Statistics,* **32**, November, 281–99.

Locke, John (1691), *Some Considerations of the Consequences of the Lowering of Interest, and Raising the Value of Money,* London: Awnsham and John Churchill. Second edition, 1696, reprinted in John Locke, *Several Papers Relating to Money, Interest and Trade, & c.,* London: A. and J. Churchill. Facsimile reprint, New York: Augustus M. Kelley Publishers, 1968. First edition reprinted together with a reprint of the first edition of J. R. McCulloch,

Principles of Political Economy, London: Alex. Murray and Son, 1870, 220–360. Page references are to the 1696 edition.

MacDougall, Donald (1957), *The World Dollar Problem,* London: Macmillan.

Machlup, Fritz (1950), 'Three Concepts of the Balance of Payments and the So-Called Dollar Shortage', *Economic Journal,* **60**, March, 46–68.

Malynes, Gerrard de (1601), A *Treatise of the Canker of England's Commonwealth,* London, printed by Richard Field for William Iohnes. Facsimile reprint, Amsterdam: Theatrvm Orbis Terrarvm Ltd, and Norwood, N.J.: Walter J. Johnson, Inc., 1977.

Malynes, Gerrard de (1622), *The Maintenance of Free Trade, According to the Three Essentiall Parts of Traffique,* London, printed by I. L.[egatt] for W. Sheffard. Facsimile reprint, New York: Augustus M. Kelley, Publishers, 1971.

Malynes, Gerrard de (1623), *The Centre of the Circle of Commerce,* London, printed by William Jones, for Nicholas Bourne. Facsimile reprint, Clifton, N.J.: Augustus M. Kelley Publishers, 1973.

McCulloch, J. R. (ed.) (1856), A *Select Collection of Early English Tracts on Commerce.* London. Printed for the Political Economy Club. Reprinted as *Early English Tracts on Commerce,* Cambridge: Cambridge University Press, 1954.

Misselden, Edward (1622), *Free Trade. Or the Meanes to Make Trade Florish,* London, printed by Iohn Leggat, for Simon Waterfon. Facsimile reprint, Amsterdam: Theatrvm Orbis Terrarvm Ltd, and New York: Da Capo Press, 1970.

Misselden, Edward (1623), *The Circle of Commerce. Or the Ballance of Trade, in Defence of free Trade,* London, printed by Iohn Dawson, for Nicholas Bourne. Facsimile reprint, Amsterdam: Theatrvm Orbis Terrarvm Ltd, and New York: Da Capo Press, 1969.

Mun, Thomas (1621), A *Discovrse of Trade, from England vnto the East-Indies,* London, printed by Nicholas Okes for Iohn Pyper. Reprinted in McCulloch (1856), 1–47. Facsimile reprint of 1621 edition, Amsterdam: Theatrvm Orbis Terrarvm Ltd, and New York: Da Capo Press, 1969. Page references are to the latter.

Mun, Thomas (1664), *England's Treasure by Forraign Trade,* London: Thomas Clark. Reprinted in McCulloch (1856), 115–209. Exact reprint of first edition, New York: Macmillan and Co., 1910. Page references are to the latter.

Nurkse, Ragnar (1953), *Problems of Capital Formation in Underdeveloped Countries,* Oxford: Basil Blackwell.

Obstfeld, Maurice (1982), 'Aggregate Spending and the Terms of Trade: Is There a Laursen–Metzler Effect?' *Quarterly Journal of Economics,* **97**, May, 251–70.

Oncken, August (1902), *Geschichte der Nationalökonomie,* Vol. 1, Leipzig: Verlag von C. L. Hirschfeld.

Petty, Sir William (1691a), *Political Arithmetick,* 2nd edition, London, printed for Robert Clavel and Hen. Mortlock.

Petty, Sir William (1691b,c), *The Political Anatomy of Ireland.* To which is added *Verbum Sapienti,* London, printed for D. Brown and W. Rogers.

Pollexfen, John (1697a), A *Discourse of Trade, Coyn, and Paper Credit: and of Ways and Means to Gain, and Retain Riches,* London, printed for Brabazon Aylmer.

Pollexfen, John (1697b), *England and East-India Inconsistent in Their Manufactures,* London.

Ricardo, David (1815), *An Essay on the Influence of a Low Price of Corn on the Profits of Stock,* London: John Murray. In Piero Sraffa (ed.), *The Works and Correspondence of David Ricardo,* Vol. 4, Cambridge: Cambridge University Press, 1951, 9–41. Page references are to the latter.

Roscher, Wilhelm (1851), *Zur Geschichte der englischen Volkswirthschaftslehre im sechzehnten und siebzehnten Jahrhundert,* Leipzig: Weidmannsche Buchhandlung. Reprinted in the *Abhandlung der philologisch-historischen Classe der königlich Sächsischen Gesellschaft der Wissenschaften,* **2**, (1857), 1–146.

Roscher, Wilhelm (1878), 'International Trade' and 'The Industrial Protective System', Appendices II and III to William Roscher, *Principles of Political Economy,* in two volumes, New York: Henry Holt & Co., Vol. II, 391–455.

Samuelson, Paul A. (1939), 'The Gains from International Trade', *Canadian Journal of Economics and Political Science,* **5**, May, 195–205.

Samuelson, Paul A. (1953), 'Prices of Factors and Goods in General Equilibrium', *Review of Economic Studies,* **21,** 1–20.

Schumpeter, Joseph A. (1954), *History of Economic Analysis,* New York: Oxford University Press.

Seligman, Edwin R. A. (1935), 'Bullionists', in Edwin R. A. Seligman (ed.), *Encyclopædia of the Social Sciences, Vol.* 3, New York: The Macmillan Co., 60–64.

Smith, Adam (1776), *An Inquiry into the Nature and Causes of the Wealth of Nations,* London: W. Strahan and T. Cadell.

[Smith, Sir Thomas – also attributed to John Hales] (1581), *A Discourse of the Commonwealth of This Realm of England,* London: T. Marshe. New edition edited by Mary Dewar from the Yelverton manuscript, Charlottesville: The University Press of Virginia, 1969.

Steuart, Sir James (1767), *An Inquiry into The Principles of Political Œconomy: Being an essay on the Science of Domestic Policy in Free Nations,* in two volumes, London: A. Millar and T. Cadell. Reprinted in Vols. I–IV of *The Works, Political, Metaphysical, and Chronological, of the late Sir James Steuart,* London: T. Cadell and W. Davies, 1805.

Stolper, Wolfgang (1950), 'Notes on the Dollar Shortage', *American Economic Review,* **40,** June, 285–300.

Suviranta, Bruno (1923), *The Theory of the Balance of Trade in England. A Study in Mercantilism,* Helsingfors, printed by Suomal, Kirjall, Seuran Kirjap, O.Y., 1923.

Svensson, Lars and Razin, Assaf (1983), 'The Terms of Trade and the Current Account: The Harberger–Laursen–Metzler Effect', *Journal of Political Economy,* **91,** February, 97–125.

Tawney, R. H. and Power, Eileen (1924), *Tudor Economic Documents,* in three volumes, London: Longmans, Green and Co.

Viner, Jacob (1930), 'English Theories of Foreign Trade before Adam Smith', *Journal of Political Economy,* **38,** June, August, 249–301, 404–457. Largely reproduced in Viner (1937), 1–118.

Viner, Jacob (1937), *Studies in the Theory of International Trade,* New York: Harper & Brothers.

Woodland, Alan D. (1980), 'Direct and Indirect Trade Utility Functions', *Review of Economic Studies,* **47,** October, 907–26.

4 The international trade system, trade blocs and US trade policies

Dominick Salvatore

Introduction

The world is today at a crossroads in international trade relations. The road taken and the reforms adopted during the next few years will shape the international trading system of the 21st century. The choice is either to move towards more protectionism, bilateralism and fragmentation into a few large trading blocs, or to move in the opposite direction towards a system of freer trade, multilateralism and a truly integrated world trading system.

Which of these diverging directions the world will take depends to a large extent on how the leading industrial nations perceive that they can best solve the major trade problems that they face today. These are the need to stimulate or protect their high-tech sectors and agriculture, as well as to reduce large trade imbalances. My main theme is that, while we cannot determine the details of the future international trading system, we can infer its main features and broad outlines from the need to solve today's international trade problems, and from the constraints imposed by what is politically feasible. It is within this context that US trade policies can best be formulated and evaluated.

The international trade system

In order to understand present US trade problems and evaluate US trade policies, it is necessary to review quickly the operation of the present trading system. The conduct of international trade under the present international economic system is regulated by the General Agreements on Tariff and Trade (GATT), the organization which was set up after World War II and to which 96 nations (including all the leading industrial nations) now belong. GATT rests on four basic principles: (1) member countries should work to lower trade barriers, especially quotas; (2) any barrier to trade should be applied on a non-discriminatory basis to all member countries (the so-called most-favoured-nations principle); (3) trade concessions cannot be rescinded without compensation to affected trade partners; and (4) trade disputes should be settled through consultation and negotiations within the GATT framework. From 1947 to 1979, GATT sponsored seven rounds of multilateral trade negotiations which cut tariffs on manufactured goods from about 40 per cent in the late 1940s to less than 5 per cent by the early 1980s. This stimulated the growth of international trade, which in turn provided a strong stimulus to the growth of the entire world economy by stimulating productivity. During the 1950s and 1960s, the merchandise trade of industrial countries grew at an average rate of about 8 per cent per year, and this fuelled a growth in world real gross domestic product of over 4 per cent per year. This period can truly be regarded as a golden age of growth and stability.

Despite these successes, several fundamental weaknesses have become evident during the past decade in the conduct of international trade within the GATT framework. The first problem arises from the increasing tendency of nations to bypass GATT rules and impose many new types of non-tariff trade barriers to international trade. These are collectively referred to as 'new protectionism' and include 'voluntary' export restraints, orderly marketing arrangements, anti-dumping measures, countervailing duties, and so on. As much as 50 per cent of world trade is now affected by this new protectionism. Since these new non-tariff trade barriers are applied discriminatorily against the exports of specific nations, they are pushing the world further away from multilateralism and freer trade, and towards bilateralism and more restricted trade. If this process continues, the leading nations may even begin to demand specific shares of each other's markets as a condition for allowing continued access into their own market. The great danger is that the continued proliferation of non-tariff trade barriers will lead to retaliation and a decline in the flow of international trade and specialization. This will result in a misallocation of resources internationally, a slowdown in structural adjustments in mature economies and in growth in developing economies, and in an increase in the spectre of a trade war in which all nations stand to lose.

A second major shortcoming in the operation of the present trade system is that only trade in commodities is regulated by GATT. Trade in services is not. Since the relative importance of services has grown rapidly during the post-war period to the point where today they account for over 50 per cent of value added in industrial countries and constitute over 20 per cent of international trade, the exclusion of services from multilateral trade negotiations represents a serious weakness of the present system. Agriculture is similarly excluded from GATT jurisdiction. As is well known, most nations have very elaborate domestic agricultural support programmes and jealously shield their agriculture from outside competition by a powerful array of subsidies, tariffs, quotas, health regulations and so on. The European Economic Community, Japan and the United States now spend over $20 billion per year on agricultural support programmes. These not only raise costs to consumers but also interfere with the international specialization of resources and lead to serious trade disputes that threaten the entire world trading system. Still another problem of the present international trade system is the slow and cumbersome dispute settlement mechanism of GATT. Cases brought before GATT can drag on for several years, and a party to a trade dispute can block the settlement recommendations.

All these problems are being taken up in the eighth round (the Uruguay round) of multilateral trade negotiations that started in 1986 and is now in the phase of being concluded (after it collapsed at the end of 1990 – the original deadline for its completion). The current round of trade negotiations is scheduled to establish rules for checking the proliferation of the new protectionism and to reverse its trend; to bring services, agriculture and foreign investments into the negotiations; to negotiate international rules for the protection of intellectual property rights; and to improve the dispute settlement mechanism by ensuring more timely decisions and compliance with GATT rulings. The successful completion of the present round would go a long way towards resolving the serious problems that face the present international trade system in general, and the United States in particular, and to restoring international confidence in the system. Success has proven extremely difficult, however. Negotiating rules of conduct to reverse the spread of the new protectionism is extremely difficult, since this often involves issues of national sovereignty. Many of the leading developing countries, such as Brazil and India, have objected to bringing services into the negotiations because of fear that with foreign competition they will be unable to develop such service industries as telecommunications, data processing, banking and insurance, which they regard as crucial to their national development. In agriculture, the European Economic Community and Japan have objected to the original US proposal to remove all farm aid programmes that interfere with international trade by the turn of the century. As will be pointed out later, however, even partial success in these negotiations is crucial to reverse the trend towards protectionism and bilateralism, and to cut the high costs and inefficiencies that result from them.

Trade protectionism and alternative trade systems
As pointed out earlier, the world faces the choice of either moving towards more protectionism, bilateralism and the creation of major trading blocs, or, alternatively, towards a more open trading system, increased multilateralism and greater international specialization. The superiority of the latter over the former system is by no means as clear-cut today as it was a decade ago. There are two reasons for this. One is that many of the new non-tariff trade restrictions are considered part of the arsenal of policies that a nation believes to be necessary in order to achieve some important domestic objective. An example of this is the protection from foreign competition and the

subsidies provided by many leading nations to their national computer and data processing industries. The second is that in recent years the very theoretical foundation of the modern theory of international trade, which for nearly two centuries has been consistently based on the alleged superiority of free trade over trade-restricted trade, is being questioned. Thus, on theoretical grounds as well as on grounds of political feasibility, the world faces a true choice between a more restricted or a more open trading system. The direction chosen during the next few years is crucial to the type of international trade order that the world will have in the 21st century.

Today all the leading countries, including Japan, impose some type of restriction on the importation of automobiles, steel, textiles, consumer electronic products and agricultural products. Practically all provide direct and indirect subsidies of their computer and data processing industries, aircraft industry and most other high-tech industries. Industrial nations regard these direct and indirect trade restrictions and subsidies as crucial either to protect employment in their large mature industries (such as automobile, steel, and textiles) or to promote the growth of high-tech industries (such as the computer and aircraft industries), which are deemed essential for international competitiveness and technological leadership in the future. These goals are promoted with a maze of policy tools in the form of tax benefits and subsidies for research, education and investments, which most nations regard as purely internal matters.

An example of this is Japan's industrial strategy. As is well known, Japan provides protection from foreign competition and a maze of direct and indirect subsidies to an industry targeted for growth. After the industry has grown and is able to meet foreign competition, the industry, with tacit approval and indirect government support, begins to dump the product (that is, to sell products abroad at below domestic production cost) on the world market on a massive scale until it has driven foreign competitors out of business. The industry then raises prices and proclaims full support for the principle of free trade, pointing to its then unprotected industry as a model of efficiency. Japan has successfully and systematically applied this policy to steel, automobiles and computer memory chips, and is now attempting to do the same in computers and financial services. Understandably, Japan is not ready to abandon an industrial strategy that has proved so successful and instrumental in turning it into a first class economic power in just a few decades.

While somewhat less aggressively and generally less successfully, the leading European countries have also used some of these same policies (for example, the Airbus and the Arianne space programme) and, to some extent, so has the United States (through the commercial applications of the technological discoveries arising from its military and space research programmes).

Thus, while the leaders of the major industrial countries pay lip-service to the great benefits and preference for a free trade multilateral trading system, they have moved more and more towards trade protectionism since the mid-1970s. Charging interference with national sovereignty, the leading industrial nations even object to providing information on these new indirect forms of trade protection to GATT. The attempt at the Tokyo round (1974–1977) to negotiate rules of behaviour to limit the uses of these new forms of protectionism and to make them more transparent (for example, by replacing them with equivalent open tariffs) has, in general, not been successful.

The more protectionist trade alternative is also characterized by more bilateral trade deals. This is demonstrated by the incessant movement towards the formation of three major trading blocs in the world today: the European Economic Community (EEC), the United States–Canada–Mexico bloc, and Japan, South East Asian countries and possibly Australia. As is known, the EEC has removed all remaining barriers to the internal flow of goods and resources as of the end of 1992. The United States negotiated a free trade agreement with Canada to remove all barriers to trade in 1988 and with Mexico in 1992. As a result, Japan is becoming increasingly concerned about being excluded by these two trading blocs and in response may set up a free trade area with some other Asian countries and Australia. One could argue along the lines of customs union theory that such free trade areas are second-best trade arrangements if a true world-wide free trade system cannot be achieved under present conditions. The formation of these trade blocs, it is argued, will lead to increased specialization in production and raise world welfare if the net effect is to stimulate trade within each bloc without reducing trade among the blocs. The latter expectation, however, may not materialize and the formation of trading blocs may in fact have a net diverting trade effect. This will impose efficiency and welfare costs on the world similar to those resulting from the oligopolization of previously near perfect competitive markets.

This protectionism and bilateral trade system is also being encouraged indirectly by the recent questioning of the clear superiority of the time-honoured free trade model of international economics by some of today's leading international trade theoreticians. Ricardo's theory of comparative advantage is attacked as being entirely static in nature and not very relevant to international trade in a world characterized by imperfect competition, technological breakthroughs, product cycles, intra-industry trade, multinational corporations and integrated capital markets. Some of these criticisms are not new, but they seem to have been given new force and legitimacy by the fact that some leading theorists are joining in the criticism of traditional comparative advantage. It is now believed that most of today's international trade is based on comparative advantages that have been created by industrial policies (which give rise to new technologies and new industries) rather than by traditional comparative advantage based on inherited international differences in factor endowments across nations.

It is interesting, however, that one of the exponents of this view, Paul Krugman (1987) of the MIT, eventually came to the conclusion that interferences with the free flow of international trade by using industrial policies to create comparative advantages may lead to even greater market imperfections and inefficiencies. Bhagwati (1971), however, pointed out that these imperfections can be corrected with appropriate policies at the source; that is, in the market where the imperfections occur. Similarly, the theory of comparative advantage can be extended to incorporate dynamic changes in the form of new products and new technologies. Furthermore, industrial policies to create comparative advantages face the serious theoretical criticism that it is often very difficult for the government to pick winners in the technological race and from the empirical fact that for each real-world success story one could probably produce a counter-example of a major failure (for example, the abandoned synthetic fuel programme in the United States, the economic losses of the Anglo-French Concorde, and the still higher cost of electricity generated by atomic power). These recent attacks on traditional trade theory in general and comparative advantage in particular, irked Paul Samuelson into stating that he has looked for and found nothing in these recent criticisms of comparative advantage that makes sense: 'They wouldn't pass peer review in any economics journal. I am afraid it's a very superficial diagnosis', and 'Comparative advantage is the only competitive theory that there is'.[1] This is also the view of Jagdish Bhagwati (1988).

The alternative to an international trade order characterized by growing protectionism, bilateralism and the formation of major trading blocs towards which the world seems to be moving, is an international trading system based on a reaffirmation of the principles of free trade and a strengthening of GATT as an institution capable of forcefully promoting such a free trade order in the future. The conclusion (even if only partially successful) of the Uruguay round of trade negotiations would go a long way towards reversing the trend towards growing protectionism and bilateralism in international trade. The current trade negotiations, however, are the most complex and ambitious trade exercise to date, and whatever their outcome they will shape the international trade order for years to come.

Trade policies and the future of the international trading system
While the outcome of the current round of trade negotiations will certainly affect the international economic order of the 21st century, I believe that the world is already locked into an international trade system. Specifically, the world has already, probably irreversibly, moved into an international trade

order characterized by three major trading blocs. The EEC is already a political and economic reality, and the United States–Canada–Mexico free trade area seems to be more or less already agreed upon; the only question is the speed with which the agreements are carried out in practice. Least developed is the Asian trade bloc around Japan. This is still in its early and tentative stage, but the dynamics of the situation are such that its formation is all but inevitable if the other two trading blocs continue to keep to their timetable for implementation.

The only other possibility is that Japan will try to link up and form a free trade area with the United States. I believe this to be unlikely, however, for either of two reasons. If Japan does not succeed in overtaking the United States during the next decade and become the leading economic power, Japan will not want to abandon the industrial policies that allowed it to be the undisputed success story of the post-war period. If Japan does succeed in overtaking the United States, it will be the United States that would not want to form a free trade area with Japan. It is always the dominant economic power of the time that pushes for free trade. This was true for the United Kingdom in the 19th century and for the US during the post-war period until the 1970s. If the United States were clearly to lose its economic predominance, it is very likely that the United States would become even more protectionistic than it is today. Therefore, in the end, the world is likely to end up with the three major trading blocs. The other nations of the world will then gravitate towards one of these blocs based on traditional and commercial links and geographic location.

What the current round of trade negotiations can do is to determine the degree of openness of trade among the three economic blocs. If the Uruguay round achieves only meagre results, commercial relations among the blocs are likely to be seriously restricted and trade frictions will be the order of the day. The total volume of world trade will fail to rise and may even decline, international specialization in production will be limited by the extent of the market of the three blocs, and the stimulating force that trade can play in the growth of the world economy will be seriously constrained. To borrow a phrase from customs union theory, the trade blocs will be for the most part a trade-diverting type. This may preclude many of the dynamic benefits that would flow from a truly free trade world trading system. On the other hand, if the Uruguay round is very successful and achieves its goals, or at least sets the framework for their future achievement, then trade frictions among the three economic blocs are likely to diminish over time, the volume of trade and the flow of resources among the blocs will increase, and many of the dynamic benefits of the truly open and free trade multilateral trade system can be achieved. Conceivably, the movement towards the formation of these trading blocs could even be reversed.

Thus, the international trade order of the 21st century is likely to consist of three major trading blocs, with the degree of openness and economic relations among the blocs determined by the degree of success in the Uruguay round of trade negotiations. Speculating about the outcome of the current multilateral trade negotiations, I would say that it is most unlikely that they will succeed in fully reversing the trend towards the new protectionism and in fully liberalizing trade in services and in agricultural products. What is possible is to negotiate for a reduction of traditional trade barriers and explicit non-tariff trade barriers and accept as inevitable the existence of some implicit non-tariff trade barriers (such as government aid to sunset and sunrise industries that nations might be unwilling to give up). Nations could counteract with appropriate domestic policies the most disturbing effects of implicit foreign non-tariff trade barriers in a manner that minimizes the resulting trade controversies. Success in these negotiations is made more difficult by the loss of the large hegemonic position that the United States enjoyed during the 1950s and 1960s. The most that can be expected from the Uruguay round is that it will succeed in: (1) reasserting the principle of an open multilateral trading system; (2) strengthening the dispute settlement procedure of GATT and raising its status to that of the International Monetary Fund and the World Bank, and (3) setting up the framework and establishing the principle for subsequent trade liberalization in trade in services and agriculture.

The movement towards the formation of three major trading blocs in the world today has been paralleled in the monetary area by the establishment of three major world currencies: the US dollar, the ECU (the European Currency Unit, as the trade-weighted average of the currencies of the EEC countries), and the Japanese yen. It is also likely that the international financial system of the future will be a hybrid system, not too dissimilar to the present system, under which balance-of-payments adjustment is achieved by allowing the various adjustment mechanisms to operate by different degrees depending on the nation and the specific circumstances. Specifically, the future international financial system is likely to be based on the establishment of exchange rate target zones with soft margins, and with each nation intervening in foreign exchange markets, adjusting its money supply, and responding to calls for adjustment policy depending on its circumstances, the domestic targets that it sets for itself, and the relative importance that the nation attaches to these domestic targets. One thing is clear – balance-of-payments adjustment (as any type of adjustment) is painful. Rather than using only one method of adjustment (such as changes in exchange rates, changes in the money supply, or fiscal and other policy changes), each nation will allow all of the mechanisms of adjustment to operate in various degrees to suit its own specific preferences.

The effect on the United States of the full integration of the European economic community in 1992

We now briefly examine the effect on the United States of the full integration of the European Common Market in 1992 and of possible increased EEC protectionism against US exports. We do this by reporting simulations of the McKibbin–Sachs Global Model (Congressional Budget Office, 1990, pp. 21–37). In order to put these effects in their proper perspective, we also report the effects of the EEC92 programme on the EEC itself.

Table 4.1:   Estimates of the effects of 1992 on the EEC and on the US

	1991	1992	1993	1994	1995	2000
EEC						
GDP	1.6	3.0	4.9	6.9	7.4	6.0
CPI	−0.7	−2.2	−3.8	−5.4	−5.8	−4.3
i	1.3	1.4	1.6	0.6	0.0	0.0
i'	0.5	0.4	0.2	0.1	0.0	0.0
R	−0.9	−2.1	−3.4	−5.0	−5.5	−5.3
X	1.9	8.7	15.8	26. 1	30.3	34.5
United States						
GDP	0.0	0.1	0.2	0.3	0.3	0.0
CPI	−0.1	−0.3	−0.4	−0.4	−0.3	−0.1
i	0.0	−0.2	−0.2	0.0	0.1	0.1
i'	0.0	0.1	0.1	0.1	0.1	0.1
R	0.4	0.9	1.5	2.0	2.2	1.8
X	−3.3	−3.9	−5.8	−6.0	−6.2	−5.7

Notes:
GDP = Real gross domestic product − percentage difference from baseline.
CPI = Consumer price index − percentage difference from baseline.
i = Real short-term interest rate − difference from baseline in percentage points.
i' = Real long-term interest rate − difference from base line in percentage points.
R = Real effective exchange rate − foreign currency/home currency.
X = Net exports − difference from baseline in billions of 1989 dollars.

Table 4.1 shows estimates of the effect of the full integration of the EEC in 1992 on real gross domestic product (GDP), consumer price index (CPI), real short-term interest rate (i), real long-term interest rate (i'), the real effective exchange rate (R – defined as the trade-weighted average of the foreign currency/home currency), and net exports (X – trade balance) on the EEC and the United States in each year from 1991 to 1995 and for the year 2000 with a neutral fiscal policy (that is, one that keeps the budget deficit of

EEC members constant in relation to GDP), and without any increase in EEC protectionism. We see from Table 4.1 that the EEC92 reform pro-gramme would raise gross domestic product in the EEC by about 6 per cent above what it would otherwise be by the year 2000 because of better utiliza-tion of economic resources and greater productivity. The spillover effects on US GDP, however, are very small, reaching a peak of 0.3 in 1994 and 1995, and petering out by the year 2000. Because of increased productivity and supply, the EEC consumer prices index will be 5.8 per cent lower than otherwise in 1995 and 4.3 per cent lower in the year 2000. As a repercussion, US prices will fall by 0.4 per cent in 1993 and 1994, but this effect will disappear by the year 2000. Real short- and long-term interest rates rise in the EEC in the short run because of increased demand for credit resulting from increased investment opportunities, but the increase is rather small in the EEC and so are the spillover effects on US interest rates. The EEC92 programme is also expected to result in a 5.3 per cent real depreciation of European currencies and a 1.8 per cent real *appreciation* of the US dollar by the year 2000. These would lead net exports to be $35 billion higher than otherwise in the EEC and $6 billion lower than otherwise in the United States by the end of the century.

From the results reported in Table 4.1, we can conclude that the effects of EEC92 on the United States are rather small. There are two reasons for this. First, the economic effects of EEC92 on the EEC itself are themselves not very large, and so we cannot expect the repercussions or spillover effects on the United States to be large either. Secondly, the United States remains the largest economic unit in the world and, as such, we would expect most outside forces not to affect it very much. But this raises a difficult question. That is, if the EEC92 does not affect the EEC very much and affects the United States even less, why then should the EEC pour so much effort be-hind achieving full integration, and why is the United States and the rest of the world so interested and concerned about what happens in the EEC? The answer may be that the EEC, the United States and the rest of the world believe that the push toward the full integration of the EEC will indeed have very significant, dynamic, long-run effects on the EEC and the rest of the world, but that econometric models, by their very nature, fail to capture the full effect of the dynamic forces at work in the long run. If this is the case, then the usefulness of simulation exercises that use econometric models is limited to showing partial and static effects rather than the full long-run dynamic effects.

Table 4.2 shows the effect on the United States of the increased protec-tionism that might be the outcome of the EEC92 programme. Increased protectionism is here assumed to take the form of holding imports from the United States and the rest of the world to the EEC constant as a proportion

Table 4.2:   *Estimates of the effects of EEC protectionism on the US*

	1991	1992	1993	1994	1995	2000
GDP	–0.1	–0.2	–0.2	–0.3	–0.4	–0.2
CPI	0.1	0.2	0.4	0.6	0.9	0.6
i	–0.2	–0.2	0.0	0.3	0.5	0.6
i'	0.4	0.5	0.5	0.6	0.6	0.4
R	–0.9	–1.2	–1.6	–1.9	–1.7	–1.0
X	3.3	5.1	7.0	9.6	12.3	10.7

Notes:
GDP = Real gross domestic product – percentage difference from baseline.
CPI = Consumer price index – percentage difference from baseline.
i = Real short-term interest rate – difference from baseline in percentage points.
i' = Real long-term interest rate – difference from base line in percentage points.
R = Real effective exchange rate – foreign currency/home currency.
X = Net exports – difference from baseline in billions of 1989 dollars.

of the EEC's GDP, as in the baseline scenario (that is, in the absence of the EEC92 programme). This type of protectionism means that none of the additional growth of the EEC's GDP resulting from the EEC92 programme is spent on US (and on the rest of the world) exports. Table 4.2 shows that the effect of this type of increased EEC protectionism on US real gross domestic product, consumer price index, real short- and long-term interest rates, real effective exchange rate, and net exports is very small indeed. Once again, however, we cannot conclude that this should not be of great concern to the United States, because this type of modelling may not capture the full long-term dynamic effects of such increased EEC protectionism. Furthermore, even if the aggregate effects are small, this does not necessarily mean that some important industries in the United States and in the rest of the world might not suffer significant detrimental effects.

US trade policies
Within the context of the present international trade and financial system, the best that the United States can do is: (1) strive to bring the present Uruguay round to a successful conclusion; (2) press for the completion of a North American free trade area stretching from Yukon to Yucatán; (3) continue aggressive multilateral negotiations through GATT to open more widely the Japanese and European markets to American products; (4) retaliate in a tit-for-tat fashion against Japan and the EEC for the persistent restrictions imposed on US exports; and (5) sponsor and contribute funding for research

and development consortia in crucial high-tech fields in order to counter foreign targeting.

Such a many-pronged trade policy programme is the most likely to establish as close to a level playing field in international trade on a world-wide basis as possible, while at the same time aggressively pursuing second-best benefits from the formation of a North American free trade area. Freeing trade unilaterally is not the answer; but neither is for the United States to withdraw further into protectionism.

At present, the United States is not doing all that it can to bring the Uruguay round to a successful conclusion. In particular, it has allowed its farm lobby to turn the Uruguay round into an all-or-nothing negotiation on eliminating farm support programmes in Europe, instead of trying to open up the European and the Japanese markets more widely to US industrial products. Secondly, while US efforts to establish a free trade area with Canada are proceeding rapidly, this is not the case with extending the free trade area to Mexico. Thirdly, the United States did pursue aggressively multilateral trade negotiations with Europe and Japan (even though success has been meagre). Fourthly, while the United States has been willing occasionally to respond in a tit-for-tat fashion to persistent foreign trade restrictions against US exports (for example, by negotiating the semi-conductor agreement with Japan to open up 20 per cent of the Japanese market to US producers), its response has generally been slow, half-hearted and often misdirected (who cares about US rice exports to Japan, when Japan consistently barred US exports of supercomputers until it developed its own?). Similarly half-hearted and humble has been the US effort to stimulate high-tech research and commercialization.

The United States, of course, has many trade restrictions against imports. But in the case of Japanese and European products, these were for the most part imposed in response to foreign strategic trade practices, and only after foreigners had gained significant market share in the United States. For example, Japan has captured 34 per cent of the US automobile market through exports and production by transplants, while the United States has less than 3 per cent of the Japanese market in telecommunications and only 6 per cent in supercomputers, despite the greater efficiency of US firms. Similarly, US ineptitude allowed the establishment and growth of Airbus industries in Europe through huge direct government subsidies, to the point where the United States no longer dominates this field. What is remarkable is that economists often argue whether the United States, Japan or Europe is the more protectionistic. The results of numerous empirical studies indicate that the degree of protectionism is similar in all three. This is nonsense. If that were true we would find that the price of traded goods would be more or less the same in all three areas, except for transportation costs. What we find instead is that prices are much lower in the United States than in Japan and Europe, even for products manufactured in Japan and Europe. This can only mean one thing – that there must be non-transparent restrictions in Japan and Europe that effectively hamper US exports.

The United States has much to learn from Europe. For example, while US automobile producers are generally more efficient than their European counterparts, US producers are incurring huge losses and rapidly losing market share to Japanese firms, while European producers are not. Europe was not even a factor in the commercial aircraft and computer fields a decade ago. Thanks to their policies, they are now competitors that American producers must reckon with. Call it naïvety, a misguided desire to impose a free trade philosophy on the rest of the world, or whatever. The truth is that the United States has lost competitiveness to Japan and Europe in one major industry after another in a very rapid and dramatic manner. Another decade like the 1980s and the United States will have lost its technological leadership in most fields to Japan, and perhaps even to Europe. Clearly, the United States must change its ways if it wants to remain a major player in the high-tech field. Unfortunately, the required changes and reorientation in trade policies only now seem to be forthcoming from the present leadership in Washington.

Summary and conclusions
In international trade, the world has already and probably irreversibly moved into an international trade order characterized by three major trading blocs. The EEC is already a political and economic reality, and the United States–Canada–Mexico free trade area seems to be more or less already agreed upon, the only question being the speed with which the agreements are carried out in practice. Least developed is the Asian trade bloc around Japan, but the dynamics of the situation are such that its formation is all but inevitable if the other two trading blocs continue to keep to their timetable for implementation.

The most that can realistically be expected from the current Uruguay round of trade negotiations is agreement on procedures to minimize trade friction among the trading blocs, check the spread of trade protectionism, achieve some liberalization in trade in agricultural products and services, and set up the framework for bringing them into GATT. Simulations with a large-scale econometric model indicate that the economic effects on the United States resulting from the full integration of the EEC in 1992 or from a rise in trade protectionism in the EEC will be small on the United States. This, however, may result from the inability of econometric models to pick up the full, long-run dynamic effects from full integration and rising protectionism in the EEC, rather than from the absence of large such effects.

The best policy response by the United States was outlined earlier. The United States, however, has been either unwilling or unable to pursue aggressively most of these policies. Without a rapid and significant reorientation in its trade and industrial policies along the lines indicated earlier, however, the United States will lose technological leadership in most fields to Japan, and perhaps even to Europe, during the present decade.

Note
1.   'The Economists Take Their Lumps,' *US News and World Report*, 13 July 1987, p. 46.

Bibliography

Bhagwati, Jagdish N. (1971), 'The Generalized Theory of Distortions and Welfare', in Jagdish N. Bhagwati (ed.), *International Trade: Selected Readings*, Cambridge, Mass.: The MIT Press, 171–89.

Bhagwati, Jagdish N. (1988), *Ohlin's Lecture in International Trade*, Cambridge, Mass.: The MIT Press.

Congressional Budget Office (1990), *How the Economic Transformations in Europe Affect the United States,* Washington, D.C.: US Government Printing Office.

Corden, M.W. (1987), *Protectionism and Liberalization: A Review of Analytical Issues*, Occasional Paper 54, Washington, D.C.: International Monetary Fund.

Council of Economic Advisors (1988), *Economic Report of the President*, Washington, D.C.: US Government Printing Office.

Hathaway, Dale E. (1987), *Agriculture and GATT: Rewriting the Rules*, Washington, D.C.: Institute for International Economics.

Krugman, Paul (ed.) (1986), *Strategic Trade Policy and The New International Economics*, Cambridge, Mass.: The MIT Press.

Krugman, Paul (1987), 'Is Free Trade Passé?', *Economic Perspectives*, **1**, Autumn, 131–44.

Organization for Economic Co-operation and Development (1985), *Costs and Benefits of Protection*, Paris: OECD.

Salvatore, Dominick (1987a), 'Import Penetration, Exchange Rates, and Protectionism in the United States,' *Journal of Policy Modeling*, **9**, Spring, 125–41.

Salvatore, Dominick (ed.), (1987b), *The New Protectionist Threat to World Welfare*, New York and Amsterdam: North-Holland.

Salvatore, Dominick (1988), 'The New Protectionism with Non-Tariff Instruments', in Christopher Saunders (ed.), *Macroeconomic Management and the Enterprise in East and West*, London: Macmillan, 155–82.

Salvatore, Dominick (1989), 'Global Imbalance and the US Policy Responses', in Christopher Saunders and Gary Bersch (eds), *East-West Economic Relations*, London: Macmillan, 37–54.

Salvatore, Dominick (1990), *The Japanese Trade Challenge and the US Response*, Washington, D.C.: The Economic Policy Institute.

Salvatore, Dominick (ed.) (1991a), *Handbook of National Economic Policies*, Westport, Conn.: Greenwood Press.

Salvatore, Dominick (1991b), 'Trade Protection and Foreign Direct Investment in the United States', *Annals of the American Academy of Political and Social Science*, July, 91–105.

Salvatore, Dominick (ed.) (1992), *Handbook of National Trade Policies*, Amsterdam: North-Holland and Westport, Conn.: Greenwood Press.

Salvatore, Dominick (ed.) (1993a), *International Economics*, 4th edn, New York: Macmillan.

Salvatore, Dominick (ed.) (1993b), *Protectionism and World Welfare*, New York: Cambridge University Press.

5   The macroeconomic effects of exchange rate instability

Steven Pressman

Economic debate over fixed versus flexible exchange has had a long and chequered history. According to Schumpeter (1954, p. 732), the classical economists found the automatic mechanisms of the fixed rate gold standard 'a moral as well as an economic ideal'. In this century, John Maynard Keynes (1971) argued for fixed exchange rates because they promoted foreign trade by reducing the cost and uncertainty of economic transactions that require crossing national borders.

Yet despite the prestige of their supporters and the power of their arguments, systems of fixed exchange rates have been subject to severe criticism. The fixed exchange rates established by the gold standard did not result in stable prices, and macroeconomic performance was not especially good when the gold standard was in effect (Cooper, 1982). Moreover, while exchange rates were relatively fixed under the Bretton Woods system, many countries experienced continual balance-of-payments problems (Friedman, 1953). Those nations running trade deficits tended to impose import restrictions which, it has been argued, hurt the world economy in the post–war era. More recently, the European Monetary System put into place a regime of relatively fixed exchange rates. However, this system has been faulted for causing 'Eurosclerosis', the slow economic growth and high unemployment rates that have plagued Europe in the 1980s (Tsoukalis, 1989).

The concern of this paper is to examine the advantages and disadvantages of fixed and flexible exchange rates in a global economy. The focus of Section 1 is on a more detailed look at the theoretical arguments for fixed and flexible exchange rates. Section 2 then evaluates the macroeconomic impact of fixed versus flexible exchange rates with a view to determining whether there has been a clear-cut gain from either of these regimes. Section 3 concludes by drawing out the policy implications of what we have learned.

Section 1

The debate over fixed versus flexible exchange rates is primarily a dispute concerning the real world consequences of both types of exchange rate regime. Advocates of flexible exchange rates (Friedman (1953), Friedman and Roosa (1967), Johnson (1972) and Haberler (1970)) have argued that flexible exchange rates would free traditional macroeconomic policies from concern about balance-of-payments problems. This would allow national policy-makers to pursue domestic economic objectives such as full employment and low inflation.

Supporters of flexible exchange rates also argue that because flexible exchange rates quickly and efficiently eliminate balance-of-payments problems they would reduce the demand for protectionism. Trade would thus grow more rapidly – to the benefit of the entire world economy. And with more trade would come greater specialization of production and hence greater productivity growth in the world economy.

The case for fixed exchange rates rests on the negative effects of volatile exchange rates and the argument that floating exchange rates quickly become volatile exchange rates. Five consequences of exchange rate volatility have been mentioned most frequently as reasons for concern.

First, wildly fluctuating exchange rates may increase the cost of foreign trade. An American importer placing an order for Japanese goods must agree on a price denominated in Japanese yen. In the short run, the importer can hedge on the future price of these goods through the purchase of Japanese yen at its 90 day forward price. But even in this case there may be real economic costs, since studies have found that the price of obtaining foreign exchange increases along with exchange rate volatility (Fieleke, 1975).

It is in the long run, however, that the costs are deadly to foreign trade. To succeed, an American importer or a foreign exporter must obtain an adequate market share. This is a long-run risk that cannot be hedged against through the purchase of foreign exchange futures. Rather, it requires making inroads into a country through competitive price and quality. When market share is important, foreign trade will be more risky the more volatile the exchange rates. If returns do not go up to compensate for the greater risk, there will be less trade. Even if returns do rise to compensate for greater risk, this too will reduce the amount of foreign trade that occurs, for it will increase the price of imported goods.[1]

A second negative consequence of volatile exchange rates is that businesses may focus on making money through exchange rate fluctuations rather than by producing goods and services more efficiently. In particular, internal firm resources may be put towards finance and speculation in foreign exchange markets rather than towards research and development. Lichtenberg and Siegel (1991) have shown that at the level of the firm, the more money spent on research and development, the faster productivity grows. The implication is that by reducing research and development spending by firms, volatile exchange rates may hinder productivity growth in the world economy.

In addition, volatile exchange rates will likely be associated with volatile sales. Fluctuating sales, in turn, mean greater fluctuations in employment. When sales are slow, firms will lay off workers, and when the economy is booming workers will have good opportunities to leave their current jobs and seek employment at higher pay elsewhere. These actions may well reduce firm incentives to provide training to their employees. This, too, may lower productivity growth.

A third problem with volatile exchange rates is that they may increase uncertainty. As Keynes (1964, p. 148) noted in the *General Theory*, uncertainty is not the same thing as risk. Uncertainty arises when individuals are unable to make probability assignments for future events – such as the price of a good many years in the future or the probability of war in the future. The investment decision involves businesses overcoming inherent uncertainty. If exchange rate volatility increases uncertainty, it will reduce investment and economic growth, and increase unemployment. In this instance, exchange rate volatility leads to stagnation in the world economy.

Volatile exchange rates may also increase uncertainty by destabilizing the economy. There is a great deal of evidence that exchange rate values since the early 1970s have been driven by speculation and have been far from the set of rates which would be necessary for balance-of-payments equilibrium (Williamson (1985), Krugman (1989), Cooper (1984)).

When speculation depreciates a nation's exchange rate, the nation exports more and imports less. Domestic production is stimulated and both GDP and employment increase. When exchange rates appreciate, a nation loses its export markets, while imports become cheaper for residents to buy than domestically produced goods. Volatile exchange rates are thus likely to contribute to a more volatile economy. Less stability in the domestic economy is bad in and of itself, but if it also increases uncertainty the damage is much greater.

Finally, exchange rate volatility may affect the relationship between capital and labour to the detriment of workers. Capital can hedge exchange rate volatility in the short run by purchasing future contracts for foreign currencies. But, more importantly, it can hedge in the long run by moving operations abroad. Labour, in contrast, can avail itself of neither of these options. When the domestic currency depreciates, workers will find goods more expensive and, in the long run, they have fewer options than producers to relocate abroad where new jobs are being created. Instead, fearful for their jobs, workers will likely agree to wage givebacks or will accept small wage increases. By contributing to both capital mobility and capital flight, exchange rate volatility is likely to change the functional distribution of income to the detriment of a nation's workers.

Table 5.1: *Exchange rate variability for the G-7 countries*

Country	Exchange rate variability 1961–87	Exchange rate variability 1961–71	Exchange rate variability 1972–87	Percentage change in exchange rate variability (from the 1961–71 period to the 1972–87 period)
Canada	0.234	0.036	0.209	481
France	0.253	0.056	0.232	314
Germany	0.335	0.054	0.255	372
Italy	0.378	0.030	0.338	1027
Japan	0.375	0.032	0.312	875
UK	0.269	0.074	0.213	188
US	0.253	0.032	0.222	594
All (Unweighted average)	0.300	0.045	0.254	

Sources: International Monetary Fund, *International Financial Statistics*, various issues.

Section 2

The previous section identified five potentially negative consequences of volatile exchange rates. Sharp exchange rate fluctuations may reduce international trade, slow down economic growth, destabilize domestic economies and reduce productivity growth, while also making the distribution of income more unequal. This section brings some empirical evidence to bear on these issues. In particular, it contrasts the fixed exchange rate regime which existed until 1972 and the regime of flexible or floating exchange rates that began at that time.

Table 5.1 sets out measures of exchange rate volatility for the group of seven (G-7) countries between 1961 and 1987. Data are presented for all G-7 countries over the entire time period, as well as for the two subperiods 1961–1971 and 1972–1987. The figures in Table 5.1 were derived by first finding the nominal rate of exchange between each set of G-7 nation pairs for each year. The coefficient of variation for each two-nation exchange rate was then calculated, and a coefficient of variation for each nation was derived by averaging the coefficient of variation between that country's exchange rate and the exchange rate of the other six G-7 nations. Figures reported in Table 5.1 are thus unweighted country averages. Using weighted averages gives slightly different figures for each country, but does not change the overall results.

Over the entire 1961–87 period exchange rates were most stable for Canada, France and the United States; they were least stable for Italy and Japan. For the first subperiod (1961–1971), exchange rates were highly stable for all countries. They were most stable for Italy, Japan, the United States and Canada; and they were least stable for the United Kingdom. In the post-Bretton Woods era, exchange rates were significantly more volatile overall. During this period exchange rates were most stable for Canada, the United Kingdom and the United States; Italy and Japan experienced the lowest exchange rate stability.

Table 5.1 also shows that, beginning in 1972, exchange rates became considerably more volatile for each of the G-7 nations. In two cases – Italy and Japan – they became extremely volatile. Italy and Japan had the most stable exchange rates in the pre-Bretton Woods era, but the least stable exchange rates in the post-Bretton Woods era.

These rather dramatic changes in exchange rate variability provide an opportunity to examine the effects of an institutional change on real economic performance. In particular, it lets us examine the real world impact of abandoning the fixed exchange rates of Bretton Woods and allowing exchange rates to fluctuate with little hindrance.

Table 5.2 begins our look at the real economic consequences of exchange rate volatility. It provides data on economic growth rates, the variability of

Table 5.2:   *Economic growth and the growth of international trade for the*
G-7 countries

Year	Average annual growth rate (exports/GDP; %)	Average annual GDP growth rate (%)	Coefficient of variation, GDP growth rate
1961–71	3.20	5.28	0.158
1972–87	2.24	2.93	0.456

Source: OECD, *National Accounts*, Volume 1, *Main Aggregates, 1960–1987*, Paris: OECD, 1989.

economic growth and the growth in foreign trade. In the Bretton Woods era exports grew (as a percentage of GDP) at an annual rate of 3.2 per cent. Since 1971, trade has grown at a much slower rate. The argument that exchange rate stability encourages foreign trade thus far seems to be supported. Likewise, economic growth was both greater and more stable in the 1961–1971 period than in the period following 1971. Consequently, the argument that exchange rate stability encourages greater and more stable economic growth receives some empirical support.[2]

An examination of the relationship between exchange rate variability and these three variables on a country by country basis, however, reveals that no similar relationships hold. The fact that a nation's currency was more stable relative to the other G-7 currencies does not mean that its exports grew (relative to GDP) more rapidly than the exports of other G-7 nations.[3] Japan and Italy, the countries with the least stable exchange rates, had the greatest export growth relative to GDP. In contrast, Canada, which had the most stable currency, had relatively poor export growth.

This lack of a relationship between exchange rate volatility and the growth of a country's exports is to be expected. For any country, the *direction* of change should be more important to export growth than the degree of change in its exchange rate. Nonetheless, a more detailed empirical investigation, employing regression analysis and controlling for the level of a nation's exchange rate, did not find this to be the case. Even when controlling for changes in real exchange rates, a more volatile currency was correlated with faster, rather than slower, export growth.[4]

Looking at country pairs also controls for changes in the level of exchange rates. If exchange rate variability does affect foreign trade, one would expect that two countries with stable exchange rates would experience a large growth in their bilateral trade, while two countries with wildly fluctuating exchange rates would experience only small trade growth. But this does not in fact appear to occur. To take just one striking example, the Canadian dollar and the British pound have been among the most stable exchange rate pairs of the 21 possible combinations for the G-7 nations. However, bilateral trade between Canada and the United Kingdom as a fraction of their joint GDP *fell* between the early 1960s and the late 1980s. Overall, there seems to be no relationship between exchange rate stability for any two of the G-7 countries and growth in their bilateral trade.[5]

What can we conclude about the relationship between exchange rate variability and the growth of trade? For any one country, or subset of the G-7 countries, no relationship seems to exist between exchange rate stability and the growth of international trade. At the level of the entire world economy it seems as though greater exchange rate stability is associated with greater growth in trade. However, it must be remembered that the number of data points that we have is relatively small, and that many things changed in the world economy beginning around 1972. The 1970s saw two major oil shocks, several recessions, a world-wide decline in productivity growth, and the end of European rebuilding following World War II. All or any of these might have been responsible for the slowdown in the growth of foreign trade. Since we cannot control for these events, and since cross sectional analysis fails to show that exchange rate volatility hinders international trade, we ought to remain sceptical regarding the claim that exchange rate stability contributes to greater international trade.

For the same reasons we must remain sceptical about the effects of exchange rate stability on economic growth. While there seems to be a direct relationship between stable exchange rates and faster economic growth at the level of the world economy, no such relationship exists at the level of individual G-7 countries. Likewise, while there seems to be a direct relationship between stable exchange rates and stable rates of economic growth at the level of the world economy, there is no evidence of such a relationship at the country level. Japan, with one of the most volatile exchange rates, had by far the best record of economic growth between 1961 and 1987. It has also had one of the most stable growth paths among the G-7 nations. In contrast, the United Kingdom, with one of the most stable exchange rates, experienced the slowest economic growth of all the G-7 countries, and had by far the greatest variation in its economic growth rate.

Table 5.3 examines the relationship between exchange rate volatility and productivity growth in manufacturing industries. During the era of stable exchange rates, manufacturing productivity grew at an annual rate of 5.7 per cent (unweighted average) for the G-7 countries. After 1971, productivity growth in manufacturing for the G-7 nations was only 4.0 per cent. An examination of the relationship between productivity growth in manufacturing and exchange rate variability for each of the G-7 nations, however,

Table 5.3:   *Productivity growth and real compensation growth in manufac-*
turing for the G-7 countries

Year	Annual productivity growth rates (%)	Annual growth in real compensation (%)	Annual growth in real compensation
			Annual productivity growth rates
1961–71	5.7	5.3	0.92
1972–87	4.0	2.7	0.67

Source: US Department of Labor, *Handbook of Labor Statistics*, Washington, DC: Government Printing Office, 1989.

reveals little correlation between these two variables. If anything, greater exchange rate variability goes hand in hand with greater productivity growth. Italy and Japan, the two nations with the most variable exchange rates, also had the best record of productivity growth over the 1961–87 period. In contrast, Canada, which had the most stable exchange rate, had very slow manufacturing productivity growth. For each of the two subperiods (1961–71 and 1972–87), there is likewise no noticeable relationship between productivity growth and exchange rate stability. Countries with more stable exchange rates have not had greater productivity growth in manufacturing.

Once again, these results should not surprise us. Economists do not understand the determinants of productivity growth or the reasons why productivity growth slowed in the world economy beginning in the early 1970s. In addition, many of the factors that affect productivity growth are likely to be national in origin – things such as pay schemes and the pace of innovation.[6]

One way to control for the effect of national institutions on productivity growth, as well as for any changes in the world economy that might have caused productivity growth to slow for all nations, is to see whether those countries experiencing the greatest increase in exchange rate volatility after 1971 also experienced the greatest productivity slowdown. Table 5.4, which should be compared with Table 5.1, addresses this issue.

Tables 5.1 and 5.4 imply that increased exchange rate volatility does not seem to contribute to declining productivity growth. Italy, the nation with the largest increase in exchange rate volatility, saw its productivity growth fall very little. In contrast, Japan, which also experienced a great increase in exchange rate volatility, saw a large decline in productivity growth. Consequently, we must also remain sceptical regarding the contention that greater exchange rate variability reduces productivity growth. While true for the

Table 5.4: Decline in productivity growth by country

Country	Annual productivity growth rates 1961–71 (%)	Annual productivity growth rates 1972–87 (%)	Percentage decline in productivity growth rates
Canada	4.4	2.6	−41
France	6.6	3.8	−42
Germany	5.7	3.6	−37
Italy	6.1	5.4	−11
Japan	10.4	6.1	−41
UK	3.8	3.6	−5
US	2.9	2.8	−3

Source: US Department of Labor, *Handbook of Labor Statistics*, Washington, D.C.: Government Printing Office, 1989.

entire world economy, this relationship does not seem to hold for individual nations.

Finally, we look at the argument that exchange rate volatility weakens the position of labour relative to capital. For a simple economy it is well known that output (Y) must equal domestic wage income (W) plus domestic profit income (P). Dividing by the number of workers employed (N) and taking rates of changes we get the following relationship:

$$\left(\frac{\dot{Y}}{N}\right) = \left(\frac{W}{N} + \frac{P}{N}\right).$$

For the distribution of income between capital and labour to remain the same over time it must hold that:

$$\left(\frac{\dot{Y}}{N}\right) = \left(\frac{\dot{W}}{N}\right) = \left(\frac{\dot{P}}{N}\right).$$

Here, labour and capital income increase proportionally, and each increases at the same rate as the domestic economy. Were the distribution of income to shift in favour of labour, it would be true that:

$$\left(\frac{\dot{W}}{N}\right) > \left(\frac{\dot{Y}}{N}\right) > \left(\frac{\dot{P}}{N}\right);$$

while if the distribution moved to favour capital:

$$\left(\frac{\dot{W}}{N}\right) < \left(\frac{\dot{Y}}{N}\right) < \left(\frac{\dot{P}}{N}\right).$$

No data exist for *P/N*, but data on real wages and economy-wide productivity exist for all G-7 nations. Moreover, data for just these two variables are relevant for the question at issue. If real wages grow by more than the growth of productivity, it follows that $\%\Delta(W/N) > \%\Delta(P/N)$; conversely, if real wages grow by less than the growth rate of productivity, it follows that $\%\Delta(W/N) < \%\Delta(P/N)$. When real compensation grows by more than productivity, workers obtain a greater fraction of national output, and when real worker compensation rises by less than productivity growth, the wage share falls.

As column 3 of Table 5.3 shows, in the period from 1961 to 1971, labour incomes grew by 92 per cent of the increase in labour productivity. The functional distribution of income thus remained relatively constant in the G-7 nations during this period. From 1972 to 1987, however, labour incomes rose only two-thirds as fast as productivity grew. As exchange rate volatility increased, the bargaining position of capital appears to have improved relative to the bargaining position of labour, with the result that labour was receiving less of its marginal output.

Table 5.5:   *Decline in labour's share of additional manufacturing output by country*

Country	Annual growth in real compensation / Annual productivity growth rate (1961–71)	Annual growth in real compensation / Annual productivity growth rate (1972–87)	Percentage change
Canada	0.71	0.58	–18
France	0.84	0.96	+14
Germany	1.25	1.02	–18
Italy	1.24	0.60	–52
Japan	0.78	0.51	–52
UK	0.96	0.84	–13
US	0.62	0.21	–66

Source: US Department of Labor, *Handbook of Labor Statistics*, Washington, DC: Government Printing Office, 1989.

Table 5.5 carries this analysis one step further by looking at each of the G-7 countries separately. These results also support the argument that greater exchange rate volatility tends to expand profit income more rapidly than labour income. Countries experiencing the greatest increases in exchange rate volatility (Italy, Japan and the United States) also experienced the greatest declines in labour's share of additional output. Conversely, the United Kingdom experienced the smallest increase in exchange rate volatility and only a small decline in labour's share of additional output. Meanwhile, Canada and Germany had moderate increases in exchange rate volatility and moderate declines in labour's share of additional output. The single anomaly – France – experienced a moderate increase in exchange rate volatility, yet labour received a *greater* share of additional output in the post-1971 period than it received between 1961 and 1971. Perhaps this was due to the election of a socialist government in France in the early 1980s, which worked to change the domestic power relationships between capital and labour. Or perhaps it was due to domestic economic policies that have kept levels of foreign direct investment by French firms among the lowest in the developed world (see Schaefer and Strongin, 1989). Alternatively, French labour may have decided to accept higher unemployment in exchange for greater wage gains (see Mishel and Teixeira, 1991, p. 29).

Whatever the reason for this anomaly, it does not detract from the close relationship between exchange rate volatility and declining returns to labour. For all the G-7 countries, the coefficient of correlation between the change in exchange rate variability and the change in labour's share of productivity growth works out at 0.75. While correlation does not prove causation, it does provide some empirical support for the theoretical proposition that greater exchange rate volatility has hurt labour and helped capital. Greater exchange rate volatility thus seems to be an important contributing factor to the rising income inequality over the past two decades.

Section 3

As a result of the breakdown of the Bretton Woods system, exchange rate volatility increased significantly after 1971. This paper has examined the macroeconomic impact of this institutional change.

At the aggregate level, greater exchange rate volatility has led to all the negative consequences that advocates of fixed exchange rates have worried about. After 1971, when exchange rate volatility increased significantly, economic growth slowed and became more variable, export growth slowed among the G-7 nations; productivity growth declined, and the functional distribution of income changed in favour of capital and against labour.

At the level of individual G-7 countries, however, only one of these relationships continues to hold. Those countries experiencing the greatest increase in exchange rate volatility also experienced the greatest decline in labour's share of output. Labour fared much better in those countries whose exchange rate remained more stable.

Firms produce goods abroad to reduce their costs and to reduce the uncertainty of production and trade. One primary cause of uncertainty in the global economy is exchange rate volatility. To protect themselves against sharp exchange rate fluctuations, businesses are more likely to set up production facilities in those countries where they sell goods. But this means moving production from their home country. In this way greater capital mobility has increased the bargaining power of capital relative to labour. Capital can be induced to stay at home, but only if labour agrees to accept much lower wage rates. This will reduce the cost of domestic production and compensate firms for the greater uncertainty of continuing production within the home economy. The policy implication of this analysis is quite clear. By reducing exchange rate volatility, domestic policy-makers can, to some extent, protect the income of most of their domestic citizens.

Notes
1. See Roosa's lecture in Friedman and Roosa (1967).
2. On these points also see Houthakker (1985).
3. On this point also see Bailey, Tavlas and Ulan (1986, 1987).
4. My cross-sectional regression results for the G-7 countries (1961–1987) were as follows:

$$XGROWTH = -0.66 + 11.328 \; XRVOL + 0.255 \; REALXR \qquad R^2 = 0.89;$$
$$\qquad\qquad\qquad (2.418)** \qquad\quad (0.096)$$

where XGROWTH = the annual percentage increase in exports as a fraction of GDP

XRVOL = exchange rate volatility (as reported in Table 5.1)

REALXR = the annual percentage change in a nation's real exchange rate relative to the other G-7 countries

(Standard errors are in parentheses and ** indicates statistical significance at the 0.01 level).
5. For a contrary view see Akhtar and Hilton (1984).
6. See Blinder (1990) and Bailey and Chakrabarti (1988).

References

Akhtar, M. A. and Hilton, R. Spence (1984), 'Effects of Exchange Rate Uncertainty on German and U.S. Trade', Federal Reserve Bank of New York *Quarterly Review*, 9, (1), Spring, 7–16.
Bailey, Martin Neil and Chakrabarti, Alok K. (1988), *Innovation and the Productivity Crisis*, Washington, DC: Brookings Institution.
Bailey, Martin J., Tavlas, George S. and Ulan, Michael (1986), 'Exchange-Rate Variability and Trade Performance: Evidence from the Big Seven Industrial Countries', *Weltwirtschaftliches Archiv*, **122**, 466–77.
Bailey, Martin J., Tavlas, George S. and Ulan, Michael (1987), 'The Impact of Exchange-Rate

Volatility on Export Growth: Some Theoretical Considerations and Empirical Results', *Journal of Policy Modeling*, **9**, (1), 225–43.

Blinder, Alan (ed.) (1990), *Paying for Productivity: A Look at The Evidence*, Washington, DC: Brookings Institution.

Cooper, Richard N. (1982), 'The Gold Standard: Historical Facts and Future Prospects', *Brookings Papers on Economic Activity*, **1**, 1–45.

Cooper, Richard N. (1984), 'Is There a Need for Reform?', *The International Monetary System: Forty Years After Bretton Woods*, Boston: Federal Reserve Bank of Boston.

Fieleke, Norman S. (1975), 'Exchange Rate Flexibility and the Efficiency of the Foreign Exchange Market', *Journal of Financial and Quantitative Analysis*, **10**, 409–26.

Friedman, Milton (1953), 'The Case for Flexible Exchange Rates', in Milton Friedman, *Essays in Positive Economics*, Chicago: University of Chicago Press, 157–203.

Friedman, Milton and Roosa, Robert V. (1967), *The Balance of Payments: Free Versus Fixed Exchange Rates*, Washington, DC: American Enterprise Institute.

Haberler, Gottfried (1970), 'The International Monetary System: Some Recent Developments and Discussions', in *Approaches to Greater Flexibility of Exchange Rates*, George N. Halm (ed.), Princeton, NJ: Princeton University Press.

Houthakker, Hendrik (1985), 'The International Agenda', *Eastern Economic Journal*, **11**, (1), January–March, 71–8.

Johnson, Harry G. (1972), *Further Essays in Monetary Economics*, London: George Allen & Unwin.

Keynes, John Maynard (1964), *The General Theory of Employment, Interest and Money*, New York: Harcourt, Brace & World.

Keynes, John Maynard (1971), *The Collected Writings of John Maynard Keynes, Vol. IV: A Tract on Monetary Reform*, London: Macmillan.

Krugman, Paul (1989), *Exchange-Rate Instability*, Cambridge, MA: MIT Press.

Lichtenberg, Frank R. and Siegel, Donald (1991), 'The Impact of R&D Investment on Productivity – New Evidence Using Linked R&D–LRD Data', *Economic Inquiry*, **XXIX**, (2), April, 203–29.

Mishel, Lawrence and Teixeira, Ruy A. (1991), *The Myth of the Coming Labour Shortage*, Washington, DC: Economic Policy Institute.

Schaefer, Jeffrey M. and Strongin, David G. (1989), 'Why All The Fuss About Foreign Investment?', *Challenge*, **32**, (3), May–June, 31–5.

Schumpeter, Joseph A. (1954), *History of Economic Analysis*, New York: Oxford University Press.

Tsoukalis, Loukas (1989), 'The Political Economy of the European Monetary System', in *The Political Economy of European Integration: States, Markets and Institutions*, Paolo Guerrieri & Pier Carlo Padoan (eds), Savage, MD: Barnes & Noble Books.

Williamson, John (1985), *The Exchange Rate System*, Washington, DC: Institute for International Economics.

6 Real exchange rates and patterns of international specialization

Fabrizio Onida

Introduction

The transition to a full economic and monetary union by EC members has already stimulated an abundant literature about monetary integration and exchange rate mechanisms, and their macroeconomic effects on fiscal and monetary convergence, growth and intra-area trade imbalances.[1] Economists have divided opinions about the 'stage approach' set by the Delors report (CSEMU, 1989), although credible alternative proposals cannot be easily found.[1]

This paper does not dwell on these macroeconomic arguments. It rather takes a more microeconomic approach to focus on the effects of monetary integration on economic structure. It will discuss whether and in which direction, in the absence of explicit regional and industrial policies and of specific 'strategic policies', patterns of industrial specialization are likely to change within the EC, as a result of persistent deviations of real intra-area exchange rates as a result of a transition to fixed exchange rates.

According to a 'Dutch disease' or 'British disease' view, a persistent appreciation of the real effective exchange rate leads to deindustrialization, increasing import dependency and ultimately to lower growth in productivity and income. According to an opposite view, which in the early 1980s has occasionally been voiced in assessing the impact of the EMS discipline on Italy's microeconomic performance, there has been a gradual and sustained appreciation of the real exchange rate (resulting from persistent inflationary differences not fully offset by occasional realignments of the central EMS parity), which has put healthy pressure on business firms to upgrade products and processes. The likely outcome will be a shift of national patterns of specialization in favour of new industries characterized by more non-price competition, more rapid technological change and faster growth in the world market.

Exchange rate pressure and patterns of industrial specialization

There is some scanty evidence *against* such expectations for Italy. Major industrial restructuring and reconversion took place in Japan and Korea during periods of undervaluation of their respective exchange rates. During the

1980s Italy has gone through a significant real exchange revaluation, and the pattern of Italian comparative advantages has basically become *consolidated* rather than changed. Many Latin American developing countries undergoing heavy real revaluations, as well as import-substituting protectionist policies, have failed to achieve any significant success in diversifying their export capacity. Thus better theoretical and empirical foundations are badly needed on this topic.

To the extent that intra-EC parity adjustments do not fully accommodate inflationary differentials, as has been the case in the second half of the 1980s and can be reasonably foreseen for the 1990s, intra-EC real exchange rates are likely to diverge (Vona and Bini Smaghi, 1988). These divergences are perceived to be permanent rather than transitory (that is, irreversible in the medium-long run, unlike the overshooting cycles of the dollar), which makes their impact on relative prices and quantities rather effective, though with well-known time-lags and hysteresis effects.

A permanent real exchange rate appreciation tends to wipe out any initial 'protection' or excess profits from previous competitive devaluations. Thus in due time it puts stronger competitive pressure on countries pursuing such policies to search for additional 'non price factors' (NPF) of competition. Symmetrically, a real exchange rate devaluation gives more leeway to price–cost competition to countries that are less inflation prone, which does *not* imply the weakening of their previously achieved NPFs (indeed NPFs are, by definition, subject to sunk costs, hysteresis and asymmetric cumulative effects).

Let us focus on countries experiencing a permanent real appreciation of their intra-EC exchange rate, of which Italy may be a good case in point. The increased competitive pressure will be felt asymmetrically across goods and sectors. It is fairly safe to assume that, as a result of the exit of weaker firms which move *out* of the market, and of the upgrading of processes and products of stronger firms which move *up* in the market, a positive effect on average performance will be felt across all sectors. But it is also reasonable to assume that the competitive pressure and the related downward pressure on profitability of exports and of import-competing production will be strongest on goods and sectors characterized by:

1. A higher price-elasticity of demand (price-taker firms).
2. A higher price-elasticity of supply (under perfectly competitive markets) and/or a lower excess capacity and a smaller market share (in the presence of downward sloping, long-run average cost curves, and related entry-barrier pricing by incumbent oligopolistic competitors).
3. A higher ratio of value added to sales, which implies a lower weight of imported inputs (which are made cheaper by a real exchange revaluation).

4.   A higher degree of openness, measured as export/production and import/domestic demand.

The foregoing effects do *not* imply that divergent real exchange rates will induce a change in the sectoral patterns of industrial specialization. In particular, they do not imply that the revaluing country will tend to upgrade its pattern of specialization towards industries characterized on average by smaller price elasticity of demand, faster technological change, more oligopolistic competition and related market power of major suppliers and so on. Symmetrically, they do not imply a sort of a 'downgrading' of comparative advantages in member countries experiencing a devaluation of their real intra-EC exchange rate.

These conclusions stem from two related considerations. First, changing specialization (in goods, sectors and markets) requires investment costs in order to restructure plants, adapt lines of business, learn new technologies, earn reputations, establish brand names, and penetrate and service new markets by developing a distributive and after-sale assistance network.[2] Firms' decisions to enter new market segments and to change their product mix imply an excess of discounted expected revenues over the current required entry costs (sunk plus maintenance costs) (Baldwin and Krugman, 1989). To the extent that a real exchange rate appreciation cuts export profits (under Marshall–Lerner conditions for demand elasticities and under assumption of constant or decreasing average costs), firms are subject to tighter constraints to their self-financed investments, including investment for export. Only lower interest rates and/or more efficient input–output combinations can restore profit, savings and investment. A greater incentive to upgrade products and to build new competitive strength does not imply *per se* a greater ability to achieve these targets.

Secondly, in the modern world of differentiated manufacturers, many inputs (physical, human, managerial, organizational and technological) are industry-specific and idiosyncratic rather than homogeneous and 'generic'. It follows that many of the above investments for export can indeed be seen as past costs (sunk costs, irreversibly sustained), and hence irrelevant for new entry decisions, so long as the firms upgrade their product mix within the production function (or along the 'value chain ', stretching from production design to final sales), with which the firm itself is already familiar. Moving into *new* industries requires a lengthy and costly search and learning process to identify the 'best practice' production and distribution function required for achieving positive net discounted profits. Needless to say, reference here is to Schumpeterian firms, moving in imperfect and oligopolistic markets, subject to uncertainty and to dynamic (cumulative) learning processes of innovation, rather than to neoclassical firms playing in perfect competition in a world where history does not matter and technology is a free good. Firms upgrade themselves more easily and find smaller entry barriers when they move within familiar industry structures and opportunities than when they are called to cross over industry boundaries. In cases of comparative disadvantage, domestic firms are more often than not price-takers (compared with their foreign rivals), enjoy ownership advantages, are further removed from best practice technologies, and face higher barriers to entry. Hence entry costs in sectors of comparative disadvantage tend to be higher.

Factor heterogeneity, complementarity and specificity tend to be ignored by econometric estimates of gains–losses from trade arising from factor cost differences (for example, Neven, 1990). This (rather common) attitude may lead to some misunderstanding of actual and potential specialization among areas broadly similar in 'factor costs', especially labour costs, but very dissimilar in terms of industrial organization and technological diffusion (for 'unorthodox' accents see Porter (1990)).

For sure, the two foregoing arguments (sunk costs for entry decision, industry-specific resources) do not prevent a process whereby a real exchange rate appreciation forces a change in the country's overall industrial specialization.[3] One has to take into account the existence of new entrants, which in each period make a choice of entry without any foregone sunk cost. But the effect of new entrants over the *average* sectoral performance takes quite some time to be felt. Therefore, it is expected that a real appreciation leads to, on balance, consolidating existing comparative advantages (with upgraded product mix and market niches within the same industries), rather than to gaining new sectoral comparative advantages.

The result may well therefore be an increased amount of intra-industry specialization along a 'vertical differentiation' process: more export of upgraded products and more import of price-elastic, relatively homogeneous products. The evolution of trade patterns of various countries subject to a sustained (though not irreversible) revaluation of their real exchange rate – such as Germany and Japan in the 1970s, the US in the first half of the 1980s, and Italy in the second half of the 1980s – gives some rough evidence on this matter. Symmetrically, countries experiencing a prolonged period of undervalued exchange rates (such as Japan until the late 1970s and again in the early 1980s, and South Korea and other dynamic Asian economies until very recently), seem to have undergone substantial changes in their industrial specialization, taking up massive investment to enter new industries (for example, Japanese cars, steel, ships, and consumer and professional electronics; Korean cars, ships, and consumer electronics) and exploiting newly conquered price *and* non-price factors.

Capital mobility, technology spillovers and intra-industry specialization
Europe 1992 implies some convergence in national demand structure, faster technological spillovers and greater capital mobility with relative labour immobility (at least *vis-à-vis* the US internal market, owing to linguistic, cultural and institutional barriers, which are much stronger within the Single Market). Do these changes in intra-EC resource mobility lead to an overall disappearance of intercountry differences in relative factor abundance and related classical inter-industrial comparative advantages, and therefore to an increase in intra-industry trade within a diminishing intra-area specialization? The answer requires a lot of qualifications.

According to Krugman (1987) the Single Market will simultaneously induce an increase in traditional inter-industry specialization (mainly due to recent and new entries of countries with significantly different relative factor endowment *vis-à-vis* the original EC) and in intra-industry specialization (following less conventional factors, such as economies of scale and oligopolistic rivalry). As Krugman concludes: 'The trade that these unconventional motives produce is similarly (usually) beneficial; however, it probably involves less conflict of interest *within* countries [that is, less classical redistribution of gains and losses among factors, in the spirit of the factor abundance model and of the Stolper–Samuelson theorem] and more conflict of interest *between* countries than conventional trade... There are bound to be sectors that are regarded as strategic by several European countries, but which tend to concentrate in only one or two. The danger is then of industrial policy war as each country attempts to secure the desired sectors for itself'.

This argument may be somewhat expanded.

Certainly, 'footloose' industries (that is, those with greater weight of homogeneous labour costs, low transport costs and absence of nation-specific externalities), will be subject to a substantial geographical relocation within a fully integrated European area.[4] Capital will move to minimize production costs across different regional and national locations. To this extent, the notion of national relative factor endowment will gradually lose its significance. Output growth of each region will increasingly depend on changing capital/labour ratios (Baldwin, 1989). This process of capital and technology diffusion may well induce new specializations in suitable peripheral areas, the more so the more these 'regions' will be able to keep favourable wage/productivity ratios, to offer land use at cheaper prices, and to provide essential infrastructure. The recent experience of Ireland and Spain may be a case in point.

In addition, while the disappearance of non-tariff barriers (NTBs) may well contribute to scrapping previous intra-area foreign direct investments (FDIs) exclusively originated by the existence of NTBs themselves (a sort of 'non-tariff factory'), the Single Market has already been triggering off a wave of FDIs (of both internal and external origin), mainly in the form of mergers and acquisitions rather than of greenfield operations. This has been aimed at exploiting convenient external economies as well as economies of scale and of scope, to minimize distributive costs within a more integrated market domain, so ensuring greater user–producer proximity under conditions of Chamberlinian product differentiation. A greater market integration encourages mergers and acquisitions also, because firms face lower costs of co-ordinating cross-country management within a multi-plant organization, lower cultural and linguistic barriers to service local markets, and easier compliance with different national and local regulations. Notice that firms of non-EC origin (such as Swiss, Swedish, American and Japanese firms) will have an equally strong incentive (perhaps a stronger incentive, under fear of some 'Fortress Europe') to relocate and expand their European multi-plant operations and their network of commercial and productive subsidiaries, in order to reinforce their role as 'insiders' in the expanding European market. Some of these multinational firms of non-EC origin may well be in a position to exploit the opportunities of the Single Market better than their EC counterparts, owing to their deep-rooted and long-lived managerial experience with processes of market globalization.[5]

Explicit consideration of inward and outward FDIs may add some further support to the idea that diverging intra-EC real exchange rates bring about a consolidation rather than a reshuffling of intra-area industrial specialization, at least in the short and medium run.

Let us consider inward FDIs first. Foreign investors are likely to perceive the inflation-prone country (subject to real appreciation) as a good local market in which to sell, rather than as an attractive location in which to produce and serve the enlarged European market, especially in those sectors where the country itself inherits comparative disadvantages. These foreign investors are likely to undertake new investments mainly to consolidate and expand their market position (market-oriented mergers and acquisitions and inter-firm co-operative agreements; a much more frequent category than cost-saving restructuring). In some cases, inward FDIs aim at subsequent lay-offs or substantial restructuring of redundant and inefficient production units.[6] Thus, market-oriented inward FDIs may contribute to a further relative deterioration of the trade balance in industries of comparative disadvantage. This is all the more true when these sectors require a substantial amount of intermediate visible and invisible inputs and local external economies. This is largely the case for Italy, which is weak in many 'science-based' and 'scale-intensive' sectors such as chemicals, telecommunications, computers and consumer electronics.

Will outward FDIs contribute towards, reinforce or weaken the revaluing country's industrial specialization? Here, again, the answer is subject to an inherent ambiguity: it all depends on which determinants of FDI will prevail.[6] According to the so-called Japanese view, suitable for explaining the Japanese patterns of overseas internationalization in the 1960s and 1970s, FDIs play the role of relocating abroad those activities in which the home country is losing its competitive advantage. From this perspective, the outward FDIs encouraged by real exchange rate revaluation (which by itself helps to buy foreign assets at cheaper prices) may indeed contribute to redeploying and transforming the country's pattern of industrial specialization. But according to more modern views, applicable to a wider set of historical and recent experiences of internationalization of national industries, FDIs are basically an instrument for consolidating and reinforcing the country's comparative advantages by playing strategic games and dynamic learning in oligopolistic markets (entry threats and responses). Some of the more obvious examples are German and Swiss chemicals and pharmaceuticals, Swedish telecommunications, German electrical engineering, British chemical and electronics, and Japanese motor vehicle and consumer electronics.[7]

Asymmetric sectoral impact of the 1992 market and national patterns of specialization

Finally, it may also be asked how asymmetries in the sectoral impact of Europe 1992 come into the picture of market integration and national patterns of industrialization. Some works since the Cecchini report have suggested which industries are likely to be most affected by the lowering of intra-EC trade barriers (Buigues and Ilzkovitz, 1988; CEC, 1989). These include industries characterized by: (1) the highest potential economies of scale; (2) high initial NTBs, mainly originated by national public procurement, technical and consumer safety standards, and/or distributive regulations; (3) high variances of prices for similar products, arising from supply fragmentation and/or product differentiation, aside from causes related to (1) and (2); and (4) relatively low intra-EC import penetration, for reasons different from (2) (for example, high penetration from extra-EC areas).[8]

The sensitive sectors are estimated to be 40 among the 120 industries classified as NACE-3 digits; these represent about 41 per cent of the EC industrial value added in 1983–84 (just about the same over the Italian industrial value added). They are grouped by the CEC (1989) into four classes: (1) tightly regulated public procurement; (2) high-tech public procurement (where a greater dependence on imports from the US can be found relative to the previous class); (3) mass consumption goods (both electronic and traditional) and some mechanical engineering, with high product differentiation and economies of scale in distribution after sale; and (4) some modern sectors open to import penetration from NIEs (consumer electronics and civilian shipbuilding). Sapir (1990) has an alternative classification according to a ranking of market share held by national producers, and shows how in each of the three groups one can find sectors of comparative advantage as well as of comparative disadvantage for Europe as a whole.

All these computations and classifications of 1992-sensitive sectors provide a rich network of indicators of supply and market structure, besides allowing interesting descriptions of past and recent trade performance. On the whole, these indicators can be seen as interesting predictors of trade opportunities (gains from trade from unexploited economies of scale, lowering of specific NTBs and so on), although they are less revealing with respect to national or regional trade patterns, either for Europe as a whole or for single member countries. Future trade patterns will depend on how European-based firms will exploit those opportunities. At most, one could guess that in those sensitive sectors countries already enjoying a competitive advantage will be better equipped to achieve further strength in their market shares (consolidating the previous pattern of industrial specialization), since under the 1992 rules there will be less scope than in the past for targeted national industrial policies (hence Krugman's 1987 warning) and related efforts to create new comparative advantages on a national basis. At any rate, this sort of prediction is subject to many caveats, including the likely effects of real exchange rate divergences, as is stressed in this paper.

As Sapir (1990) and other studies reveal, 1992-sensitive industries include a wide spectrum of European industries that enjoyed comparative advantages (electricity generation and transmission, railway equipment, pharmaceuticals, domestic appliances, motor vehicles, rubber, food and beverages, and several mechanical engineering industries), and some that have disadvantages (computers, electronic components, consumer electronics, medical equipment, aerospace and shipbuilding and so on). Thus, 1992 trade opportunities may well favour European imports as well as European production by non-EC multinational firms, with rather different impacts on European trade patterns.

The enlargement of the Single European Market by itself, contrary to expectations of 'Fortress Europe', carries with it potential gains from trade not only for firms of European origin, but also for European-located multinationals and for non-European exporters as well. This also has something to do with the perspectives of Europe's weaker countries and regions, which are less able to exploit opportunities of static and dynamic economies of scale in oligopolistic markets, and to upgrade their product mix according to 'vertical' differentiation in imperfectly competitive markets.

Conclusions
Persistent deviations of the real exchange rate from a given initial level are likely to induce not only various phases of macroeconomic adjustment, but

also a series of microeconomic responses to the changing competitive environment. When an inflationary-biased country enters a semi-fixed exchange rate system, its patterns of industrial specialization and trade are likely to be affected by a persistent real appreciation of the exchange rate. This paper has argued that the most likely impact, at least in the initial phase, will be a consolidation of inherited sectoral comparative advantages, with an upgrading of products and processes, rather than a push to abandon previous specialization in order to acquire new comparative advantages at industry level. The argument takes into account the standard effects of exchange rate changes on demand and supply (based on price elasticities), under imperfectly competitive and oligopolistic markets, in the presence of sunk costs (investment for exports) and of industry-specific human and organizational resources. Therefore the pressure of a real revaluation may well induce an increase in intra-industry rather than inter-industry specialization, pushing domestic firms to move up market within their technological and organizational domain, while at the same time the import of lower segment products within comparative advantage industries will grow. Intra-industry trade patterns may also be encouraged within the economic and monetary union, since intra-area mergers and acquisitions increase the scope for multi-plant enterprises relocating across the larger integrated market, and for horizontal as well as vertical product differentiation.

Notes

1. The paper largely draws from another paper, 'Europe 1992: Macroeconomic Sustainability and Implications for Patterns of Industrial Specialization', CESPRI Working Paper no. 38, September 1990.
2. Among the recent literature see Bini Smaghi (1990), CEC (1990), De Cecco and Giovannini (1989), Eichengreen (1990), Giavazzi, Micossi and Miller (1988), Giavazzi and Pagano (1988), Giavazzi and Giovannini (1989), Guerrieri and Padoan (1988), Gros and Thygesen (1990), Padoa Schioppa (1990), and Spaventa (1990).
3. This has become a popular idea in the modern literature on sunk costs, hysteresis and the macroeconomics of flexible exchange rates (for example, Krugman, 1989; Dixit, 1989), but its background can be found in Linder (1961) and in some early literature on intra-industry trade.
4. The concept of nation-specific externalities is crucial in Porter (1990).
5. The ranking of motivations for European mergers and acquisitions, according to the most recent survey of 383 operations (CEC, 1989, table 7, p. 189), has 'improving market position' at the first place, far ahead of 'complementarity', 'restructuring' and 'diversification'. Over 111 joint venture operations, on the contrary, R&D–production–marketing complex motivation is the main motivation.
   On the relative position of non-EC firms within the Single Market, see Onida (1990). Strategies aimed at rationalizing distributive networks and at ensuring the best product adaptation along user–producer relations play a crucial role in Porter (1990), as in his previous well-known works.
6. Remember that, according to Article 58 of the Treaty of Rome, foreign-owned subsidiaries cannot be discriminated, being fully 'nationals'.
7. Within the extremely wide literature on FDIs, one can still usefully refer to the lucid survey by Caves (1982). More recent assessments incorporating modern game-theoretic

approaches to strategic investment decisions can be found in Buckley (1989), Dunning (1988) and Cantwell (1991). Careful analyses of the US outward and inward experience can be found in Lipsey and Kravis (1987), Morgan Guaranty Trust Company (1989) and Graham and Krugman (1989). The most recent world-wide empirical coverage is in UNCTC (1988).

8. Let us keep in mind that an enlargement (integration) of the European market carries with it a double welfare effect: (1) better resource allocation through a greater exploitation of scale economies; and (2) a pro-competitive effect which counterbalances the risk of worsened allocative efficiency stemming from greater exploitation of monopolistic firms' economies of scale and greater product differentiation.

Notice that the standard definition of potential scale economies (ratio of existing plants to some estimate of minimum optimum scale plant) looks only at the production phase, leaving out other crucial scale economies in the upstream and downstream phases of the 'value chain'; from R&D–design to distribution/after-sale assistance/brand name. Notice that arguments popular in the current literature on 'new trade theories', such as dynamic competition effects in imperfectly competitive markets; external economies and capital mobility benefits from integration technology spillovers; and regional disequilibria and problems of fiscal and social policy harmonization, are far from having been neglected by old authors. As examples of outdated but still penetrating contributions on these topics, see Scitovsky (1958) and, of even more 'impressive' current interest, Balassa (1961).

Appendix

Exporting firms are assumed to set prices in domestic currency, and a complete 'pass through' of exchange rate changes into sellers' price tends to take place. Figures 6.1a), 6.1b), 6.1c) and 6.1d) show the standard effect of a revaluation on export and import. In the short-medium run, the hysteresis effect may well induce zero or partial shifts of the relevant demand and supply curves, but in the medium-long run (when extra profits are necessarily offset by free entry and exit), the assumption of a complete 'pass through' appears most plausible.

As Branson (1972) shows, elasticities of trade prices in foreign currency (where * indicates foreign currency) relative to exchange rates (e) are given by:

$$\frac{dp_x^* / p_x^*}{de / e} = \frac{1}{1 - d_x / s_x} \quad \text{for export prices } p_x^* \text{(Fig. 6.1a)} \tag{1}$$

$$\frac{dp_m^* / p_m^*}{de / e} = \frac{1}{1 - s_m / d_m} \quad \text{for import prices } p_m^* \text{ (Fig. 6.1c),} \tag{2}$$

and similarly for elasticities of trade prices in *domestic* currency:

$$\frac{dp_x / p_x}{de / e} = \frac{1}{1 - s_x / d_x} \quad \text{for export prices } p_x \text{(Fig. 6.1b)} \tag{3}$$

$$\frac{dp_m / p_m}{de / e} = \frac{1}{1 - d_m / s_m} \quad \text{for import prices } p_m \text{ (Fig. 6.1d),} \tag{4}$$

where d = demand elasticity
       s = supply elasticity.

For instance, equation (1) suggests that, under assumption of a perfectly elastic export supply curve ($s_x \rightarrow \infty$), export prices denominated in foreign currency (p_x^*) will rise by the full amount of the revaluation. The same conclusion holds if export demand is perfectly inelastic ($d_x = 0$).

Export

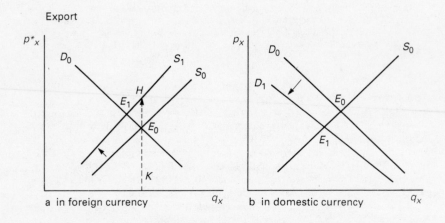

a in foreign currency

b in domestic currency

Import

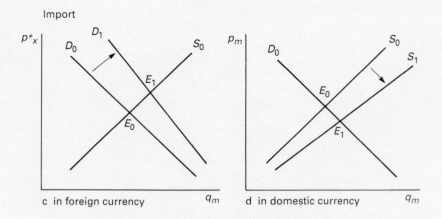

c in foreign currency

d in domestic currency

Figure 6.1:   Effects of a revaluation on export and import

Export prices in foreign currency will be unchanged following a revaluation (devaluation) if export demand is perfectly elastic ($d_x \rightarrow \infty$) or export supply is perfectly inelastic ($s_x = 0$).

Figure 6.2 shows alternative effects on prices and quantities, given different price elasticities. A revaluation induces an upward shift of the export supply curve (from S_0 to S_1) denominated in foreign currency, or a downward shift of the export demand curve (from D_0 to D_1) denominated in domestic currency. Assuming a perfectly elastic foreign-currency export demand schedule (D_0), no 'pass through' of the revaluation on foreign currency export prices can be accommodated, hence the impact of the revaluation will be fully felt on lower quantities of export (from q_0 to q_1)

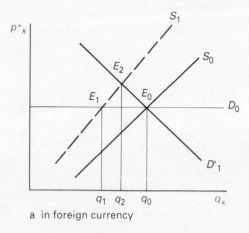

a in foreign currency

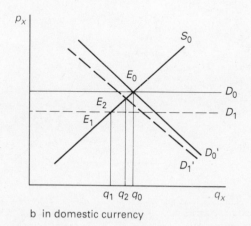

b in domestic currency

Figure 6.2:   *Effects of a revaluation on export given different price elasticities*

and on greater export profit margins. Under a less-than-infinitely elastic export demand, export quantities undergo a smaller decrease (from q_0 to q_2), as export prices in domestic currency reflect a limited amount of 'pass through'.

Hence, one may conclude that an exchange rate revaluation induces a greater fall in domestic export price and profitability, and a greater contraction of export quantities, along an upward-sloping export supply curve; the more price-elastic is the demand schedule faced by domestic exporters, the smaller the market power enjoyed by domestic exporters.

Figure 6.3 considers an oligopolistic market with economies of scale described by non-linear long-run falling average cost curves (LAC). A real revaluation is the

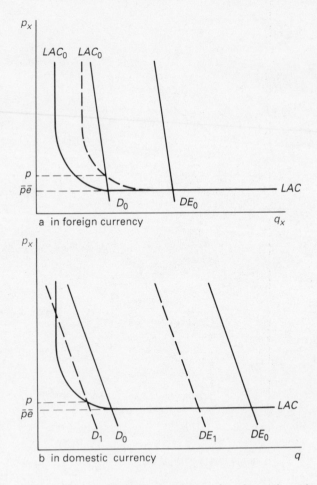

Figure 6.3:   *Effects of a revaluation on export under oligopoly with barriers to entry*

more likely to price domestic exporters out of the market, the higher are fixed costs (LAC lying high and rightward in Figure 6.3a) and/or the smallest is the market share of domestic exporters (demand curve D lying leftward in Figure 6.3b). If foreign competitors already enjoy large market shares (DE curves), an upward shift of the cost curve, LAC, in foreign currency (Figure 6.3a) or a downward shift of export demand curve in domestic currency do not prevent them from keeping their entry-preventing price $\overline{pe}$. Symmetrically, domestic exporters endowed with smaller initial market shares (D curves lying on the left) are forced by revaluation to supply equilibrium prices, p. Therefore their entry is prevented by foreign competitors' price $\overline{pe}$.

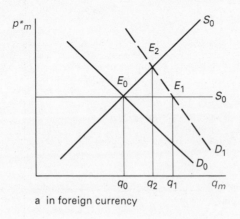

a in foreign currency

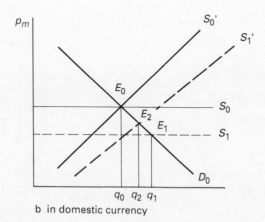

b in domestic currency

Figure 6.4:   Effects of a revaluation on imports given different price elasticities

Figure 6.4 shows the effect of revaluation on imports, again with import prices in foreign currency (p_m^* in Figure 6.4a) or in domestic currency (p_m in Figure 6.4b). The exchange revaluation will induce a greater fall in domestic currency import price p_m (a lower increase in foreign currency import price p_m^*) the more price-elastic is the foreign supply: hence a greater increase in imported quantities (from q_0 to q_1, rather than to q_2 when the foreign supply curve is less than infinitely elastic).

An infinitely elastic foreign supply curve of import will be associated with a small size of the importing country.

The impact of a real revaluation on import of intermediate inputs should also be taken into account, leading to better cost-competitiveness of domestic producers: the more so, the higher is the import dependency, that is the lower the ratio of value added to the value of final production.

Bibliography

Balassa, B. (1961), 'The Theory of Economic Integration', London: Allen & Unwin.

Baldwin, R. (1989), 'The Growth Effects of 1992', *Economic Policy*, October, 247–81.

Baldwin, R. and Krugman, P.R. (1989), 'Persistent Trade Effects of Large Exchange Rate Shocks', *Quarterly Journal of Economics*, November, 635–54.

Bini Smaghi, L. (1990), 'Progressing Towards European Monetary Unification: Selected Issues and Proposals', *Banca d'Italia, Temi di Discussione*, **133**, April.

Branson, W. (1972), 'The Trade Effect of the 1971 Currency Realignment', *Brookings Papers on Economic Activity*, 1, 15–69.

Buckley, P.J. (1989), *The Multinational Enterprise. Theory and Applications*, London: Macmillan.

Buigues, P. and Ilzkovitz, F. (1988), *The Sectoral Impact of the Internal Market*, EEC Doc. II 335/88.

Cantwell, J. (1991), 'A Survey of Theories of International Production', in C.N. Pitelis and R. Sugden (eds), *The Nature of the Transnational Firm*, London and New York: Routledge.

Caves, R.E. (1982), *Multinational Enterprise and Economic Analysis*, Cambridge, Mass.: Cambridge University Press.

CEC (Commission of the European Communities) (1989), 'The Effects of the Internal Market. Sensitive Sectors', *European Economy*, November.

CEC (Commission of the European Communities) (1990), 'One market, one money. An evaluation of potential benefits and costs of forming an economic and monetary union', Bruxelles, October.

CSEMU (Committee for the Study of Economic and Monetary Union) (1989), *Report on Economic and Monetary Union in the European Community*, Luxembourg: Office for Official Publications of the EC.

De Cecco, M. and Giovannini, A. (eds) (1989), *A European Central Bank? Perspectives on Monetary Union After Ten Years of the EMS*, Cambridge: Cambridge University Press.

Dixit, A. (1989), 'Intersectoral Capital Reallocation Under Price Uncertainty', *Journal of Political Economy*, 309–25.

Dunning, J.H. (1988), *Explaining International Production*, London: Allen & Unwin.

Eichengreen, B. (1990), 'One money for Europe? Lessons from the US Currency Union', *Economic Policy*, **10**, April, 117–87.

Giavazzi, F. and Giovannini, A. (eds) (1989), *Limiting Exchange Rate Flexibility: The European Monetary System*, Cambridge, Mass.: MIT Press.

Giavazzi, F. and Pagano, M. (1988), 'The Advantage of Tying One's Hands. EMS Discipline and Central Bank Credibility', *European Economic Review*, June.

Giavazzi, F., Micossi, S. and Miller, M. (eds) (1988), *The European Monetary System*, Cambridge, Mass.: Cambridge University Press.

Graham, E.M. and Krugman, P.R. (1989), *Foreign Direct Investment in the US*, Washington, DC: Institute for International Economics.

Gros, D. and Thygesen, N. (1990), *From the EMS Towards EMU: How to Manage in the Transition*, Bruxelles: CEPS.

Guerrieri, P. and Padoan, P.C. a cura di (1988), *L'Economia Politica dell'Integrazione Europea*, Bologna: Il Mulino.

Krugman, P.R. (1987), 'Economic Integration in Europe: Some Conceptual Issues', reprinted in A. Jacquemin and A. Sapir (eds), (1989), *The European Internal Market. Trade and Competition*, Selected Readings, Oxford University Press.

Krugman, P.R. (1989), '*Exchange Rate Instability*' (the Lionel Robbins Lectures), Cambridge, Mass.: MIT Press.

Linder, S.B. (1961), 'An essay on trade and transformation', New York: J.Wiley. (Tr.ital. del cap. 3 in R. Franco and C. Gerosa, *Il commercio internazionale. Teorie e problemi*, Etas Libri, Milano, 1980).

Lipsey, R. and Kravis, I.B. (1987), 'The Competitiveness and Comparative Advantage of US Multinationals 1957–84', *BNL Quarterly Review*, June, 147–65.

Morgan Guaranty Trust Company (1989), 'Foreign Direct Investment in the US', *World Financial Markets*, Issue 2, June 29.

Neven, D.J. (1990), 'Gains and Losses from 1992', *Economic Policy*, April, 13–62.

Onida, F. (1986), 'Tassi di Cambio, Vantaggi Comparati e Struttura Industriale', in T. Padoa Schioppa (a cura di), *Il sistema dei cambi oggi*, Collana Società Italiana degli Economisti, Il Mulino, Bologna.

Onida, F. (1990), 'Technological Competition, Structural Change and International Integration of the Single European Market', in C. Barfield (ed.), *US and Europe in the 1990s*, Washington: American Enterprise Institute (forthcoming).

Padoa Schioppa, T. (1990), 'Financial and Monetary Integration in Europe: 1990, 1992 and Beyond, Group of Thirty', Occasional Paper 28, New York; London.

Porter, M.E. (1990), *The Competitive Advantage of Nations*, London: Macmillan.

Sapir, A. (1990), 'Does 1992 Come Before or After 1990? On Regional vs. Multilateral Integration', in R.W. Jones and A.O. Krueger (eds.), *The Political Economy of International Trade. Essays in Honor of Robert E. Baldwin*, Oxford: Blackwell.

Scitovsky, T. (1958), *Economic Theory and Western European Integration*, California: Stanford University Press.

Spaventa, L. (1990), 'The Political Economy of European Monetary Integration', *BNL Quarterly Review*, March, 3–20.

UNCTC (United Nations Centre on Transnational Corporations) (1988), *Transnational Corporations and World Development*, Fourth survey, New York.

Vona, S. and Bini Smaghi, L. (1988), 'Economic Growth and Exchange Rates in the European Monetary System: Their Trade Effects in a Changing External Environment', in F. Giavazzi, S. Micossi and M. Miller (eds) (1988), *The European Monetary System*, Cambridge, Mass.: Cambridge University Press.

7 Italian joint ventures abroad: country-, industry- and firm-specific requirements

Francesca Sanna-Randaccio[1]

Introduction

The choice made by a multinational company (MNC) between joint ventures and wholly owned subsidiaries is affected by two major sets of factors. It depends, on the one hand, on the firm's preference, which in turn is a function of the costs and benefits of the alternative ownership modes. It is influenced, on the other, by government policies, in particular by the restrictive regulations imposed by the host country on the level of foreign ownership allowed in local firms.

The purpose of this paper is to test the relative influence of these determinants of ownership choice using data on the foreign activities of 100 Italian multinationals operating abroad in the manufacturing and extractive industries. By providing an empirical investigation for non-US multinationals, this study aims to contribute to a better understanding of a phenomenon which has been analysed focusing on US firms. In order to capture the effect of the parent and subsidiary's characteristics, firm-level data are used instead of industry-level proxies (other authors have used the latter due to lack of relevant information). This specification is more consistent with the theory than those adopted in previous works.[2]

Following an examination of the data, the estimation procedure used in testing the hypotheses is explained, and the empirical results are presented as a basis for reaching the main conclusions of this study.

Costs and benefits of alternative ownership structures

The economic factors that lead a profit-maximizing firm to establish a joint venture abroad may be analysed by assessing the additional costs and benefits of joint venture creation, as compared to full ownership, from the viewpoint of the foreign investor. The reasons for entering into a co-operative venture are varied (increasingly so in recent years); thus useful suggestions for such an analysis may be drawn from different theoretical approaches, namely transaction cost theory and strategic behaviour economics. Other studies provide a comprehensive analysis of the literature (Contractor and Lorange, 1988; Hennart, 1988). Only a few major aspects of this phenomenon are recalled here.

The costs associated with joint ownership may be classified in two main categories:

1. *Costs of sharing decision-making.* In a joint venture the decision-making process becomes more laborious, as the partners frequently disagree over various aspects of the subsidiary's activities. Such conflicts are most likely to arise when there are strong positive or negative interactions between the joint venture's activity and the other parent firm's operations (Hladik, 1985). The parent company seeks to maximize world-wide profits, and this objective (in the case of spillovers) may diverge from profit maximization for the joint venture alone.

The costs of sharing administration, therefore, will be particularly pronounced when the parent company pursues a strategy of rationalization of production which requires a policy of global co-ordination of activities. This hypothesis has found empirical support in the works of Stopford and Wells (1972), Gomes-Casseres (1985, 1989) and Kobrin (1988).

2. *Costs of sharing technical knowledge.* In order to transfer proprietary knowledge to a jointly owned subsidiary, the MNC must agree with the other partner(s) on the value of these intangible assets. As is well known, owing to imperfections in the market for technology, the costs of negotiating this exchange are very high. The firm must face not only the *ex ante* transaction costs of negotiation, but also the *ex post* costs of legal enforcement of the contract (Williamson, 1986).

Furthermore, the foreign investor must take into account the risk that the transfer of proprietary knowledge to an only partially controlled subsidiary may result in fostering future competition. The know-how is more likely to be disseminated to third parties and, if the joint venture is dissolved, the partner may turn into a dangerous competitor. Similar developments will be particularly damaging in production areas of strategic importance for the parent firm, which therefore will be rather unwilling to share core technologies (Harrigan, 1986).

The benefits associated with a joint venture may stem from:

1. *Access to technology and technical know-how.* The foreign investor may look for a partner in order to gain access to new technologies or technical abilities complementary to its own. The joint venture will thus become a vehicle for pooling together different abilities needed in high technology industries. The development of such joint projects has been an increasingly important feature in the 1980s, in particular in the US market (Harrigan, 1986; Kogut and Singh, 1988). Often these ventures have been formed by

large firms in association with smaller producers operating in fast developing sectors such as robotics, biotechnology and solar energy (Doz, 1988).

2.   *Exchange of other complementary resources.* The need for a foreign partner is likely to be felt particularly by small and medium sized firms. These enterprises are constrained in their foreign expansion by the limited managerial and financial resources at their disposal, but at the same time face competitive pressures to become international. Several studies have in fact indicated that, when compared with larger competitors, small firms show a higher propensity to expand abroad by forming joint ventures (Stopford and Wells, 1972; Gomes-Casseres, 1985). *Ceteris paribus,* the propensity to share ownership is also influenced by the international experience of the investing firm.

The lack of knowledge of foreign markets is an important obstacle to the development of foreign operations and may represent a reason for associating with a foreign firm in a joint venture. By establishing activities abroad, however, the firm sets in motion a cumulative process of knowledge development that will result in a greater ability to search for information on foreign markets and to manage geographically dispersed activities. For this reason, the propensity to form joint ventures will tend to fall. We may note that, when discussing the role of firm size, the attention is directed to the managerial resources available to the firm. Here, instead, the emphasis is placed on the services provided by a given managerial staff. These services increase as a consequence of the experience accumulated in the course of previous foreign expansion (Johanson and Vahlne, 1977).

3.   *Risk reduction. A* joint venture may be established in order to reduce the riskiness of a particular operation. The risk-sharing function of a co-operative venture may take different forms. In some cases, similar resources are pooled together to spread the risks of a large project over more than one firm; in others, the investor associates with a local partner to limit the political risks of the foreign operation.

4.   *Ability to influence the structural evolution of the market.* Several types of joint venture fall into this category (Contractor and Lorange, 1988). In a mature industry, for example, a joint venture may be formed in order to help restructure production by eliminating excess capacity. The joint venture may, in addition, be used for collusive purposes. In emerging industries, furthermore, joint ventures are sometimes established to control the direction of the structural evolution of the market. The spider's web joint ventures analysed by Harrigan (1986) are examples of such a strategy.

Host country policies

Institutional factors also play a crucial role in the choice between partial and full ownership. Government measures may affect a firm's ownership policy in different ways. For instance, Mowery (1991) stresses the importance of non-tariff barriers as a factor inducing joint venture formation, in particular in the high technology sectors in the developed countries. According to this author, several joint ventures recently formed by US and EC firms have been stimulated by the restrictions which various governments have imposed on the participation of foreign firms in publicly financed research projects.

However, the policies that influence a firm's ownership choice the most are those directed to limiting the equity participation allowed to foreign firms in domestic activities. The effect of government regulations and requirements on the ownership policy of US multinationals has been analysed by several authors (for example, Gomes Casseres, 1990; Contractor, 1990). When the choice in favour of shared ownership is determined by these institutional constraints, joint ventures become a second-best option for the investing firm.

The data used

This study is based principally on information from the database on Italian multinationals at the *Dipartimento di Economia Pubblica*, University of Rome. The database covers the period 1974–86, and is the result of an ongoing project begun ten years ago to collect, through questionnaires and interviews, detailed data on Italian parent companies and foreign subsidiaries.[3] The methodology and the range of available information on parent and subsidiary characteristics are illustrated in Acocella (ed.)(1985).

The present work focuses on subsidiaries active in 1986. Following Stopford and Wells (1972) and Gomes-Casseres (1989, 1990), a joint venture is defined as a subsidiary in which the parent owned, in 1986, less than 95 per cent of the equity. A broad definition of joint venture is thus adopted, which will include not only newly formed enterprises jointly owned by two or more partners, but also cases of partial acquisition. The reasons why the theoretical framework elaborated for joint venture, narrowly defined, can be extended also to partial acquisitions have been examined by Gomes-Casseres (1989).

A total number of 436 foreign units (owned by 141 Italian parents) was found to exist in 1986. However, the information required to test equations 1 and 2 is available only for a subset of these foreign companies (288 and 231 respectively) and of the parents (100 and 94). These smaller samples, nonetheless, include a fairly diversified group of subsidiaries in terms of the geographical and industrial composition of their operation, and cover the activities of all the major Italian multinationals.

The estimation procedure

The estimation procedure followed in order to analyse the choice between a joint venture and a wholly owned subsidiary will now be illustrated. The dependent variable is a dummy equal to one when the subsidiary is a joint venture, that is, when the parent owns less than 95 per cent of the subsidiary equity, and zero otherwise. The actual ownership level was not used, as firms are likely to see differently changes in the ownership percentage which are of an equal amount, but which take place at different points of the ownership range, for example, the change between 100 per cent and 80 per cent or between 80 per cent and 60 per cent. For similar reasons, a qualitative dependent variable has been used by other authors (Gomes-Casseres, 1989, 1990; Hennart, 1991).

Since the dependent variable is dichotomous, the estimation problem may be formulated in terms of the probability of the event (joint venture) occurring.

For the ith subsidiary, we have:

$$y_i = \begin{cases} 1 & \text{if joint venture (the subsidiary's equity} \\ & \text{owned in 1986 by the parent is} < 95 \text{ per cent)} \\ \\ 0 & \text{if wholly owned (the subsidiary's equity} \\ & \text{owned in 1986 by the parent is} \geq 95 \text{ per cent)} \end{cases}$$

and $P_i = \Pr(y_i = 1) = f(\mathbf{x}'_i\mathbf{b})$,

where $\mathbf{x}'_i$ is the vector of observations on the set of explanatory variables. The first element in $\mathbf{x}'_i$ is unity, as a constant is included.

Two functional forms of the postulated relationship between P_i and the explanatory variables are estimated. P_i is first assumed to be a linear function of the explanatory variables. The linear probability model is estimated by using ordinary least square (OLS). Such a procedure presents two main difficulties: in general the error terms are heteroskedastic and the estimated probabilities are not in the $(0,1)$ range.

As an alternative the logit model, based on the logistic cumulative distribution function, is considered. The joint venture probability then becomes:

$$P_i = \Pr(y_i = 1) = 1/(1 + \exp(-\mathbf{x}'_i\mathbf{b})).$$

The model is not linear in its parameters, thus it must be estimated by using maximum likelihood techniques. A positive sign for an estimated coefficient indicates that an increase in the corresponding variable has a positive effect on joint venture probability.[4]

Both OLS and maximum likelihood logit estimates were reported to check the sensitivity of the results to the choice of the estimation methods.

The hypotheses

The model estimates the probability that a subsidiary is a joint venture as a function of a set of explanatory variables. The hypotheses considered, which are based on the analysis in Section 2, and the variables actually tested will now be described.

Intra-firm co-ordination

We saw that the potential for conflicts between partners – and thus the costs of sharing ownership – are likely to be greater when the MNC parent, by creating an integrated network of subsidiaries, follows a strategy of global co-ordination. In order to measure the integration of the subsidiary's activity with the other parent's operations, the dummy INTRAFT is introduced. INTRAFT was set equal to one when more than 25 per cent of the subsidiary's production was exported to Italy.[5] Although for lack of appropriate data it is not possible to distinguish between export to parent and to other firms, this indicator is the best available proxy for the intensity of intra-firm trade.[6] The variable is expected to exercise a negative influence on the probability that a foreign subsidiary is a joint venture.

Transfer of technology

When analysing the effect of technology on ownership policy, one must try to separate the instances in which the firm expands overseas to transfer its know-how from the investments designed to acquire new skills abroad. The firms most likely to undertake the first type of expansion (leading to a transfer of know-how) are undoubtedly the leading producers in each sector. To capture this firm-specific effect I have considered the technological competitiveness of each parent company (TECHCOMP), measured as R&D over sales for each firm divided by the R&D intensity of the corresponding sector in Italy. As an indicator of the likelihood that the firm will invest abroad to transfer technical capabilities, I preferred TECHCOMP to the non-normalized value (the absolute value of each parent's R&D intensity), as this last variable, more than a firm-specific effect, captures an industry characteristic which, on the contrary, may be associated with investment directed to technology acquisition. I expect TECHCOMP to exercise a negative influence on joint venture probability.

Access to technology

To estimate the effect of technology acquisition on ownership policy, the variable IR&DINT*USA has been introduced. This is the multiplicative interaction between IR&DINT (the R&D intensity of the subsidiary's industry, measured with data for the corresponding industry in Italy) and a dummy equal to one for subsidiaries located in the USA, and zero otherwise.

As no direct measure is available, IR&DINT*USA is adopted as a proxy for technology acquisition on the basis of the following considerations. Technical rivalry is particularly fierce in high technology sectors. In such industries, to keep up in the competitive race, firms have increasingly favoured joint venture creation to obtain access to new technical resources, either by acquiring participation in small innovating firms, or by pooling resources with major partners in new R&D projects. Such a phenomenon has concerned, in particular, the USA, which is not only the leading country as far as many high technology sectors are concerned, but is also comparatively more liberal *vis-à-vis* inward foreign investments. It is thus expected that Italian MNCs that expand into US high technology sectors will prefer to share ownership with local producers in order to obtain access to their technical resources. In other words, when other effects (in particular that of technology transfer) are taken account of separately, I expect IR&DINT*USA to promote joint venture.

Foreign firms' abilities

In only a few studies (Hladik, 1988) have variables been introduced which measure directly the characteristics of foreign partners. In general, some indicator of the host country's level of development is adopted as a rough proxy for local firms' abilities, and thus for potential benefits of co-operation. Following this convention, GNP/N (GNP per capita)[7] is considered in order to test the hypothesis that the presence of highly skilled local producers will increase the likelihood of joint venture. These considerations lead to the prediction of a positive coefficient for GNP/N.

However, GNP/N may also capture other effects. For instance, we know that 'cultural distance' is an important element in leading to a higher use of joint venture, and as far as Italian firms are concerned, this distance is greater with less developed markets than with more advanced ones. This effect will result in a negative relationship between GNP/N and joint venture likelihood.

Internal resources constraint

The choice of partial ownership may also be explained by internal resources constraint. Various aspects may be considered in this regard:

Size   A negative relationship between the parent's size and the likelihood of joint venture was found in several studies. According to these authors, due to managerial constraints smaller firms are more likely to seek a foreign partner than larger competitors. Two formulations of this hypothesis are considered. The effect of absolute size is tested with LSIZE, the log of the parent's domestic sale; and the effect of normalized size with LNSIZE, the log of the ratio of the parent's domestic sales to those of the 40 largest Italian companies operating in the same industry.[8]

The effect of size on ownership choice may, however, be non-linear. In a study of major UK companies, for instance, Cantwell and Dunning (1986) showed that parent size was positively correlated with joint venture involvement. It would thus appear that when only large firms are compared, size may have a positive effect on the probability of a joint venture occurring. To take into account the possibility of non-linearity in this relationship, a second order term was introduced ($LSIZE^2$, $LNSIZE^2$). With such a quadratic formulation it is possible to test a hypothesis advanced, in a different context, by several authors (Penrose, 1959; Porter, 1986). They suggest that small, medium large, and very large firms are distinct strategic groups, competing in separate environments and adopting different strategies.

Experience   The variable INTEXP is introduced to test the hypothesis that the experience accumulated in the course of the firm's foreign expansion lowers the information costs associated with foreign operations and results in a greater ability to co-ordinate geographically dispersed activities, thus decreasing the need for a foreign partner. International experience is here measured by the number of subsidiaries each parent has created up to 1986, thus including divestments. An alternative indicator of experience is represented by the 'age' of the firm as foreign producer. However, INTEXP was chosen because it captures the learning process associated with the creation of each additional subsidiary. It is also highly correlated with the geographical dispersion of the parent's foreign productive activities, and thus with its knowledge of different markets.

On the other hand, high values of INTEXP may be expected to exercise a different effect on ownership policy. High values of this indicator are, in fact, associated with a thorough knowledge of the complexities of managing foreign activities, of the characteristics of foreign markets and of their legal environment. While initially a rise in experience affects mostly the need of a foreign partner's resources, at higher levels further increases in INTEXP may instead result in a greater ability to capture the benefits of co-operation. A second order term ($INTEXP^2$) was introduced to account for this possibility.

Finance   The presence of a financial constraint may be another important reason to favour the formation of a joint venture instead of a wholly owned subsidiary. PROFIT/S is added to account for the effect of a liquidity constraint. This variable measures profitability as a percentage of sales revenue. It is equal to the ratio between net domestic profits (gross profits less depreciation provisions, interest payments and taxation) and domestic sales. To average the effect of profit fluctuation, as data for 1981 and 1986 were available, the average value for these two years is considered.

This indicator is a reasonable, though rough, proxy for finance by internally generated funds. It also assumes that, once size differences are controlled for, external finances will be highly correlated to the firm's profitability as measured here. It can be expected that PROFIT/S has a negative influence on joint venture probability.

Risk reduction

Several dimensions of the risk reduction function of shared ownership have been highlighted in the literature (Contractor and Lorange, 1988). Here I focus on one of these aspects, specifically the spreading of the risk of a large project. The greater the size of the foreign operation compared to that of the parent company, the more risky the investment and thus the greater the likelihood of a joint venture. This consideration is reflected in LRELSZ, the log of the ratio between the parent's domestic size (measured by sales) and the subsidiary's sale size. A negative coefficient is expected. This variable is also strictly connected with the internal resources constraint effect, and for this reason, too, its coefficient is predicted to be negative.

Host government restrictive policies

The host country's laws and regulations may impose limitations on the firm's ownership choice. To control for these institutional constraints the dummy GOVRES is added, set equal to one for restrictive host governments and to zero otherwise. As such restrictions have been particularly prominent in the developing world, the country classification adopted follows the results of a recent OECD study (1989) on restrictive measures introduced by developing countries. The restrictive governments considered here are those countries which have set limitations on foreign ownership participations in all sectors of the economy (Bolivia, Colombia, Ecuador, India, Indonesia, Kuwait, Malaysia, Mexico, Mozambique, Nigeria, Paraguay, Peru, the Philippines, South Korea, Sri Lanka, Tanzania, Thailand, Togo, Tunisia and Venezuela). The fact of considering only restrictive developing countries does not appear to be a serious limitation. Restrictions in developed markets, in fact, had mostly been removed by the early 1980s and, furthermore, aimed to deter the penetration of world leading producers, such as the American firms, rather than that of followers, such as the Italian MNCs.

Control variable

The variable YEARSUB, which is equal to the year of entry of each subsidiary in the parent system, is introduced to detect whether more recent subsidiaries show a different ownership structure from older ones. As the dependent

Table 7.1:   *Determinants of the probability that a subsidiary is a joint venture (dependent variable: MNC ownership < 95 per cent)*

Independent variable	1a Logit	1b OLS linear probability	2a Logit	2b OLS linear probability
INTRAFT	-1.576^a (0.556)	-0.292^a (0.093)	-1.646^a (0.571)	-0.272^a (0.091)
TECHCOMP	-0.020 (0.015)	-0.0017^b (0.0008)	-0.018 (0.013)	-0.0018^b (0.0007)
IR&DINT*USA	0.236^b (0.113)	0.047^b (0.023)		
GNP/N	-0.148^a (0.035)	-0.030^a (0.006)	-0.124^a (0.031)	-0.024^a (0.005)
LSIZE	-2.492^b (1.254)	-0.449^b (0.208)		
LSIZE^2	0.091^c (0.048)	0.017^b (0.008)		
INTEXP	-0.120^b (0.052)	-0.024^a (0.009)	-0.113^b (0.044)	-0.023^a (0.008)
INTEXP^2	0.0022^a (0.0008)	0.0004^a (0.0001)	0.0018^b (0.0008)	0.0003^b (0.0001)
PROFIT/S	-4.458^b (2.186)	-0.797^b (0.370)	-5.853^a (2.263)	-0.962^a (0.351)
LRELSZ			-0.214^b (0.108)	-0.028 (0.018)
GOVRES	0.627 (0.437)	0.108 (0.075)	0.837^c (0.501)	0.138^c (0.082)
YEARSUB	0.018 (0.011)	0.0035^c (0.0020)	0.021 (0.013)	0.0038^c (0.0022)
CONSTANT	17.253^b (8.153)	3.583^a (1.325)	0.857 (1.008)	0.652^a (0.174)
R^2	0.22^d	0.26	0.25^d	0.29
$\chi^2 (11)^e$	88.32^a	$\chi^2(9)$	79.56^e	

Notes:
Standard errors in parentheses. Number of observations: 1a and 1b 288; 2a and 2b 231
a: Significant at the 0.01 level (two-tail test).
b: Significant at the 0.05 level (two-tail test).
c: Significant at the 0.10 level (two-tail test).
d: Pseudo-R^2, see Judge *et al.* (1988), p. 794.
e: Likelihood ratio test, see Judge *et al.* (1988), p. 794.

variable measures the ownership structure in 1986, and not at the moment of entry, the sign of the coefficient of YEARSUB may be interpreted in various ways. A positive coefficient may indicate that the preference for joint venture has increased in recent years or that joint ventures are subject to a greater mortality than wholly owned subsidiaries. No prediction is made as to the sign of this relationship.

Empirical results

The statistical results are shown in Table 7.1. Two different specifications of the theoretical model are considered and each is estimated by using both logit and linear probability form. In equations 1a and 1b the non-linear effect of absolute size is analysed. The relative size (parent/subsidiary) influence is instead tested in equations 2a and 2b. In these last two equations, due to the lack of data on the subsidiary's sales, the number of observations falls from 288 to 231. Sale data were not available for most of the subsidiaries in US high technology industries, therefore IR&DINT*USA could not be included among the explanatory variables in equations 2a and 2b.

The results of the four equations tested show a remarkable similarity as far as the sign and level of significance of the coefficients are concerned. This similarity can be taken as evidence of the robustness of the results.[9]

Let us now turn to the individual variables. The negative and highly significant (0.01) coefficient of INTRAFT confirms the hypothesis that, when the parent follows a strategy of global co-ordination, it is less likely to form a joint venture. Similar results were found by Stopford and Wells (1972), Kobrin (1988), and Gomes-Casseres (1989) for American firms, and by Rolli (1988) in an earlier study on Italian multinationals.[10]

As expected, the coefficient of TECHCOMP is also negative but, in the logit equations, it is not significant. Thus, differently from what was found by Gomes-Casseres (1989), the transaction cost argument (that the transfer of know-how has a negative effect on the likelihood of shared ownership) is not fully supported by the results. It is interesting to note that, for the firms studied, this indicator assumes the highest value in the case of two textile firms and a producer of furniture. In other words, the gap between the technological abilities of the leaders, on one side, and of the average firm, on the other, appears to be greater in these Italian industries than in other sectors. This result is not really surprising when we consider the well-known competitiveness of the Italian textile multinationals. Furthermore, it reflects the pattern of specialization of Italian industry. These firms are, however, leading producers in relatively low technology industries. Presumably this is one of the reasons why technology transfer has a more limited influence on ownership policy for Italian than for US firms. The latter group in fact enjoys leading positions in high technology sectors.

The hypothesis that the acquisition of technology has a positive influence on joint venture probability finds support in the positive and significant (0.05) sign on IR&DINT*USA. This result is highly influenced by the strategy of Olivetti, one of the major Italian MNCs, which in the 1980s followed an aggressive policy of technology acquisition in the USA, through cooperation with small local firms (Sanna-Randaccio, 1989). The decisive influence of individual investors on the overall results reflects one of the most important characteristics of the Italian case: the existence of only a limited number of foreign investors, and in particular of major MNCs (Acocella (ed.), 1985; Sanna-Randaccio, 1987; Onida and Viesti (eds), 1988; Acocella and Schiattarella (eds), 1988; Cominotti and Mariotti (eds), 1989).

A negative and highly significant (0.01) coefficient is found for GNP/N, thus apparently contradicting the hypothesis that the presence of highly skilled local producers increases the likelihood of a joint venture occurring.[11] This result is in contrast with the finding of Gomes-Casseres (1985).[12] The negative sign of GNP/N seems to lend some support to the counter-hypothesis. That is, that the greater 'cultural difference' existing with developing countries appears to increase the probability that shared ownership will be chosen.

The role of internal resources constraints in encouraging joint venture is fully confirmed by the results. There is a significant U-shaped relationship between size and joint venture probability. Both LSIZE and $LSIZE^2$ are significant (equation (1a)). The turning point is estimated at 884 billion Lit. In 1986, out of 100 parents considered, 15 had domestic sales higher than the value just mentioned. Thus, at least initially, as size increases, the likelihood of joint venture falls. This result conforms to earlier findings (Stopford and Wells, 1972; Gomes-Casseres, 1989) and gives credence to the hypothesis of the managerial constraint. It also gives support to one aspect of the idea of external finance constraint. In fact, once we control for profitability, size is likely to be inversely associated with the availability of external sources of finance.

The positive sign of $LSIZE^2$ is consistent with the interpretation that large firms represent a separate strategic group. These companies operate in international oligopolistic industries which in recent years have been undergoing profound changes, while medium sized firms are more frequently niche producers. According to this line of reasoning, $LSIZE^2$ captures the effect of a competitive environment which is conducive to joint venture formation for strategic reasons not otherwise accounted for in the model.[13]

A significant U-shaped relationship is found also in the case of INTEXP and $INTEXP^2$. Therefore, initially the accumulation of experience seems to lead to a decrease in joint venture probability. This result is in line with earlier findings from studies based on data from the 1960s and 1970s. In addition, this research shows that, at least in the case of Italian MNCs, once a high level has been accumulated, further increases in experience lead to a greater likelihood of joint venture formation.[14] The positive and significant coefficient of INTEXP^2 is interpreted as an indication that highly experienced firms are in a better position to exploit the benefits of co-operation.

The negative and significant (5 per cent or 1 per cent level according to the equation) coefficient on PROFIT/S fully confirms the role of the financial constraint. A firm's profitability has in fact a negative effect on the probability of a joint venture occurring.

Furthermore, the risk reduction function of shared ownership finds support in the results. The hypothesis is tested in equations 2a and 2b. The negative and significant coefficient (at the 0.05 level) on LRELSZ indicates that the riskiness of the operation, which is negatively related to LRELSZ, encourages shared ownership.

Turning to the effect of the government constraints, GOVRES is correctly signed but is significant only in equation 2. Gomes-Casseres (1989) found instead that in the case of US firms this variable was highly significant. A possible interpretation of this result is that restrictive regulations are applied more strictly in the case of US than of Italian MNCs. An alternative explanation is that the data of Gomes-Casseres reflect a period (the 1960s and 1970s) during which host government policies were considerably more restrictive than in the 1980s. As these policies have undergone profound changes (United Nations, 1988) the impact of this variable is now less pronounced.

As to the control variable, the coefficient on YEARSUB is not significant. This seems to suggest that in recent years Italian MNCs have not shown an increased preference for joint venture.

The values of the likelihood ratio test statistic calculated for each equation show that the logit regressions 1a and 2a are statistically significant at the 1 per cent level. The pseudo-R^2 (ρ^2) reported in Table 7.1 may be interpreted as a measure of the percentage of the 'uncertainty' in the data explained by the empirical results (Fomby, Hill and Johnson, 1984). It is thus a measure of the model explanatory power. The ρ^2 values for equations (1a) and (2a) are considerably higher than those obtained in similar studies.[15] However, they are still rather low, suggesting that further research is needed on the determinants of joint venture probability.

Conclusions

The model tested captures different facets of the joint venture phenomenon. The role of the internal resources constraint is fully confirmed by the results, but the importance of co-operative motivations (as in IR&DINT*USA) is also vindicated. Furthermore, institutional constraints, too, seem to have affected the ownership choices of Italian multinationals, although in a more limited fashion than in the case of US firms.

Notwithstanding the fact that a comparison with other studies is rather difficult, for lack of homogeneity in model specification and the time period considered, the following remarks can be made. It appears that several results conform by and large to earlier findings. This is the case for INTRAFT, LSIZE, INTEXP and LRELSZ. However, some new phenomena are detected, such as the U-shaped relationships between joint venture probability, size and experience. These results are likely to be a consequence of new patterns of ownership policy that emerged in the 1980s, rather than of peculiarities of the Italian case. The peculiarity of the Italian case seems to rest more in the small number of foreign investors rather than in the strategies of the firms operating abroad.

Notes

1. Financial support from the University of Rome 'La Sapienza' (ricerca di Ateneo) is gratefully acknowledged.
2. Notable exceptions are represented by Rolli (1988) and Hennart (1991).
3. A first project was conducted in association with IRM and covered the years 1974–81 (Acocella (ed.), 1985). The data were later updated to 1986 (Acocella and Schiattarella (eds), 1988).
4. It is important in interpreting the results to remember that 'while the sign of the coefficient does indicate the direction of the change, the magnitude depends upon $f(x'_i b)$, which, of course, reflects the steepness of the cumulative distribution function at $x'_i b$' (Fomby, Hill and Johnson, 1984, p. 351).
5. Like all other data, when not otherwise specified, these figures refer to 1986 and are drawn from the University of Rome database.
6. In some cases, while data on the percentage of the subsidiary's production exported to Italy were not available, information was available on the percentage of production sold in the local market (PSLM) and on the factors which had stimulated the investment. It may be recalled that the low cost of labour in the host country (CLCH) is an important locational determinant in the case of vertical integration obtained via runaway subsidiaries. In these additional cases, INTRAFT was set equal to one when PSLM was < 50 per cent *and* CLHC was mentioned as a determinant of local production.
7. The source used is World Bank, *World Development Report 1988,* Oxford: Oxford University Press. The data refer to 1986.
8. The data are taken from Mediobanca (1987), *Le Principali Società Italiane,* Milano: Mediobanca.
9. The diagnostic tests on equations 1b and 2b show that the assumptions of normality of residuals (in both equations) and of absence of heteroskedasticity (in equation 1b) are violated. Thus, when reporting the results, I will refer to the logit regressions.
10. Rolli, in her interesting research, considered the ownership structure of the foreign subsidiaries of Italian multinationals in 1981. The results, however, are not fully comparable with the ones reported here as the specification of the theoretical model tested is different.
11. It must be recalled, however, that this indicator is a poor proxy for local firms' capabilities.
12. However, this author uses a different proxy, namely the size of the host country's industrial sector. Hladik (1988) also found that GDP per capita has a positive and significant influence on the likelihood of joint venture, but she confined her study to R&D joint ventures.

13. Equations 1a and 1b have also been tested with normalized size (LNSIZE, LNSIZE^2), as this indicator is more in line with the proxies used in other studies (Stopford and Wells, 1972; Gomes–Casseres, 1985). The first order term was negative as expected, but not significant, while the coefficient on LNSIZE^2 was positive and significant, although at a lower level (10 per cent instead of 5 per cent). This change had no major effect on the other variables.
14. It must be noted that only one firm has a higher experience than the one associated with the turning point (between 27 and 31 subsidiaries, depending on the equation).
15. In Gomes-Casseres (1989), notwithstanding the much higher number of observations, the values of ρ^2 lie between 0.12 and 0.13.

Bibliography

Acocella, N. (ed.) (1985), *Le Multinazionali Italiane,* Bologna: Il Mulino.

Acocella, N. and Schiattarella, R. (eds) (1988), *Teorie dell'Internazionalizzazione e Realtà Italiana,* Napoli: Liguori.

Cantwell, J.A. and Dunning, J.H. (1986), 'New Forms of International Involvement of British Firms in the Third World', *mimeo,* University of Reading.

Cominotti, R. and Mariotti, S. (eds) (1989), *Italia Multinazionale,* Milano, il Sole 24 Ore.

Contractor, F. (1990), 'Ownership Patterns of US Joint Ventures Abroad and the Liberalisation of Foreign Government Regulations in the 1980s: Evidence from the Benchmark Surveys', *Journal of International Business Studies,* First Quarter, **21** (1), 55–73.

Contractor, F. and Lorange, P. (eds) (1988), *Cooperative Strategies in International Business,* Lexington: Lexington Books.

Doz, Y.L. (1988), 'Technology Partnership Between Larger and Smaller Firms: Some Critical Issues', in Contractor and Lorange (1988), 317–38.

Fomby, T.B., Hill, R.C. and Johnson, S.R. (1984), *Advanced Econometric Methods,* New York: Springer-Verlag.

Gomes-Casseres, B. (1985), *Multinational Ownership Strategies,* Unpublished doctoral dissertation. Harvard University, Graduate School of Business Administration, Boston.

Gomes-Casseres, B. (1989), 'Ownership Structures of Foreign Subsidiaries', *Journal of Economic Behaviour and Organisation,* **11**, 1–25.

Gomes-Casseres, B. (1990), 'Firm Ownership Preferences and Host Government Restrictions: An Integrated Approach', *Journal of International Business Studies,* First Quarter, **21** (1), 1–22.

Harrigan, K.R. (1986), *Managing for Joint Venture Success,* Lexington: Lexington Books.

Hennart, J.F. (1988), 'A Transaction Cost Theory of Equity Joint Ventures, *Strategic Management Journal,* Jul./Aug., **9**, 36–74.

Hennart, J.F. (1991), 'The Transaction Cost Theory of Joint Ventures: An Empirical Study of Japanese Subsidiaries in the United States', *Management Science,* (forthcoming).

Hladik, K.J. (1985), *International Joint Ventures: An Econometric Analysis of US Foreign Business Partnerships,* Lexington: Lexington Books.

Hladik, K.J. (1988), 'R&D and International Joint Ventures', in Contractor and Lorange (1988), 187–204.

Johanson, I. and Vahlne, J.E. (1977), 'The Internationalisation Process of the Firm: A Model of Knowledge Development and Increasing Foreign Market Commitments', *Journal of International Business Studies,* **8**, 23–32.

Judge, G.G., Hill, R.C., Griffiths, W.E., Lutkepohl, H. and Lee, T.C. (1988), *Introduction to the Theory and Practice of Econometrics,* New York: Wiley & Sons.

Kobrin, S.J. (1988), 'Trends in Ownership of US Manufacturing Subsidiaries in Developing Countries: An Interindustry Analysis', in Contractor and Lorange (1988), 129–42.

Kogut, B. (1989), 'The Stability of Joint Ventures: Reciprocity and Competitive Rivalry', *Journal of Industrial Economics,* **XXXVIII** (2), 183–98.

Kogut, B. and Singh, H. (1988), 'Entering the United States by Joint Venture: Competitive Rivalry and Industry Structure', in Contractor and Lorange (1988), 241–52.

Mowery, D. (ed.) (1988), *International Collaborative Ventures in US Manufacturing*, Cambridge, Mass.: Ballinger Publishing Company.

Mowery, D. (1991), 'Public Policy Influences on the Formation of International Joint Ventures', *mimeo*, University of California, Berkeley.

OECD (1989), *Investment Incentives and Disincentives: Effects on International Direct Investment*, Paris: OECD.

Onida, F. and Viesti, G. (eds) (1988), *Italian Multinationals*, London: Croom Helm.

Penrose, E.T. (1959), *The Theory of the Growth of the Firm*, Oxford: Basil Blackwell.

Porter, M.E. (1986), 'Competition in Global Industries: A Conceptual Framework', in M.E. Porter (ed.), *Competition in Global Industries*, Boston: Harvard Business School Press.

Rolli, V. (1988), 'Le joint venture internazionali delle imprese italiane: una verifica econometrica', *Quaderni Sardi di Economia*, **XVII**, 183–225.

Sanna-Randaccio. F. (1985), 'Quote di proprietà, joint ventures e soci: l'esperienza delle imprese multinazionali italiane', in Acocella (1985), 105–36.

Sanna-Randaccio. F. (1987), 'Note sull'internazionalizzazione produttiva delle imprese italiane', *Economia e Politica Industriale*, **XIV** (55), 219–33.

Sanna-Randaccio, F. (1989), 'Gli investimenti diretti italiani nei paesi industrializzati: il caso degli Stati Uniti', in Acocella and Schiattarella (1988), 339ff.

Stopford, J.M. and Wells, L.T. (1972), *Managing the Multinational Enterprise: Organisation of the Firm and Ownership of the Subsidiaries*, New York: Basic Books.

United Nations (1988), *Transnational Corporations in World Development*, New York: United Nations.

Williamson, O.E. (1986), *Economic Organisation: Firms, Markets and Policy Control*, Brighton: Wheatsheaf Books.

8 The impact on Spanish industry of accession with the European Economic Community

Susan Wolcott

Introduction

There has been a shift in the opinions of developing countries' policy-makers concerning the links between trade and growth. Though it has yet had only a small impact on the global trading network, its effect will accelerate in coming years. After World War II, many developing countries felt they would do best to turn inward and rely upon protected domestic markets to generate growth. This strategy proved unworkable and so they looked to increase trade, but in an asymmetric fashion. Developing countries sought reductions in barriers to their products while keeping their own trade restrictions intact. Now, the momentum is towards free trade associations and mutual reductions of barriers between developed and developing countries. The expansion of the European Community to include Greece, Portugal and Spain was the first example of such a union. The Community may soon furnish other examples. Turkey has long petitioned for entrance, and the newly democratic East European countries appear poised to add their requests. Mexico, barring political difficulties in the US, will soon join in the North American Free Trade Association with the US and Canada. Other Latin American countries have expressed a desire to do likewise. The South East Asian countries are considering the merits of forming a union with Japan.

In the midst of this general rush, it is appropriate and useful to examine the impact of one such union. Only the expansion of the EC has advanced beyond the negotiation stage. Of its three new members, Spain's experience is the most revealing. Portugal and Greece had negotiated away virtually all trade barriers with the EC by 1970. Only Spanish goods still faced substantial impediments. When two entities with dissimilar endowments, such as Spain and the previous nine members of the EC (the EC9 – Belgium, Denmark, France, Great Britain, Ireland, Italy, Luxemburg, Holland and West Germany) mutually lower trade barriers, according to the Heckscher–Ohlin theory, there should be a realignment of both entities' industrial production and exports towards those industries which use their relatively abundant factors most intensively. By examining the changes in composition and volume of disaggregated trade flows, and subtracting industrial trade losses from trade gains, it should be possible to infer the extent of the impact on aggregate industrial production and, through it, on income and employment. To conduct such a study, data on bilateral trade flows between Spain and the EC9 were converted from the Standard International Trade Classification (SITC) commodity categories to International Standard Industrial Classification (ISIC) industrial categories. The results were somewhat surprising. Not only did accession lead to a sharp decrease in Spain's overall bilateral trade balance – going from a surplus of over one billion US dollars to a deficit of over ten billion US dollars, but also the trade balance deteriorated for every major Spanish export industry. The few industries in which the net trade balance improved were insignificant in terms of the value of net exports.

This paper has three sections. The first examines the pre-accession trade barriers between Spain and the EC9, and the basic structure of their bilateral trade. The second catalogues post-accession changes in the disaggregated trade flows. The third questions just how surprising and problematic these changes truly are.

The basic structure of bilateral trade: pre-accession bilateral trade restrictions

Though accession has stimulated trade, the pattern of trade does not appear to have altered in any significant way. Table 8.1 lists the five industries which, in terms of value, were the most important to Spanish exports and imports in 1980, 1985 and 1988. The year 1988 is the most recent post-accession year for which data are available; 1985 was the last pre-accession year; and 1980 was included for perspective. The composition of important importing industries (industrial chemicals, transport equipment, basic iron and steel, electrical machinery and machinery, n.e.c.) has not changed over the period. For exports, three industries always predominate: transport equipment, basic iron and steel, and machinery, n.e.c.; and industrial chemicals was among the five most important industries in both 1985 and 1988. Two points can be drawn from table 8.1. First, at least regarding trade between the EC9 and Spain, the most important Spanish exporting industries are also the most important EC9 exporting industries. Secondly, though both exports and imports increased for all five industries between 1985 and 1988, the increase in imports was much more dramatic.

This last point is especially interesting given the pre-accession structure of trade barriers between Spain and the EC9. The trade-weighted averages of the basic duties applied to the products of each industry are listed in Table 8.2. Average EC tariffs are uniformly much lower than average Spanish tariffs. This is not only because their customs duties are, in general, lower than Spanish duties, but also because the EC granted Spanish imports a 60 per cent reduction in duties in a 1970 agreement.

Table 8.1:   *The five most important Spanish exporting and importing*
industries by value of the trade flow (millions of US dollars)
1980, 1985 and 1988

1980				
Exporting industries			Importing industries	
ISIC code		Value	ISIC code	Value
384	Transport Equipment	2504	382 Machinery, n.e.c.	1578
371	Basic iron and steel	1214	351 Industrial chemicals	1239
382	Machinery, n.e.c.	670	384 Transport equipment	1192
372	Basic non-ferrous metals	494	371 Basic iron and steel	797
381	Metal products	429	383 Electrical machinery	788
Total		5311	Total	5594
Total for all exports		9624	Total for all imports	9944

1985				
Exporting industries			Importing industries	
ISIC code		Value	ISIC code	Value
384	Transport equipment	3494	382 Machinery, n.e.c.	1804
371	Basic iron and steel	1431	384 Transport equipment	1469
353	Petroleum refineries	968	351 Industrial chemicals	1203
382	Machinery, n.e.c.	900	371 Basic iron and steel	760
351	Industrial chemicals	599	383 Electrical machinery	667
Total		7392	Total	5903
Total for all exports		11924	Total for all imports	10281

1988				
Exporting industries			Importing industries	
ISIC code		Value	ISIC code	Value
384	Transport equipment	7245	384 Transport equipment	7745
371	Basic iron and steel	2890	382 Machinery, n.e.c.	5388
382	Machinery, n.e.c.	1741	371 Basic iron and steel	2867
351	Industrial chemicals	1106	351 Industrial chemicals	2819
383	Electrical machinery	1047	383 Electrical machinery	2394
Total		14029	Total	21213
Total for all exports		22521	Total for all imports	32585

Note:
The SITC commodity trade flows were converted to ISIC industry classifications according to
the methods described in Appendix I.

Source: United Nations Trade Statistics.

Table 8.2 also identifies the extent to which EC9 and Spanish imports from each other were expected to increase by the end of 1988 if the new enlarged quotas proved to be binding, that is, if Spanish imports of goods from these EC9 industries, and EC9 imports from Spain, increased as much as quota limits. Once again, it is the Spanish industries which lose protection. In particular, note the case of the textile industry, about whose competition the EC9 countries were especially worried, as one might well expect. Table 8.2 suggests that the lowering of quota barriers would benefit the EC9 textile industry more than any other. Both the EC9 and Spain initially had quotas on these products which were scheduled to be phased out by the end of 1989. But the Spanish quota limits expand to a greater extent. In fact, between 1985 and 1988, Spanish net exports to the EC9 of textile industry products fell 150 per cent![1] In general, because Spanish trade barriers were initially higher than the comparable EC9 barriers, the apparent similarity of trading industries meant that when the countries began to drop their mutual trade barriers, Spanish exports from these industries were not stimulated in proportion with Spanish imports.[2]

Post-accession changes in bilateral trade
Table 8.3 reflects the impact accession has had on the growth of Spanish exports to the EC9 countries for each of the 32 three-digit ISIC industrial classifications. Table 8.4 lists similar measures for EC9 exports to Spain. The column of tables 8.3 and 8.4 headed 'Trend growth rate in quantity' lists the annual compound growth rate of export quantities over the pre-accession period, 1968–1985. Looking at Table 8.3 the first point to notice is that the fastest growing industries – tobacco (314), beverages (313), rubber products (355), professional goods (385) and transport equipment (384) – are, with the exception of the last, not yet among the largest exporting industries. Another significant observation that relates to this column is that 23 of the entries bear positive signs, which contrasts markedly with the next column, in which an equal number are negative. With the exception of industrial chemicals (351), the positive signs relate to industries that are insignificant in terms of bilateral export value. This column, headed 'Difference $(g-\hat{g})$', lists the difference between the actual growth rate between 1985 and 1988 and the predicted rate based on the pre-accession trend. The implication of these negative values is that, instead of speeding up Spanish export growth to the EC9, accession seems to have slowed it down!

This is similarly the implication of data relating to another measure of Spain's export success: import share that is included in consumption. A country's share in the apparent consumption of another is defined as the value of the first country's imports divided by the value of apparent domestic consumption of the second country. Apparent domestic consumption is

Table 8.2: Community and Spanish trade barriers

ISIC code	Weighted average tariff rates		Predicted impact on imports of relaxing quotas	
	Spain	EC9	percentage increase by 1988 of EC9 imports	percentage increase by 1988 of Spanish imports
210 Coal mining	12.50	0.00		
220 Petroleum and gas	11.16	2.36		
230 Metal mining	0.00	0.00		
290 Other mining	4.47	0.45		0.44
313 Beverages	28.23	7.91		
314 Tobacco	36.30	18.40		
321 Textiles	19.13	3.42	7.3	14.42
322 Apparel	26.27	4.29	12.7	186.67
323 Leather manufactures	5.88	1.06		
324 Footwear	15.29	4.08		
331 Wood Products	7.56	2.83		
332 Furniture	15.76	1.91		22.85
341 Paper and paper manufactures	10.88	2.01		
342 Printing and publishing	11.41	1.76		
351 Industrial chemicals	12.54	3.22		3.70
352 Other chemicals	14.57	2.90		2.49
353 Petroleum refineries	11.63	2.52		0.10
354 Petroleum and coal manufactures	10.65	1.35		
355 Rubber products	14.76	2.59		0.88

356	Plastic products	21.12	3.91	36.82
361	Pottery, china and so on	21.41	3.18	
362	Glass products	24.19	3.18	
369	Non-metal products	10.81	1.50	
371	Basic Iron and steel	17.34	3.72	0.01
372	Basic non-ferrous metals	9.82	1.12	
380	Scrap metal	4.67	0.00	
381	Metal products	12.54	2.15	3.41
382	Machinery, n.e.c.	10.02	1.64	16.17
383	Electrical machinery	15.68	1.88	13.83
384	Transport equipment	27.14	4.04	3.10
385	Professional goods	14.62	2.12	
390	Miscellaneous Manufactures n.e.c.	11.96	2.80	3.80

Note:
To construct the average industry weights, I first computed an unweighted average rate for each four-digit commodity classification. Using the SITC-NIMEXE correlation tables published by the EC, I assigned customs duties to four-digit SITC classifications. When more than one NIMEXE code was contained in an SITC classification, I took the unweighted average of the customs duties. Then I used a concordance linking SITC to ISIC published by the UN to assign customs duties to the three-digit ISIC classifications. I first, however, weighted the customs duty of the four-digit SITC code in the calculation by that codes value share in the relevant three-digit ISIC code in 1985. To determine the impact of relaxing quotas, I took the percentage increase in the quota given by the treaty for a four-digit NIMEXE category, translated it into a SITC category, and then determined the percentage increase in the three-digit ISIC category from the given percentage increase in its SITC component, again using 1985 weights.

Source: The European Community Commons Customs Tariff are from the *Official Journal of the European Communities.* The Spanish tariffs, the *Arancel de Aduanas,* are from *Boletin Oficial del Estado.* The information on quotas is from the Treaty of Accession, *Official Journal of the European Communities,* L 302, vol. 23, November 15, 1985. The EC concordance is from the European Community, 'SITC-NIMEXE Correlation Tables,' *Official Journal of the European Communities,* December 30, 1985, pp. 564–78. The UN concordance is from the United Nations, *Classification of Commodities by Industrial Origin (Links Between the Standard International Trade Classification and the International Standard Industrial Classification),* series M, no. 43, rev. 1, 1972.

Table 8.3: Growth of Spanish exports to the EC9 since accession

ISIC code		Value of exports 1987 (million $)	Trend[a] growth rate in quantity (1000 tonnes)	Difference $(g-\hat{g})$ 1985/88	Share in trend coefficient 1987	Trend[b] growth of share	Difference $(t-\hat{t})$ 1985/87
Total		22521.3	-0.09	0.16	0.70	0.07[a]	-0.32
210	Coal mining	0.9	2.20	-1.78	0.00	-0.00[a]	-0.00
220	Petroleum and gas	100.6	1.46	-1.32	0.27	0.04[a]	-0.05
230	Metal mining	54.5	0.65[c]	-0.62	3.06	0.25[a]	-2.40
290	Other mining	155.3	-0.67[c]	0.77	0.95	0.09[a]	0.40
313	Beverages	380.3	2.11[c]	-2.18	0.58	0.05[a]	-0.34
314	Tobacco	1.3	2.04[d]	1.45	0.00	0.00	-0.00
321	Textiles	790.5	-0.12	0.31	0.64	0.06[a]	-0.37
322	Apparel	216.0	0.49[c]	-0.41	0.36	-0.00	-0.02
323	Leather manufactures	382.6	0.50[c]	-0.48	3.63	0.17[a]	-0.30
324	Footwear	268.9	1.17[c]	-1.10	1.32	0.05[a]	-0.22
331	Wood products	257.2	-0.56[c]	0.30	0.58	0.07[a]	-0.68
332	Furniture	97.7	1.21[c]	-1.07	0.19	0.01[a]	-0.02
341	Paper and paper manufactures	607.6	-0.41	0.53	0.61	0.06[a]	-0.18
342	Printing and publishing	335.7	0.73[c]	-0.55	0.28	-0.01[b]	0.01
351	Industrial chemicals	1105.9	-0.25	0.40	0.52	0.05[a]	-0.26
352	Other chemicals	203.0	0.21	-0.15	0.11	0.00[a]	-0.06
353	Petroleum refineries	535.9	-0.23	0.21	0.64	0.21[a]	-1.01

354	Petroleum and coal manufacturing	53.9	-0.34	0.31	0.13	-0.02[a]	-0.04
355	Rubber products	632.7	1.88[c]	-1.80	1.46	0.04[a]	-0.28
356	Plastic products	601.0	0.27	-0.09	0.64	0.04[a]	-0.15
361	Pottery, china and so on	93.8	1.33[c]	-1.23	0.87	0.03[a]	0.22
362	Glass products	382.6	1.10[c]	-0.96	1.12	0.10[a]	-0.33
369	Non-metal products	394.0	0.71[c]	-0.49	0.45	0.01[b]	-0.09
371	Basic iron and steel	2890.3	0.73[c]	-0.56	1.90	0.20[a]	-0.56
372	Basic non-ferrous metals	543.8	-1.42[c]	1.30	0.60	0.08[a]	-0.86
380	Scrap metal	55.2	-1.44[c]	2.06	e	e	e
381	Metal products	762.2	1.20[c]	-1.11	0.35	-0.01	-0.07
382	Machinery, n.e.c.	1741.4	1.03[c]	-0.95	0.48	0.04[a]	-0.22
383	Electrical machinery	1046.7	1.42[c]	-1.30	0.29	0.02[a]	-0.08
384	Transport equipment	7244.6	1.70[c]	-1.67	1.59	0.21[a]	-1.04
385	Professional goods	217.8	1.86[c]	-1.73	0.51	0.02[a]	-0.03
390	Miscellaneous manufactures, n.e.c.	368.0	0.90[c]	-0.75	1.45	0.04	-0.02

a: This is the compound annual rate of growth of quantity (1 000 metric tonnes) of Spanish exports to the EC9 over the period 1968 to 1985, correcting for variations in EC9 GDP. I used quantities rather than values as there were no appropriate deflators for the separate industries. As long as the intra-group composition was relatively stable, this should be a meaningful indication of growth. I call the estimated rate ĝ. The 'difference' is then between the actual compound annual growth rate between 1985 and 1988 and the estimated rate.

b: This is the simple trend growth in the percentage share of apparent consumption between 1979 and 1985. Because it is a share, no correction for income or price variation is necessary. See the text for the definition of the share measure. The detrended post-accession change is the actual change between 1985 and 1987 in the percentage share, less the change we would have expected due to the previous trend.

c: Statistically significant at the 5 per cent level.

d: Statistically significant at the 10 per cent level.

e: This ISIC group is not a true industry. It was created because certain SITC categories originated in too many ISIC groups to apportion them with any degree of accuracy. See Appendix I for a full discussion of the concordance techniques.

Source: United Nations trade statistics.

Table 8.4: *Growth of EC9 exports to Spain since accession*

ISIC code		Value of exports 1987 (million $)	Trend[a] growth rate in quantity (1000 tonnes)	Difference (g–ĝ) 1985/88	Share in trend coefficient 1987	Trend[b] growth of share	Difference (t–t̂) 1985/87
Total		32585.3	0.18	−0.03	18.32	0.71c	5.26
210	Coal mining	2.5	4.35c	4.46	0.12	−0.14c	0.31
220	Petroleum and gas	184.0	4.67a	−4.55	69.14	0.58	19.27
230	Metal mining	13.2	0.95	−1.33	5.31	−1.52c	0.75
290	Other mining	103.5	−0.54c	0.69	9.77	0.20	0.59
313	Beverages	438.0	0.67	−0.23	5.05	0.15c	2.11
314	Tobacco	21.9	0.67	−0.73	1.06	0.02	−0.34
321	Textiles	906.6	−0.44	0.72	10.93	0.55c	3.18
322	Apparel	259.2	0.18	−0.14	5.97	0.24c	2.44
323	Leather manufactures	204.9	−0.01	0.23	14.23	0.28c	8.53
324	Footwear	21.7	0.08	−0.01	1.75	0.09c	0.55
331	Wood products	232.4	−1.16c	1.31	5.85	0.24c	0.90
332	Furniture	121.2	−0.24	0.55	4.28	0.15c	1.87
341	Paper and paper manufactures	535.8	0.34	−0.11	8.66	0.33c	2.64
342	Printing and publishing	605.3	0.28	−0.10	12.25	0.17c	4.11
351	Industrial chemicals	2818.9	−0.50c	0.74	24.20	0.45d	6.94
352	Other chemicals	634.8	0.08	0.07	6.46	0.11c	1.50
353	Petroleum refineries	393.3	0.58	−0.38	5.73	0.05	2.43

354	Petroleum and coal manufactures	133.3	−0.56	0.67	12.20	0.10	−3.45
355	Rubber products	570.3	−0.12	0.43	20.86	0.94[c]	6.27
356	Plastic products	938.1	0.47	−0.25	20.01	0.94[c]	4.36
361	Pottery, china and so on	60.1	−1.03[c]	1.35	11.45	0.13	3.12
362	Glass products	549.2	−0.04	0.31	32.36	1.58[c]	6.66
369	Non-metal products	256.5	0.49	−0.39	4.11	0.10[c]	0.92
371	Basic Iron and steel	2867.2	0.04	0.32	27.73	0.66[c]	13.62
372	Basic non-ferrous metals	570.2	0.19	0.00	14.12	0.36[c]	4.19
380	Scrap metals	554.0	1.13	−1.22	e	e	e
381	Metal products	1460.2	−0.14	0.43	14.36	0.63[c]	4.04
382	Machinery, n.e.c.	5387.7	−0.06	0.46	38.03	1.29[c]	7.02
383	Electrical machinery	2394.2	0.07	0.16	17.96	0.61[c]	4.08
384	Transport equipment	7744.8	0.20	0.17	30.75	1.81[c]	8.33
385	Professional goods	1115.2	0.19	0.06	58.26	1.27[c]	8.30
390	Miscellaneous manufactures, n.e.c.	487.6	0.18	−0.04	32.01	0.24	7.72

a: This is the compound annual rate of growth of quantity (1 000 metric tonnes) of EC9 exports to Spain over the period 1968 to 1985, correcting for variations in Spanish GDP. I used quantities rather than values as there were no appropriate deflators for the separate industries. As long as the intra-group composition was relatively stable, this should be a meaningful indication of growth. I call the estimated rate ĝ. The 'difference' is then between the actual compound annual growth rate between 1985 and 1988 and the estimated rate.

b: This is the simple trend growth in the percentage share of apparent consumption between 1979 and 1985. Because it is a share, no correction for income or price variation is necessary. See the text for the definition of the share measure. The detrended post-accession change is the actual change between 1985 and 1987 in the percentage share, less the change we would have expected due to the previous trend.

c: Statistically significant at the 5 per cent level.

d: Statistically significant at the 10 per cent level.

e: This ISIC group is not a true industry. It was created because certain SITC categories originated in too many ISIC groups to apportion them with any degree of accuracy. See Appendix I for a full discussion of the concordance techniques.

Source: United Nations trade statistics.

defined as domestic production plus total imports, less total exports.[3] The Spanish industries that have a relatively large share of the EC9 market include leather manufactures (323), metal ore mining (230), basic iron and steel (371), transport equipment (384), and rubber products (355). This list seems reasonable, though there is limited overlap with either the fastest growing or the largest exporting industries.

The column of Table 8.3 headed 'Trend growth of share' identifies the trend coefficient on the share measure over the period 1979 to 1985. Almost every element is positive, which suggests that even prior to accession Spain was becoming an increasingly important supplier of industrial goods to the EC9. But, once again, accession seems to have slowed the trend. The last column of Table 8.3 lists the difference between the actual and detrended change in the share measure since accession. The measure has grown below trend for all but two of the industries.

Table 8.3 should be compared to Table 8.4, which shows the impact of accession on EC9 exports to Spain. The situation is reversed. Since accession, exports from EC9 industries to Spain have increased above trend for all but the relatively insignificant industries. The share of EC9 imports in Spanish consumption has likewise increased at a rate greater than trend.

This situation is not surprising, given the relative size of pre-accession trade barriers between the EC9 and Spain. The significant and positive trend coefficients of Spanish exports to the EC9 and the share measures attest to the benefit Spain has received from the preferential treatment the European Community has granted to her over the past two decades. The consumption measure over the entire period cannot be constructed because of the lack of production data. However, Figure 8.1 plots Spain's share of the EC9's total *imports* of the total of these 32 industries' products between 1968 and 1987.[4] Spain's share has gone from just over 2 per cent to 6.5 per cent. Of the countries considered, only Japan's share has grown by a greater proportion over this period.[5] The periods of the Spanish share's most rapid growth were from 1970 to 1972 and from 1982 to 1984. The first growth spurt could well be explained by the lowering of EC9 trade barriers, while the second is more properly explained by the Spanish recovery from the fall in her competitiveness due to the 1979 oil shock.[6] Beginning in 1984, growth slowed noticeably, which is a bit surprising. Though EC9 trade barriers were low, they did exist. One would have thought that their disappearance would have led to some increase in Spain's share in consumption. The fall might reflect Spain's own improving domestic demand, which picked up sharply in 1985.[7]

Table 8.3 also facilitates examination of the experience of several 'sensitive industries'. European manufacturers and policy-makers were worried about a flood of cheap Spanish goods from industries which use low-skilled labour relatively intensively, which would have exacerbated existing problems

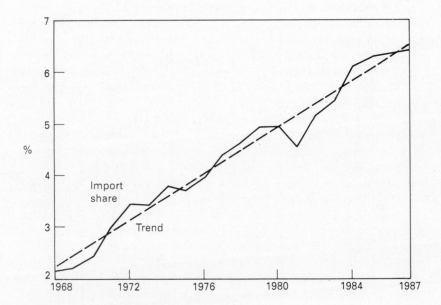

Note: See the text for a definition of the share measure.
Source: United Nations trade statistics.

Figure 8.1: Spain's share of total EC9 imports

of overcapacity in the EC. Their concerns about the textile industry have already been noted. Other industries considered vulnerable were the footwear, iron and steel, and the shipbuilding industries.[8] In a study which, among other things, attempts to predict industries in which Spain would have a competitive advantage, Robert Hine suggests that Spanish wages relative to German wages are especially low in the rubber, textiles, miscellaneous goods, footwear, minerals, timber, leather and food industries (Hine, 1989, p. 12).[9] There is substantial overlap between this set and the set of Spanish industries which are relatively important EC9 suppliers, and with the group of industries which concerned EC9 policy makers. Of these latter four, accession has led to a growth in Spanish net exports for footwear only; this is thus the only industry which could have been harmed among the EC9 countries by Spanish accession. In the other three, it appears to be the Spanish industries which suffered.

Though it appears that, in terms of net exports, the aggregate Spanish economy has suffered more than the aggregate EC9 economy, this pessimis-

Table 8.5: Value share of the five largest SITC groups contained in selected ISIC groups in 1985 and 1988

The five most important SITC groups contained in ISIC group 351 (industrial chemicals):

1985	Spanish exports to the EC9			Spanish imports from the EC9	
5121	Organic chemicals	18.46	5128	Organo-inorganic and heterocyclic	12.90
5128	Organo-inorganic and heterocyclic	11.21	5127	Nitrogen function compounds	8.53
5812	Products of polymerization	8.45	5125	Acids and their derivatives	8.42
5125	Acids and their derivatives	5.55	5812	Products of polymerization	7.69
5127	Nitrogen function compounds	5.04	2312	Synthetic rubber	7.50
1988	**Spanish exports to the EC9**			**Spanish imports from the EC9**	
5812	Products of polymerization	12.69	5127	Nitrogen function compounds	11.04
5121	Organic chemicals	8.15	5812	Products of polymerization	10.63
5128	Products of polymerization	7.30	5125	Acids and their derivatives	8.88
5127	Nitrogen function compounds	6.84	5128	Products of polymerization	8.15
5122	Alcohols, phenols, glycerine	6.23	5811	Products of condensation	5.28

The five most important SITC groups contained in ISIC group 371 (basic iron and steel):

1985	Spanish exports to the EC9			Spanish imports from the EC9	
6732	Bars and rods of iron or steel	26.68	6727	Iron or steel coils	32.03
6734	Angles, shapes and sections	14.09	6743	Plates and sheets, < 3mm thick, uncoated	11.79
6743	Plates and sheets, < 3mm thick, uncoated	9.71	6747	Tinned plates and sheets	8.62
6741	Universals and heavy sheets or plates	6.52	6750	Hoop and strip of iron or steel	7.59
6715	Other ferro alloys	5.57	6748	Plates and sheets, < 3mm thick, coated	7.57
1988	**Spanish exports to the EC9**			**Spanish imports from the EC9**	
6732	Bars and rods of iron or steel	23.39	6727	Iron or steel coils	25.69
6743	Plates and sheets, < 3mm thick, uncoated	15.78	6743	Plates & sheets, < 3mm thick, uncoated	15.00
6734	Angles, shapes and sections	11.88	6748	Plates and sheets, < 3mm thick, coated	11.16
6725	Blooms, billets and slabs	7.76	6742	Medium plates and sheets	5.75
6741	Universals and heavy sheets or plates	5.03	6731	Wire rod of iron or steel	5.22

The five most important SITC groups contained in ISIC group 382 (machinery, n.e.c.):

	1985 Spanish exports to the EC9		1985 Spanish imports from the EC9	
7143	Statistical machines	39.01	Office machines, n.e.c.	22.17
7149	Office machines, n.e.c.	10.76	Statistical machines	19.70
7250	Domestic electrical equipment	6.26	Pumps and centrifuges	5.81
7151	Machine tools for working metals	5.87	Road rollers, mechanically propelled	5.61
7192	Pumps and centrifuges	5.58	Machines and mechanical appliances, n.e.c.	4.11

	1988 Spanish exports to the EC9		1988 Spanish imports from the EC9	
7143	Statistical machines	23.36	Statistical machines	14.97
7149	Office machines, n.e.c.	15.35	Office machines, n.e.c.	8.38
7192	Pumps and centrifuges	8.04	Road rollers, mechanically propelled	6.58
7151	Machine tools for working metals	6.41	Pumps and centrifuges	6.13
7250	Domestic electrical equipment	6.35	Machines and mechanical appliances, n.e.c.	5.96

The five most important SITC groups contained in ISIC group 383 (electrical machinery):

	1985 Spanish exports to the EC9		1985 Spanish imports from the EC9	
7294	Auto electrical equipment	20.37	Auto electrical equipment	17.10
7250	Domestic electrical equipment	13.45	Electrical circuit makers, etc	16.84
7222	Electrical circuit makers, etc.	13.42	Telecommunications equipment	10.86
7231	Insulated wire and cable	12.27	Electrical machinery n.e.c.	9.28
7221	Electrical power machinery	9.21	Thermionic equipment etc.	9.06

	1988 Spanish exports to the EC9		1988 Spanish imports from the EC9	
7294	Auto electrical equip.	21.71	Electrical circuit makers, etc.	16.35
7222	Elec. circuit makers, etc.	12.34	Thermionic equipment, etc.	13.74
7250	Domestic electrical equipment	10.55	Auto electrical equipment	11.90
7231	Insulated wire and cable	10.35	Telecommunications equipment	10.30
7221	Electrical power machinery	9.31	Electrical power machinery	7.90

The five most important SITC groups contained in ISIC group 384 (transport equipment):

1985	Spanish Exports to the EC9		1985	Spanish Imports from the EC9	
7321	Passenger motor cars	77.19	7328	Bodies, chassis, frames	34.86
7328	Bodies, chassis, frames	13.57	7321	Passenger motor cars	27.05
7115	Combustion engines	4.90	7115	Combustion engines	19.49
7349	Airships and balloons	1.16	7199	Machine parts, n.e.c.	3.30
7199	Machine parts, n.e.c.	0.94	7192	Pumps and centrifuges	3.01
1988	Spanish exports to the EC9		1988	Spanish imports from the EC9	
7321	Passenger motor cars	67.65	7321	Passenger motor cars	47.97
7328	Bodies, chassis, frames	14.53	7328	Bodies, chassis, frames	18.77
7115	Combustion engines	6.31	7115	Combustion engines	13.27
7341	Aircraft, heavier than air	4.64	7325	Road tractors	4.69
7349	Airships and balloons	4.02	7341	Aircraft, heavier than air	2.69

Note: The concordance between the SITC groups and the ISIC groups is discussed in Appendix I.

Source: United Nations trade statistics.

tic conclusion would not necessarily hold if the broad industry classifications were masking significant differences in the composition of Spanish
exports and imports. What appears in the trade statistics as inter-industry
trade could simply be attributed to Spain importing inputs from the EC9
which are assembled in Spain for re-export as a finished product to the
EC9.[10] To the extent that assembly trade dominates the bilateral trade flow,
the increased EC9 imports are not actually competing with Spanish goods in
the domestic market. An important example of this type of trade is in the
automobile industry. The Spanish industry, which is run by five multinationals, now produces more than the United Kingdom's industry and exports
over half of the cars it manufactures. Three of the four largest non-oil-
exporting companies in Spain are Ford, General Motors and Renault. The
fourth is IBM. All are also among Spain's largest importers.[11]

According to a USITC study in 1984, the EC imported 1.4 billion US
dollars worth of goods after outward processing in Spain. Of this, 94 per
cent were motor vehicles, 1 per cent motors, generators, transformers and
related equipment, and another 1 per cent other machinery and equipment.
The remainder was distributed among several industries.[12]

An examination of the SITC trade flows which the concordance assigns to
the important ISIC industry classifications suggests that this type of assembly trade could be very important in the bilateral Spain–EC9 trade flow.[13] It
also suggests that even where assembly trade does not dominate, describing
the trade flows as 'inter-industry' may still be inappropriate. Table 8.5 lists
the contributions of the five most important SITC groups to the trade flows
for the five most important ISIC industry groups in 1985 and 1988.[14] Especially for ISIC groups 383 and 384 – electrical machinery and transport
equipment, respectively – the disaggregated SITC components appear to fit
the list given by the USITC. And given IBM's prominence as an exporter
and an importer, the prominence of statistical machines (SITC group 7143)
in ISIC group 382 – machinery, n.e.c. – suggests that assembly trade might
be important here as well.

The dominance of auto-related products in Table 8.5 is impressive. The
Spanish auto industry has been expanding rapidly in the last few years.
However, the huge post-accession jump in Spanish imports of fully assembled cars – from $3.5 billion in 1985 to $31 billion in 1988 – suggests that it
is in for stiff competition.

In the other cases, it is not obviously the case that the right hand elements
that relate to imports from the EC9 are inputs into the left hand elements that
comprise Spanish exports to the EC9. That does not necessarily imply that
they are equivalent goods. Even at this more disaggregated level, it is difficult to distinguish between inter- and intra-industry trade. Exports and imports
share similar commodity classifications, but it is just as easy to believe in

many cases that the products traded are of very different quality (even though belonging to the same SITC group) as it is to believe that they are truly examples of inter-industry trade. Without more specific knowledge of the actual trade flows, it is not clear that distinctions based on trade statistics can be made regarding the type of trade flow.

Though difficult to observe empirically, the distinction between intra- and inter-industry trade is important on welfare grounds. If the trade flows represent substantially different industries combined in one relatively broad statistical category, there is room for inter-industry trade gains. If the trade flows are intra-industry, the welfare results are ambiguous. Hine suggests that the greater the similarity of industrial structures among trading partners, the greater the opportunity for increases in inter-industry trade, and so the greater the potential for gains from accession. But if the traded goods are in direct competition – as between domestic and foreign produced automobiles – the similarity of the pattern of exporting industries, coupled with Spain's initially higher barriers, could mean that many of Spain's exporting firms are now at risk.

Assessing the risks of accession

Thus far, accession appears to have rendered Spain's industries less competitive; but appearances may be deceptive, especially at this early stage. It may be that the import surge only represents the natural build-up of capital in a country that is re-tooling prior to launching an export market attack. Proponents of this view can point to the impressive increase in foreign direct investment in Spain (which has doubled as a percentage of GDP from 1 to 2 per cent since 1986), and argue that the current account deficit is only the natural corollary to the capital account surplus. Accordingly, there will be trade gains from accession that will only appear in later years.

But there might be a link between accession and foreign investment completely separate from expected future exports. Investment, especially foreign investment, has been the engine driving Spain's recent exceptional GNP growth.[15] The data presented in this paper, however, suggest that static trade effects are a minimal part of the story. Nor is trade *per se* likely to be supremely important in the future: as Tables 8.6 and 8.7 illustrate, foreign investment has been concentrated increasingly on industries committed to serving the Spanish economy. Because accession did not change foreign access to this market, the new interest in the internal market suggests that the gains from accession will come from the associated internal reorganization of the moribund Spanish economy.

This point is recognized by Spanish government analysts. In a recent publication, Antonio Carrascosa Morales (the Director General of External Transactions) states that the accession stimulated investment flows in two

Table 8.6:   *Authorized foreign direct investment in Spain by industrial*
sector

Year	Percentage share of foreign direct investment								
	1982	1983	1984	1985	1986	1987	1988	1989	1990
Agriculture	2.70	1.94	9.74	1.27	1.73	1.47	1.19	4.40	0.97
Energy and mining	0.14	0.84	0.57	0.01	0.44	0.31	2.00	0.04	3.48
Manufacturing	69.11	61.29	52.85	63.40	61.43	52.60	36.67	39.43	34.60
Services	28.05	35.93	36.84	35.32	36.41	45.62	60.13	56.14	60.94

Source: *Boletin Economico de Informacion Comercial Española*, various issues.

Table 8.7:   *Authorized foreign direct investment in Spain by national*
origin

Year	Percentage share of foreign direct investment							
	1983	1984	1985	1986	1987	1988	1989	1990
EC	58.90	40.40	47.00	64.53	66.10	71.62	71.65	83.45
US	13.33	14.73	25.69	10.18	7.43	5.21	5.63	2.94
Japan	3.06	6.57	5.91	3.15	6.16	2.02	2.60	2.38
Others	24.71	38.30	21.40	22.14	20.31	21.15	20.12	11.23

Source: *Boletin Economico de Informacion Comercial Española*, various issues.

ways, of which only the second stems from the market's tendencies to allocate resources efficiently in an integrated area in order to achieve factor price equalization.[16] The first impact he points to is through the internationalization, and hence stabilization, of Spanish politics. He brings this point to the fore again when he discusses the present surge in investment by multinationals. Such companies follow a general strategy of having interests in many markets simultaneously in order to reduce risk. Despite this inclination, he suggests, they had limited their exposure in Spain relative to other Western European countries, until there was the consolidation of democracy associated with the accession.

The Director General also briefly alludes to a specific change in Spanish law which has encouraged investment. Various laws have been enacted since 1986 which have liberalized and *dotado de mayor transparencia* [made more transparent] the capital market. These include a basic change in the intent of the laws which substituted a requirement that the government authorize and approve all foreign investment for the requirement that the government be notified. More specific changes included a reduction in the number of 'strategic sectors' – sectors for which the government retained the right to authorize investment. In addition, the legal definition of 'direct investment' was brought into accordance with that developed in the Treaty of Rome (the document which initiated the EC), and the laws covering investment in the *Bolsa* – the Spanish stock market – were brought more into line with other EC countries' rules.[17]

The introduction of flexible labour contracts is another legal change which has induced investment in Spain.[18] When Franco outlawed unions in order to safeguard workers' rights, he simultaneously enacted laws which made it extremely difficult for firms to lay off full-time workers. The government has not eliminated these laws, but it has lessened their impact by introducing fixed term contracts and various special contracts for young people which combine fixed terms with decreases in the required Social Security contributions. These contracts have become so popular that they now comprise 30 per cent of all wage contracts.[19]

What is important to point out about these policy changes is that they were not necessarily connected to accession. They could have taken place without the accession, and accession could have proceeded without them. Their only connection to trade liberalization is that all three types of policies stem from the government's new strategy of freeing the workings of market forces.

One area in which change was necessitated by accession was monetary policy. Historically, Spain's inflation has been considerably higher than that of her European neighbours. The authorities began as early as 1982 to reduce inflation levels so that Spain could eventually join the European Monetary System, with its restricted band of variation among member currencies. The strong recent growth in domestic demand has meant that in order to keep inflation in check, authorities have had to keep monetary policy tight. The resulting high real interest rates have been another reason for the inflow of foreign capital. There has been another, less beneficial result. The high real rates have kept the peseta near the top of its allowed range in the EMS, thus decreasing the competitiveness of Spanish goods and compounding the direct ill-effects that the high rates are having on operating costs.

The complications of monetary policy highlight the double-edged nature of the benefits of accession. On the one hand, integration into the European Community has meant the opportunity to share the technical knowledge and financial resources of a more developed partner. On the other, Spain has had to give up much of her autonomy over trade, monetary and, in part, fiscal policies.[20] She is now much more vulnerable to external forces. Presently, many Spanish-made goods are not competitive with West European goods – a fact indicated by the great influx of imports post-accession. But because of the resources Spain possesses – primarily a well-trained and still relatively low wage work-force – there is every reason to expect that that would change if firms operated more efficiently. If greater efficiency can be brought about, Spain will gain enormously from her new opportunities. If she fails in this task, however, the new vulnerability can only bring eventual hardship.

The government, having given up the right to foster Spanish industry by shielding it from competitive risk, has undertaken a new strategy of improving the conditions in which firms operate. This is the rationale for the policies designed to liberalize the labour and capital markets that were described earlier. The government has also embarked on an ambitious programme to improve the country's infrastructure, increase vocational training, and reduce excess capacity in certain industries. But ultimately, it will be up to the firms themselves to reorganize. Spanish exporters experienced a substantial drop in profits in the first post-accession year.[21] There were extenuating circumstances: the decrease in US demand, the increase in domestic demand, the increase in the peseta and the decrease in subsidies to exporters. But at least part of the problem appears to have been the unwillingness of Spanish firms to change their habits and engage actively in external markets. They doubt they can compete either because these markets seem to be too difficult to break into, or because the firms have the perception, possibly correct, that their products are inferior. One hopeful sign for the future, however, was an international workshop organized by firms in October of 1986. There, the message was stressed that the progressive abandonment of protectionism ought to reinforce external competitiveness as it replaces previous government policies which had only been aids to inefficiency. Their apparent enthusiasm to accept responsibility for competitiveness – despite the already apparent problems of openness – may be the best reason to hope for the future of Spanish exports.

Conclusion

What lesson does Spain have to teach other less developed countries contemplating entry into a customs union with a developed partner? The most obvious is that there are potential gains, but they will not be realized without substantial changes in production practices. Further, the responsibility for success lies almost entirely with the private sector. If the firms fail to take advantage of the new opportunities, the government can assist them only in limited ways. By the act of accession, the government signs away the right to engage in protectionist policies. In a sense, this may be the most important benefit of such a union. Accession allows government to commit credibly to a policy of non-intervention. If this is what the businesses of these countries now want, as appears to be the case, then there has truly been a revolution in accepted development strategies since World War II.

Notes

1. The elimination of quotas was not the only factor negatively affecting the Spanish textile industry. A report prepared in 1985 by the Consejo Intertextile estimated that the imposition of the 11 per cent VAT levy, coupled with the end to a 12 per cent export tax rebate, would have an 18.98 per cent negative impact on the sector's commercial balance. 'Scaling Heights and Plumbing the Depths', *Financial Times*, 18 January 1986, survey article.
2. The pre-accession similarity of Spanish and EC production was also pointed out by Robert C. Hine, 'Customs Union Enlargement and Adjustment: Spain's Accession to the European Community', *Journal of Common Market Studies*, **28**, 1989, 9–10. He takes the more optimistic view that this similarity suggests that the accession will create opportunities to reap economies of scale.
3. It was impossible to consider all other countries when creating these measures at disaggregated levels. Consequently, I limited the 'rest of the world' to major trade partners. The countries of the EC9 are relatively open economies, and have significant trade links with many partners. As criteria for 'important', I required that the value of a country's total non-agricultural imports to the EC9 in 1985 had to be greater than one billion US dollars, and that the majority of the imports could not be petroleum related. In addition to Spain, 31 countries met that criteria. They were the US, Japan, the countries of the European Free Trade Association: Austria, Finland, Norway, Sweden and Switzerland; the other two recent entrants to the European Community: Greece and Portugal; an applicant to the Community, Turkey; the East European countries: Czechoslovakia, East Germany, Hungary, Poland, Romania and Yugoslavia; several members of the British Commonwealth: Australia, Canada, India and South Africa; and the newly industrializing countries: Hong Kong, Malaysia, Singapore, South Korea and Taiwan. Brazil, China and Israel also met the criteria. (Portugal was also a member of the EFTA prior to accession to the EC. To avoid double-counting, I never include it in that group.) The criteria for choosing Spain's major trade partners was that imports in 1985 had to be greater than 500 million US dollars, and that the majority of imports could not be petroleum related. Other than the countries of the EC9, only the US and Japan met the criteria. Because of their special significance in this question, I also included Greece and Portugal in the analysis.
4. 'Total imports' are again defined relative to the countries listed in the previous note.
5. Between 1968 and 1987, Spain's share of EC9 imports grew by 200.18 per cent (from 3.21 to 6.42 per cent). Japan's share grew by 283.99 per cent (from 5.23 to 14.86 per cent). The group which experienced the next largest growth after Spain was the NIC, the share of which grew by 137.63 per cent (from 6.20 to 8.53 per cent).
6. Augusto Lopez-Claros, 'The Search for Efficiency in the Adjustment Process: Spain in the 1980s', IMF Occasional Paper 57, February 1988, 4–5.
7. Lopez-Claros, 'The Search for Efficiency,' Table 2.
8. See, among others, Guido Ashoff, 'The Textile Policy of the European Community towards the Mediterranean Countries: Effects and Future Options', *Journal of Common Market Studies*, **22**, (1), September 1983, 17–45; Antonio Da Silva Ferreira, 'The Economics of Enlargement: Trade Effects on the Applicant Countries,' ibid., **17**, (2), December 1978, 120–42; Christian Deubner, 'The Southern Enlargement of the European Community: Opportunities and Dilemmas from a West German Point of View', ibid., **18**, (3), March 1980, 229–45; Ansgar Eussner, 'Industrial Policy and Southward Enlargement of the European Community: The Case of Shipbuilding and Repairs', ibid., **22**, (2), December 1983, 147–72; and Hine, 'Customs Union Enlargement and Adjustment'.

9. Note that this study does not attempt to analyse post-accession changes in trade for the food industry due to the great complexity of bilateral negotiations covering the Common Agricultural Policy.
10. I am indebted to Greg K. Schoepfle of the US Department of Labor for bringing this point to my attention.
11. David White and Ian Rodger, 'Everybody Wants it Made in Spain', *Financial Times*, 18 March 1986, p. 24.
12. United States International Trade Commission, *Production Sharing: US Imports Under Harmonized Tariff Schedule Subheadings 9802.00.60 and 9802.00.80, 1985–1988*, USITC Publication 2243, Washington, December 1989, Table 9–3.
13. Trade flow data are recorded according to the SITC (Standard International Trade Classification) system. Industry data on production and employment are recorded according to the ISIC (International Standard Industrial Classification) system. I have assigned the trade flow data to ISIC classifications using a concordance system described in Appendix I.
14. Note that it is possible for an SITC group to contribute to more than one ISIC group. For example, SITC group 7192, pumps and centrifuges, contributed $1.05 billion to Spanish imports of ISIC group 382 in 1985, and $391 million to ISIC group 384. The concordance between the SITC and ISIC groups is discussed in detail in Appendix I.
15. Simulations from the OECD INTERLINK model for Spain suggest that the growth in foreign investment has been responsible for one-third of the growth in GDP and employment between 1986 and 1988. OECD, *Economic Surveys: Spain*, 1988/89, Annex Table 1.
16. Antonio Carrascosa Morales, 'Inversiones extranjeras directas: Algunas motivaciones economicas de las ampliaciones de capital', *Boletin Economico de Informacion Comercial Española*, n. 2,128, April 4/10, 1988.
17. 'Nuevo régimen de inversiones extranjeras', *Boletin Economico de Informacion Comercial Española*, n. 2,043, July 7/13, 1986.
18. Josè Hernandez Delgado, 'Situacion industrial e incentivos a la inversion en España,' *Boletin Economico de Informacion Comercial Española*, n. 2,052, September 29/October 5, 1986.
19. Banco de España, *Economic Bulletin*, October 1990, p. 24.
20. Spain has now adopted the Community's VAT taxing system. Previously, she had had a 'cascading tax' system which, because exporters could receive rebates, had essentially subsidized exports. This change had a once and for all effect of raising Spanish prices, and so decreasing competitiveness, just as protectionist barriers were coming down. Ascension Calatrava Andres, 'El sector exterior ante la Union Aduanera: Anàlisis cuantitativo a nivel sectorial de la perdida de proteccion', *Boletin Economico de Informacion Comercial Española* n. 2,027, March 17/23, 1986. More recently, the need to control inflation has led to a general tightening of fiscal policy. Banco de España, *Economic Bulletin*, October 1990, p. 17.
21. Fancesc Granell, 'Las rentas de las empresas exportadoras en 1986,' *Boletin Economico de Informacion Comercial Española*, n. 2088, June 8/14, 1987.

Appendix I: Concordance

The commodity trade data were converted to industry classifications according to a schedule derived from the United Nations publication, *Classification of Commodities by Industrial Origin* (Links Between the Standard International Trade Classification and the International Standard Industrial Classification), series M, no. 43, rev. 1, (1972). There are 484 four-digit SITC classifications. These aggregate to form 32 three-digit ISIC groups. I did not follow the published schedule completely. A perfect concordance requires not only SITC data at the five-digit level, but also further unpublished divisions of some categories into parts 'A', 'B', 'C', and so on. When a four-digit SITC code appeared in more than one ISIC category, I split the

SITC classification. I assumed each part of the five-digit classification had an equal share in the four-digit classification. I attributed to the ISIC code the same share of the four-digit SITC classification as it had five-digit parts. I made a similar assumption concerning letter divisions.

There is one other problem with the concordance. The UN publication has a distinct, three-digit ISIC category, '380'. It refers to this group as metal products, machinery and equipment. The SITC codes which comprise '380' are various waste metals, and originate in all of the ISIC 38 categories. The UN created the 380 category as it was impossible to distinguish their exact origin.

9 Globalization and new forms of industrial organization

Klaus Weiermair

Introduction

Throughout the last decade and in the wake of intensified international competition, heightened technological change and uncertain macroeconomic conditions, firms, industries and whole jurisdictions have been subjected to massive industrial restructuring. To a large extent the restructuring exercise has been motivated by the desire of firms to restore competitiveness and profitability, and has been facilitated by their ability to adjust to the dictates of a changed and more turbulent market-place. By itself this observation would hardly be worth any further discussion or economic analysis. For throughout time, firms and markets have adjusted to shifts in demand or production, thereby changing the organizational structure and make-up of the 'efficient' organizations that survive the competitive race. According to this 'orthodox' school of thought, varying institutional arrangements such as, for example, different forms of work organization, may be regarded as trivial aspects of the market setting. However, this attitude of complacency regarding institutional phenomena in mainstream economics has given way to a renewed interest in studying institutional variety. Particular attention has, in this context, been given to two areas. One of these is the relationship between different organizational and technological features of firms and countries, and their consequences for patterns of trade and international competitiveness (Porter, 1990; Cantwell, 1989). The second is the diffusion of organizing principles in a more global economy (Kogut, 1985; Teece, 1987).

This paper is linked to both areas of inquiry. At the same time it explores the nature of technological and organizational 'trajectories' and, relatedly, 'trajectories in international competitiveness' for different industries and countries. It is organized as follows: Part 1 describes and defines the process of globalization in various industrial settings; and Part 2 examines the diffusion of two new industrial organizing principles, specifically flexible 'manufacturing' and 'network organization'. In Part 3 we conclude and speculate on the future organizational trajectories of diverse industrial and country settings.

The process of industrial globalization

Globalization and/or 'to globalize' are widely used terms in many academic and popular journals alike. But just as the word 'competition' conveys a fair degree of conceptual ambiguity, so globalization means different things to different authors (Ghoshal, 1987). According to Porter, who was one of the first to use the terms 'globalization' and 'global competition', a global industry is defined as: 'one... in which a firm's competitive position in one national market is appreciably affected by its competitive position in another national market.' Hence, global competition implies that firms compete against each other on a truly world-wide basis, drawing on competitive advantages that grow out of their world-wide network of activities (Porter, 1986).

Typically, advantageous interactions between a firm's position in different markets may arise from sharing costs and resources (for example, learning benefits) across different markets. Diverse strategic actions by individual firms have also been a factor. Favourable conditions for globalization in some industries have derived from technological changes that yield lower costs of global management and control. Hence it is probably not useful, and it may be impossible, to classify industries *ex ante* into those which are multidomestic in nature and those which have a global reach. Most industries are not born global, but may have global integration and activities thrust upon them in the course of time through entrepreneurship and technical change.

Thus it seems that globalization represents at least in part the dynamic adjustment of market and enterprise behaviour to changes in the fundamental socio-economic characteristics of economies in diverse regions.

In some cases, for example in steel, glass, aeroframe and aeroengines, production scale economies are sufficiently large for global integration to offer advantages over time, irrespective of the more or less efficient allocative processes at work at each point in time. Put differently, the global distribution of production, foreign investment and trade is not simply a derivation of nationally and regionally varying factor endowments and/or factor prices, but is determined by the way in which those factors are utilized in the specific and internationally varying socio-economic settings of firms and industries. A few illustrations may serve to clarify the point. Italy's success in becoming the largest exporter of textiles and clothing in the industrialized world has not been attributable to low wages, big economies of scale or cheaper and more abundant general purpose technologies in textiles and clothing. Rather, success and international competitiveness have resulted from the way in which industry- and firm-specific skills have been created through specialized schooling and training in textile (clothing) fashions and technology. This is evident within firms and local schools, and in the way in which organizational and technical 'know-how' has been developed across firms within industrial districts (Weiermair, 1991). Specific skills similarily account for Denmark's success in enzyme production (which reflects a base of sophisticated scientific knowledge of fermentation) and her success in furniture (dependent on a pool of university-trained furniture designers) (Porter, 1990). Analogously, Germany's apprenticeship system in such specified fields as automative assembly, printing or tool-making has been widely acclaimed as contributing to her competitive position in these sectors (Daly *et al.*, 1985; Sengenberger, 1984). The interplay of a sophisticated home demand and robotics manufacture in Japan has been attributed to the rising success and international competitiveness of Japanese robotics producers (Sadamoto, 1981).

Globalization of economic activity therefore has to be seen within the context of a continuously and dynamically shifting competitive advantage of firms and nations (regions), with the latter two being interrelated through complex interpenetrating socio-economic and technical systems of production and distribution. The latter would have to include not only prevailing forms of market organization and domestic supplies of factors of production, but has equally to include national systems of learning and schooling; the social context of production; the system of industrial relations; socio-cultural factors shaping both patterns of production and consumption; government–business relations, notably, the relative *savoir faire* in industrial policy-making; and the domestic and international embeddedness of industries and firms with respect to related and supporting firms and industries.

Adapting a systems view, as cumbersome as it might be, is analytically better for explaining, for example, the sudden emergence of Japan and her multinational enterprises in world trade and foreign direct investment *vis-à-vis* the USA or Europe, just as it is superior for explaining the international competitiveness of specific sectors and industries in specific regions.[1] The systems view should not only help us understand the shifting location of international economic activity within a framework of 'globalization' but, more importantly, by portraying the varying international and intersectoral institutionally grounded patterns of technological and organizational learning and experimentation, the systems view facilitates a better understanding of technological trajectories, diffusion and evolving future comparative advantages.

The next section examines two novel organizing principles associated with technical change. It discusses their national and international diffusion and implications for the future international competitiveness of firms and industries.

The rise and fall of the 'Fordist' principle of production

Fordist production principles were introduced in the first quarter of this century. They are probably better known as Taylorism, by the name of their intellectual founder. Taylor promulgated three guiding principles of production:

1. The freeing of the labour process from the skills of workers (simplification of jobs and the routinizing of tasks opened the work process for unskilled workers which made management less dependent on skilled, and hence 'powerful', workers).
2. The separation between conception (design) and execution. This, in essence, left the shop floor with the mere execution of managerially predetermined, tightly enforced production plans and schedules.
3. A centralization (monopolization) of production knowledge at the management level, thereby leading to control of the entire labour process through formal rules and procedures.

Thus, the decline in the foreman's former empire went hand in hand with the rise of the managerial organization, initially characterized by large increases in the employment of engineers and, later, an army of professional managers. Expanding markets and associated technologies meanwhile created the need for the organizational transformation of the firm. High volume technologies and production methods required large-scale organizations and a massive and continuous flow of material in both production and distribution. Predicated on major technological advances in transportation, communication, distribution and production, the new managerial organization and hierarchies integrated mass production and mass distribution within a single business enterprise (Chandler, 1977). But, as noted by Piore and Sabel, the large investments in highly specialized equipment and the employment of narrowly trained workers upon which mass production depended, required stable markets for standardized products. Forward and backward vertical integration and diversification enabled firms to create entry barriers, and thereby stabilized their market share and sales growth (Piore and Sabel, 1984, p. 49).

The basic operating framework of modern industrial organizations was further extended by multinationalization of business activities. With the objective of enlarging and stabilizing markets, enterprises began to move to foreign countries. The process began in the 1920s and was intensified in the post-World War II period during the 1950s and 1960s. It was predicated on the multidivisional structure of the firm, first introduced in the management model in the 1920s. By freeing top management from everyday responsibilities, which became delegated to a new class of 'middle management' (division heads), it had become possible to concentrate more head office efforts on strategic planning, the development of new management methods and the evaluation of the various divisions. These in turn were able to pursue a greater degree of product and geographical diversification than had previously been possible with earlier functional forms of organization.

In the post-war period, the multi divisional structure became the dominant basis for organizing large-scale manufacturing. Of equal importance for the rise of managerial capitalism was the labour–capital accord in the form of evolved tacit informal understandings and collective bargaining practices between the typically large oligopolistic mass production industries and the barely legitimized industrial unions. Within this framework, unions became bureaucratic, conservative and inflexible. Firms' ability to pay on account of their market position furthermore made them sure targets for unionization drives; unions in turn provided management with much needed stability and predictability in the form of multi-year collective agreements (Aronowitz, 1974, pp. 411–412). This labour–capital accord focused mainly on the extrinsic factors of motivation and pay, and thus on distributional practices. It thereby helped to develop an industrial relations system which was based on the proliferation of clear job demarcations and classifications and strict work rules. Bureaucratic controls predicated on seniority and job classification schemes became the dominant feature of human resource policies among large American industrial firms. Thus, the system of industrial organization and industrial relations which had evolved particularly in the USA in the immediate post-war period had been successful and was accepted by all social partners. It helped to avoid the extremes of the business cycle and encouraged high levels of productivity and growth. At the work-place, more money and steady work replaced earlier values of individual achievement and greater opportunities for individual advancement. In the aggregate society, emphasis shifted from production to consumption. The aforementioned stylized description of environmental conditions and consequences is chiefly reflective of the US experience. As will be discussed later, not all industrialized countries went through the same evolutionary process, but rather adapted Fordist principles to existing and varying social, economic and political conditions.

From the early 1970s onwards the Fordist principles of production were exposed to a series of tensions which eventually led to their demise. A first social unrest against narrowly defined assembly-line work came in the form of workers' rebellion through 'wildcat strikes' in the French and Italian car industries. The US variant of the Fordist malaise manifested itself in a more subtle way through a secular rise in absenteeism, turnover and/or lower levels of worker productivity (both in terms of output and quality of work). Social unrest had furthermore been nurtured by differences between the rising work expectations of increasingly better educated workers and the deskilling tendencies of scientific management. In some jurisdictions industrialists have reacted to these trends, and still continue to react, with further standardization, automation and the employment of unskilled labour in the form of youth, women and/or immigrants and guest workers. However, despite increases in the capital/output ratio and starting well before the first oil shock in 1973, neither labour nor total factor productivity increased. This could be taken as further evidence regarding the ineffectiveness of traditional Fordist production principles. The deep 1974/1975 and 1981 recessions finally brought to light another weakness of Taylorism: specifically, an excessive rigidity of the mass production system in the face of unexpected variations in demand. Thus, for the first time, a need for significant revisions in engineering principles has became apparent. In addition, a number of product market developments have since further increased the demand for more flexible forms of manufacturing. Among these we may particularly note the following:

1. Increased levels of wealth and income have led to a saturation of markets for standardized mass products. This has provoked customers to ask increasingly for differentiated products. The replacement demands for consumer durables such as automobiles, sports equipment or consumer electronics are good examples.
2. The increase of free trade, the deregulation of capital markets and globalization have dismantled and dislocated national oligopolistic market structures and processes. Price wars have erupted as a consequence of new market entry and/or imports, and associated higher levels of underutilization of capacities in a number of regions. In turn this has spurred firms to seek 'first mover' advantages with respect to the incorporation of new designs and technologies into market products, thus making competition much more technology-driven.
3. As the cluster of innovations in mature industries such as engineering, chemistry and aerospace became progressively exhausted towards the end of the 1970s, new innovations and industries, centred around electronics and software, came to the forefront. Many of these innovations negated Fordist principles and signalled a possible shift in paradigmatic organization (Skinner, 1988; Walton and Lawrence, 1985). Information technologies have certainly enhanced the technical flexibility of production at no extra cost, thereby permitting the simultaneous achievement of flexibility and efficiency.

The new model of management, work organization and networking
Just as the production system has to be interpreted and understood via its congruent and constituent parts, that is standardization of products, mass

marketing, economies of scale, strong division of labour, clear demarcation of jobs, emphasis on extrinsic rewards, and autocratic management, the new management paradigm should similarly be grasped through a systems perspective.[2] The most important new parts of the system are:

1. The creation of long-term manufacturing strategies.
2. The development of co-operative and multi-functional inter-firm relationships.
3. The establishment of new and different organizational structures, decision-making and human resource management systems.
4. A constant nurturing of technical change and the effective blending of the human element in setting up productive organizations.

A first integral part of the new model is the firm's internal nurturing of a strategic vision with respect to manufacturing technology. This tends to reflect, or is at least influenced by, the firm's assessment of existing and potential strategic advantages in product markets. A company that believes that it can meet competition through price only will revert to the old model of standardized mass production. On the other hand, if the assessment of potential competitive advantage calls for satisfying or creating new market niches through new product design and product differentiation, a much more active stance with respect to both the level and frequency of technological change and the maintenance and development of manufacturing strategies will emerge. Inter-firm and intercountry comparisons regarding competitive response and product histories can help illustrate this point. In the automobile industry, for example, American producers until very recently have reacted to a changed demand for smaller as well as more differentiated cars with cheaper, stripped-down versions of large cars (a typical reaction for a manufacturer of standardized products). European and Japanese producers have responded with model changes and product differentiation. While, however, the strategic perspective of GM and Ford was to produce a single standardized design on a global scale at the cheapest possible cost, Japanese car-makers saw their future as lying in more careful export-oriented style changes and other forms of product differentiation (Kamiya, 1976; Abegglen and Stalk, 1985).

Similarly, Citibank had to make a strategic choice between mass production and a flexible system of production. A large increase in new financial products and new customers implied the need for a new organization of the entire operation to respond quickly to shifting customer needs. Thus, Citibank eventually replaced its functional organization design, based on standardized products and clients, by a product and design with decentralized data processing (Walters, 1982). A case study involving Olivetti has equally pointed towards the congruence between the company's perception and vision of changing customer demands in the direction of more individualized, service-oriented products and the establishment of flexible manufacturing strategies. According to Skinner (1969, 1988), poor or non-existent strategic choices have frequently been associated with personal inadequacies of CEOs in matters of technology (notably modern information technologies) and the associated premature delegation of decision-making, or alternatively have stemmed from a lack of awareness regarding choice and trade-offs among different technological options.

Another element of the new model concerns the evolution of new strategies towards suppliers and any other market organizations which bear on the vertical or horizontal aspects of production. According to the old industrial organization paradigm, standardization and heavy investment in specialized machines dictate unchanging parts requirements, and hence fostered arm's-length relationships with suppliers. It also prevented possible joint venturing and co-operation in R&D across the market-place on account of appropriability problems. Rapid product line changes and heavy product differentiation, on the other hand, demand a much closer co-operation between primary production units and parts firms and other suppliers and sub-suppliers, particularly in areas such as design and production access to central firms and, vice versa, the tapping of new ideas in supplying firms through the central unit. Thus, the total inter-organizational network can consist of affiliated supply and sales organizations, independent manufacturing and parts processing firms, and an R&D network in which company- and government- or university-owned organizations can entertain co-operative relationships.

The network form of organization has become particularly useful, if not necessary, wherever an interactive process of information creation and learning is required, and where 'information condensed though the network is "thicker" than that condensed though the market, but is "thinner" than that in the hierarchy' (Imai, 1989). Cases in point are the fusion and fission of technologies through continuous interactive innovation by linkages across, rather than within, the borders of specific industries and firms (for example, machatronics involves the fusion of mechanical engineering and electronics).

Networks do not stop at the border of countries. To the contrary, there has recently been a mushrooming of cross-border networks, particularly in information technology-related markets, where systemic innovation is best carried out through fusion and fission of core technologies using co-operative networks. Networks often require a rich and thorough exchange of information and personnel between firms, based on the need to develop and build jointly new products and to create new information. Creation of the socio-economic context for the generation of new information constitutes a very process-oriented and entrepreneurial act in contrast to the planned control mechanism of the traditional organization. For a network organization to be effective, it is necessary that the links maintain a long-term, semi-fixed relationship with a full sharing of information based on 'mutual trust and mutual dependency'.

Probably the most important ingredient of the new management model, and hence the area where changes are needed the most in laggard companies (jurisdictions), concerns the ways in which new configurations of technology and human resources are perceived, designed and executed. The crisis of manufacturing in some advanced countries stems either from an incongruence of new technologies and obsolete organizations (Hayes and Jaikumar, 1988) or from the fact that tool-makers and computer companies fail to offer more than small chunks of a company's total technological system's needs (Skinner, 1988: Hayes and Jaikumar, 1988, p. 277). This is a fact which is enhanced in a market environment where co-operative inter-firm linkages are absent and risk aversion dictates narrow specialization. Finally, the new system of flexible production changes skill requirements and power shifts within companies (conferring more power to system designers, co-ordinators and/or trouble-shooters, and taking it away from discipline, control-oriented supervisors and line managers). Flexibility requires a new complex, informal system of work knowledge within which workers can respond to changes in the conditions of production (the nature and composition of inputs, mechanical maintenance, and so on). Just as standardization previously led to deskilling, increased hierarchy in the factory, and loose, price-oriented supplier contacts, the transition towards the new model of industrial leadership is largely hampered by prevailing rules of corporate capital budgeting and financial management, as well as the prevalence of traditional reward/punishment practices (Skinner, 1988).

What is needed from management now is a process of 'reconceptualization', which should lead to revival in industries generally thought to be at the end of their product life-cycle. Industries which had generally been thought of as relatively mature only a decade ago (for example, textiles, shoes, steel, automobiles, railroads or banking) have shown that reversals are possible through new technologies and organizational innovation, for example, new forms of management (OECD, 1988). Mature industries became mature in the first place because management strived to put into place established markets, established production competencies, established dealer networks and existing hardware, and tried to make it work with high volumes, low margins, and standardized products and processes. There was also a tremendous reluctance on the part of management, towards change. Reconceptualization poses real challenges to management, not only because this is difficult in itself but, more importantly, because today's changes appear very different from the kind of tasks and work which management has become accustomed to. Although well described in a mushrooming literature on the management of change (for example, Morgan, 1988), industrial practice is still lagging behind. Alternatively, change has become managed in a sub-optimal manner and still reflects Fordist/Taylorist principles in which organizational design such as CIM is simply superimposed (driven by staff specialists) on existing structures, reward systems, skill distributions, and existing decision-making structures.

The more successful approach towards restructuring, reorganization and maturity reversal operates from within the production system. It is facilitated by management's delicate balancing of stability and instability, reciprocal mutual dependence, information-sharing among all members of the organization, and a climate of rapid individual and organizational learning which ideally involves supplier and sub-supplier systems. The aforementioned constitute the ideal applauded by many writers in both the academic and popular management literature over the past decade (Adler, 1986, 1988; Tushman *et al.* 1986; Ouchi, 1981; Jaikumar, 1986; Gunn, 1987; Peters, 1988; Abernathy, 1982; Schonberger, 1986; Business Week, 1989a, 1989b; The Economist, 1987). Yet, as alluded to earlier, in some jurisdictions (notably the USA but also the UK and France), management has not been able to obtain the kinds of flexibilities promised in the literature.

The prevalent Western system seems to aim at the pursuit of economic efficiencies realizable through the professional control over specialized operational tasks. In the Japanese case, there appears to be a greater 'semi-autonomous problem-solving capability (information processing capacity) among workers, thus making the intra-firm demarcation between control and operating tasks rather ambiguous' (Aoki, 1988). However, if post-Fordism forms of production and management are as important and efficient as claimed, free trade, foreign direct investment and/or globalization should diffuse this new form of organization across industries and jurisdictions. In the final section we will speculate on the possible future of the new industrial organization paradigm in different sectors and jurisdictions.

Globalization and the diffusion of the new organizing principles

Pressures to reorganize industrial production now exist in most industrialized countries on account of the aforementioned changes in educational attainment, technologies and customer demands for higher quality and more diversity at a reasonable price. It is through a new international environment of relatively unrestricted foreign investment and free trade that these new production philosophies and principles begin to penetrate markets on a global scale. With unrestrained competition this is also what one would expect: for example, those companies which can translate customers' needs for higher quality and service, low price and product diversity into a coherent and rational production and management system will be the ones who will eventually remain as sole survivors in the market-place.

The extent and speed of the diffusion process in various sectors and regions will be determined by the trade and foreign investment exposure of a given sector, a region's initial infrastructure with respect to technology and human capital, and finally management and firms' capabilities and willingness to adopt strategic changes where necessary. A relatively simple and straightforward hypothesis can be constructed with respect to the first determinant of diffusion, that is, the strength and level of international competition in a particular sector or region. The more protected or the less exposed a particular industry or sector, the less likely will there be changes in methods of production or distribution, particularly when such changes emanate from abroad. Similarly, we would expect those sectors to have been less affected by organizational innovations in the past. Industries which might fit this multidomestic mode of operation are usually traditional, supplier-dominated industries such as agriculture, housing, traditional manufacturing or private services. By and large these are sectors which also in the past have neither seen the rapid introduction of Fordist principles nor the spread of the MD form organization (Chandler, 1977; Maddison, 1982).

On the other hand, the consequences of international trade, investments and changes in competitive advantage on account of factor endowment are much more difficult to predict because of the interdependencies between industrial production and the generation of new opportunities (production and products) through organizational and individual learning. Such learning in the form of learning by doing or search activities such as R&D occur in fields of firms and industries related to their current know-how. A fair amount of this know-how is furthermore of an accumulative and tacit nature and rests embodied in organizations and people. As such it suggests that:

1. Initial factor endowment, and particularly its initial deployment and utilization in institutionally (efficiency) varying forms, can give rise to vicious or virtuous cycles of industrial, national or organizational economic development, irrespective of subsequent patterns of trade and foreign investment.
2. Technology transfer, to the extent that it does take place, can in this case only be effectuated through the transfer of property rights pertaining to whole organizations.[3]

The above imply also a new and different form of intermediate market organization in the form of industrial districts or parks, or other boundary-crossing network organizations. These will enhance co-operation and technology transfer in the face of high costs and risks of rent appropriation.

Regions or jurisdictions which provide industrial system synergies or agglomeration economies can therefore lay the foundation for technological trajectories in such new information, sensitive industries as banking and insurance, or such emergent industries as electronics, machatronics, computers and telecommunications.

Most important and arching over to all these considerations and conditions for shaping comparative advantages through new forms of industrial organization are the ability and willingness of firms and management to accept and implement the implied strategic changes with respect to their organizations. Some authors have identified the decline of countries, regions, industries and firms with the ossification of economic and organizational structures due to conflict and adversarial relationships among interest groups, none of which are powerful enough to enhance the welfare of their constituents (Olson, 1982; Ouchi, 1984; Thurow, 1982). Viewed in this context, Japan and its system of management appear to have temporarily outperformed the rest of the world, contrary to North America and Europe where the movement towards the new paradigm appears still to be met with considerable social resistance.

Japan's far wider-reaching consensus has enabled a new system of social and industrial organization that contains the aforementioned configuration of 'hardware, software and humanware' which constitutes the J-form of management in Japanese manufacturing, both at home and in their wholly owned foreign subsidiaries (Shimada and MacDuffie, 1987; Yoshida, 1987; Shibagaki *et al.*, 1989; Dunning, 1986; Womak, 1988). Given its productivity imperatives, the J-form will eventually spread across the globe just as the Fordist principle did 60 years ago. There will, however, be large intercountry differences in adaptation, just as the Fordist principle was not copied perfectly by every country (OECD, 1989). By then it may very well be that Europe has adopted a common approach regarding these changes, so that one might truly speak of a 'European system of management'.

Notes

1. This is not the place to discuss the relative merit of orthodox versus systems views in explaining trade. Such a discussion would constitute another paper.
2. As with the Fordist system different industries and jurisdictions will likely evolve different versions of the new management system. For heuristic purposes we first describe the new paradigm as an ideal-type system.
3. As there is no ready market for organization-specific human or technological capital, purchasers of know how are required to buy whole firms as opposed to pieces of knowledge or information.

References

Abegglen, James C. and Stalk, George, Jr (1985), *Kaisha The Japanese Corporation*, New York: Basic Books.

Abernathy, William (1982), *The Productivity Dilemma*, Cambridge, MA.: MIT Press.

Adler, Paul (1986), 'New Technologies, New Skills', *California Management Review*, **24**, (1), 9–28.

Adler, Paul (1988), 'Managing Flexible Automation', *California Management Review*, **30**, (2), 34–56.

Aoki, M. (1988), 'A New Paradigm of Work Organization: The Japanese Experience', Wider: Working Paper No. 36.

Aronowitz, Stanley (1974), 'Trade Unions in America', in: B. Silverman and M. Yanovich (eds), *The Worker in Post-Industrial Capitalism*, New York: Free Press.

Business Week (1989a), 'Agenda for Change', *Business Week*, Special Issue, 170–73.

Business Week (1989b), 'Managing Innovation', *Business Week*, Special Issue on Innovation in America, 104–10.

Cantwell, John (1989), *Technological Innovations and Multinational Corporations*, Cambridge MA.: Blackwell.

Chandler, Alfred, Jr (1977), *The Visible Hand: The Management Revolution in American Business*, Cambridge, MA.: Harvard University Press.

Daly, A., Hitchens, P. and Wagner, K. (1985), 'Productivity, Machinery and Skills in a Sample of British and German Manufacturing Plants', *National Institute Economic Review*, No. 111, February, 48–61.

Dunning, J. (1986), *Japanese Participation in the UK Industry*, London: Croom Helm.

Economist (The) (1987), 'Factory of the Future', May, Supplement, The Economist.

Ghoshal, Sumantra (1987), 'Global Strategy: An Organizing Framework', INSEAD, Fontainebleau, France, in: *Strategy Management Journal*, **8**, (5), 425–40.

Gunn, Thomas G. (1987), *Manufacturing for Competitive Advantage: Becoming a World Class Manufacturer*, Cambridge, MA.: Ballinger.

Hayes, Robert and Jaikumar, Ramchandran (1988), 'Manufacturing's Crisis: New Technologies, Obsolete Organizations', *Harvard Business Review*, No. 5, 77–85.

Imai Ken-ichi (1989), 'Innovation and Cross-Border Networks', *Int. Seminar on Science, Technology and Economic Growth*, Paris: OECD.

Jaikumar, R. (1986), 'Post-Industrial Manufacturing', *Harvard Business Review*, **64**, (6), 69–76.

Kamiya, Shotoro (1976), *My Life With Toyota*, Tokyo: Toyota Motor Sales.

Kogut, B. (1985), 'Designing Global Strategies: Profiting from Operational Flexibility', *Sloan Management Review*, **26**, autumn, 29–38.

Maddison, A. (1982), *Phases of Capitalist Development*, Oxford: Oxford University Press.

Morgan, Gareth (1988), *Riding the Waves of Change*, San Francisco: Jossey Bass.

OECD (1988), *Industrial Revival Through Technology*, Paris: OECD.

OECD (1989), 'Technological Change as a Social Process. New Directions in Management Practices and Work Organization', Conference Proceedings of Helsinki Conference, December 11–13, 1989, Paris: OECD.

Olson, M. (1982), *The Rise and Decline of Nations: Economic Growth, Stagflation and Social Rigidities*, New Haven: Yale University Press.

Ouchi, W.G. (1981), *Theory Z*, Reading, MA.: Addison Wesley.

Ouchi, W.G. (1984), *The M-Form Society: How American Teamwork Can Recapture the Competitive Edge*, Reading, MA.: Addison Wesley.

Peters, Tom (1988), *Thriving on Chaos: Handbook for a Management Revolution*, New York: Perennial Library.

Piore, M.J. and Sabel, Charles F. (1984), *The Second Industrial Divide: Possibilities for Prosperity*, New York: Basic Books.

Porter, M.E. (1986), *Competition in Global Industries*, Boston: Harvard University Press.

Porter, M.E. (1990), *The Competitive Advantage of Nations*, New York: Free Press.

Sadamoto, Kuni (ed.) (1981), *Robots in the Japanese Economy*, Tokyo: Survey Japan.

Schonberger, R. (1986), *World Class Manufacturing*, New York: The Free Press.

Sengenberger, W. (1984), 'Locational Worker Training, Labour Market Structure and Industrial Relations in West Germany', The Keizai Gaku, Annual Report of the Economic Society, Tohoku University, **46**, (2), 23–37.

Shibagaki, *et al.* (eds) (1989), *Japanese and European Management: Their International Adaptability*, Tokyo: University of Tokyo Press.

Shimada, H. and MacDuffie, J.D. (1987), 'Industrial Relations and Humanware – Japanese Investments in Automobile Manufacturing in the United States', International Motor Vehicle Program, MIT, Cambridge, MA.: MIT.

Skinner, W. (1969), 'Manufacturing – Missing Link in Corporate Strategy', *Harvard Business Review*, **47**, (3), 136–45.

Skinner, W. (1988), 'Wanted: Managers for the Factory of the Future', in F. Hearn *et al.* (eds), *The Transformation of Industrial Organization: Management, Labor and Society in the United States*, Belmont, CA: Wadsworth.

Teece, D.J. (1987), *The Competitive Challenge. Strategies for Industrial Innovation and Renewal*, Cambridge, MA.: Sallinger.

Thurow, L.C. (1982), *The Zero-Sum Society: Distribution and the Possibilities for Economic Change*, New York: Penguin Books.

Tushman, M., Newman, W. and Romanelli, E. (1986), 'Convergence and Upheaval: Managing the Unsteady Pace of Organizational Evolution', *California Management Review*, **29**, (1), 1–16.

Walters, Roy (1982), 'The Citybank Project: Improving Productivity Through Work Design', in R. Zager and M. Rosow (eds), *The Innovative Organization: Productivity Programs in Action*, New York: Pergamon Press.

Walton, R. and Lawrence, P. (1985) (eds), *Human Resource Management Trends and Challenges*, Boston, MA.: Harvard Business School Press.

Weiermair, Klaus (1991), 'Restructuring, Regrouping, Adjusting: The Case of Canadian Textile and Clothing Industries', OCIB, Toronto, working paper, No. 427.

Womack, J. (1988), 'Multinational Joint Ventures in Motor Vehicles', in D.C. Mowery (ed.), *International Collaborative Ventures in US Manufacturing*, Cambridge MA.: Ballinger.

Yoshida, M. (1987), *Japanese Direct Manufacturing Investment in the United States*, New York: Praeger.

10 Globalization and the international debt trap

Omar F. Hamouda*

Introduction

The puzzle of the world economic imbalance is that while the creditor countries as a group (mostly the industrialized countries), have a relative surplus balance on current account, when in fact they should have a deficit and if they expect to be reimbursed they will have to open their domestic market to their debtors, the debtor countries as a group (mostly LDCs) have a deficit on their balance on current account, when they should have a surplus and access to foreign markets in order to be able to reimburse their debt. There are three points to be argued in this paper: (1) the debt crisis was created by the restrictive economic policies of the developed countries, and to a degree it can only be resolved with their participation; (2) the policy options put to the LDCs by the IMF with the benediction of the developed countries are more likely to deepen the crisis than to resolve it, and that, in the end, if no collaborated solution to the problem is found, the world economy as a whole will suffer; and (3) even if credit is made available to the LDCs, as long as the restrictive trade policy pattern of the 1980s prevails it is unlikely that the problem of debt will be resolved by reimbursement. Solutions must be considered in the context of the new economic globalization and international macroeconomic polarization.

The current state of the debt of the LDCs

If one looks at the figures for the debt of the last three years, one can clearly see that they have climbed at a rate of about 2 to 3 per cent per annum. Figure 10.1 shows the climbing trend. There is continually more capital flowing out of the LDCs than is going in. Even though, in some cases, the economic performance of many LDCs is above the critical level, the weight of international debt is still a fact of their economic lives.

Attitudes towards the international debt problem can be reduced to two sets of simplistic views: the dominant conservative view, and the view of the 'sceptics'. From the conservative point of view (that of international bodies such as the IMF), the LDCs should, by policy restraint, use their resources to resolve their debt problem on their own. For the sceptics, the debt is thought to have reached crisis proportions which individual debtor countries simply cannot handle, at least not within the time constraints set by the creditors.

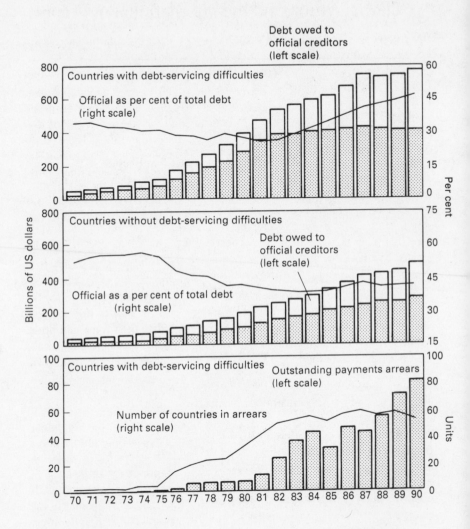

Figure 10.1:   Percentage of countries having external debt, 1970–90 (US dollars)

From their point of view, the complexity of the situation and the amount of money involved demands the collaboration of both creditors and debtors. From either perspective, economic prosperity, be it engineered by the industrialized economies or created domestically by the LDCs, is the necessary condition for any reasonable solution to the debt problem.

Following the conservative view, is it possible for the LDCs to solve the debt problem on their own? In the past some countries, such as South Korea and Taiwan, have indeed managed to deal with their debt. However, these countries contracted their debts during the period of high prosperity of the post-World War II period that was enjoyed up to the mid-1960s. The overall debt size of world debt at that time was relatively small and manageable. In addition to actual loans, these countries were also often assisted financially and materially from external sources. A non-negligible amount of aid, predominantly military related, did not have to be repaid. Parallels between the debt experience of these countries and of those of the present day, drawn for purposes of comparison, do not shed much light.

It is argued from the conservative viewpoint that the remedy to the actual debt is not any different from that used in the past. If only debtor countries would tighten their belts with sufficient self-discipline, the argument goes, they could find a solution to their debt. The suggested appropriate policy is, therefore, for them to lower imports, increase exports, tighten their money supply, reduce government spending, and to liberalize their trade and price mechanisms. Incidentally, these are the same policies that most industrialized countries find more and more difficult to implement for their own economies (witness the last GATT meeting's quarrels and the ongoing domestic political debates on government deficits).

Assume, nonetheless, for a moment that, in order to turn their deficit balance on current account into a surplus, it were possible for the debtor countries to lower their imports by structural adjustment (and not by introducing heavy tariffs, as recommended by the IMF) and also to make an effort to increase their exports. One necessary condition for an increase in the exports of the LDCs is access to the markets of the creditor countries. If both the LDCs and the creditor countries find themselves competing in the same commodity market, the increase in LDC exports could directly affect production and employment in the creditor countries, unless their governments adopt policies to create new markets at home for the additional imports. Decrease in the LDCs' imports from the creditor countries would also mean a decrease in production and employment in the creditor countries unless, again, new domestic markets were created. Governments of the creditor countries would most likely resist both any deliberate deficit in the balance of their current account and the direct intervention in the domestic market which would be required for such an LDC export increase to occur.

Furthermore, a creditor-country deficit implies the transfer of international financial reserves into the hands of the debtor countries. The creditors' financial reserves will, nonetheless, also have to be maintained for the period of time required to complete the process of reimbursement. For political reasons for some and economic reasons for others, such transfers of financial power into the hands of the LDCs may be objectionable to bankers and governments in the creditor countries.

Creditor countries acting individually thus have reason to be reluctant and to resist a policy entailing deficit for them. The corollary, given the *status quo*, is that the LDCs on their own would be helpless. Their task of turning deficits into a surplus would be more difficult without access to their creditors' markets. Under such circumstances, the solution to the international debt is clearly not attainable by the debtors alone.

The alternative view is based on the recognition that the international debt crisis started in the 1970s, at a time when the world economy experienced one of its most volatile periods since World War II. As economic growth began to slow in the industrialized countries and their markets began to shrink, the LDCs seemed at first the obvious target market, and banks, at the time, were willing to supply funds. The recession of 1982 and the subsequent unprecedentedly high interest rates marked the beginning of a new era. By the early 1980s it became clear that the financial strength and reimbursement ability of many of the indebted countries was in doubt. A policy of easy money quickly turned into one of tight money. Many LDCs which had previously planned a series of ambitious investment projects had to revise their plans downwards to incorporate a sharp decrease in their imports and a foreseeable loss of export markets. Not only did it subsequently become difficult for many LDCs to find credit funds but, since their export earnings were falling, the size of their debt began to accelerate, making it increasingly difficult for them to catch up.

Some economists realized that the only way out of the global economic stagnation of the early 1980s was to re-ignite reasonable growth in the industrialized countries. This would enhance world trade and provide recovery for the rest of the world. The Baker plan, for example, recognized that the debt crisis can be resolved only if growth is generated. Such growth did not materialize, however, in the 1980s, since most governments in the OECD followed a policy of tight money and high interest rates to contain inflation, seemingly their only major preoccupation. Many of the other plans for confronting the debt problem have suggested encouraging the big banks to ease credit, or at least persuading them to postpone repayment, and involving the governments of the creditor countries, to some extent, in resolving the debt crisis. Indeed, some capital did flow into many LDCs in the 1980s, but often this capital was lent in order that the countries might pay towards their outstanding interest payments. Under pressure exerted by the IMF, there has been continually more capital flowing out of than into the LDCs, draining these countries of all of their international reserves.

So far most of the plans advanced, including the Baker plan, have been based on the voluntary actions and goodwill of individual countries and banks. To succeed, each plan has required the participation of all parties concerned. Unfortunately, however, parties often renege on their responsibility. In the US Treasury and Morgan Guaranty Trust Company proposal, for example, it was suggested that part of the government securities of indebted countries held by banks be resold at less than their face value to the issuer; the plan was designed most specifically for the case of the indebted government of Mexico. Most holders of these securities preferred, however, to let other banks start the process in the hope that when the supply of these securities eased, they would get a better possible value for their own shares. In the end the plan failed because most players preferred the waiting strategy.

Banks are generally unwilling to take big losses on the debts they hold, and they are reluctant to grant additional credit, especially to their most heavily indebted borrowers. Even though the banks of the industrialized countries instigated the debt crisis in the first place by their ill-conceived policy of overlending, it is unlikely that the solution to the crisis will be resolved by them alone.

What is the solution to the debt crisis?
To a large degree the solution to the debt crisis lies not so much in making credit available to the LDCs, but in maintaining a prosperous world trade economy and in opening up markets. As long as the current high unemployment rates in the advanced countries are politically acceptable, however, the balance of advantage, from the standpoint of the conservative governments in the leading OECDs, lies in continuing their current macroeconomic pattern of low inflation and low growth. If expansionary policies were to be followed, and the world rate of economic growth were to rise and be sustained, based on the experiences gathered in the days of prosperity at a near-to-gold level in the 1950s and 1960s, industrialized countries' conservatives fear another ensuing rise in the power of unions as well as a sharp upward lift in world commodity prices, including that of oil. These changes in turn are predicted to rekindle inflation.

For conservative policy-makers, the only perceived benefit of a trend which increases the rate of growth of the world economy would be its positive effect on resolving the LDC debt. Since, however, this benefit would be reaped at the potential cost of fuelling inflation and of changes in oil prices and in the economic and political balance of world power, it is unlikely that any developed countries under the leadership of a conservative government would foster expansion of the world economy for this reason alone.

For a short while after the oil price shock of the mid-1970s, the OECD tried to restore an institutional consensus for growth by following an expansionary policy. This attempt was, however, not successful, especially in trying to keep inflation low. Its policy was then replaced by a contractionary one. Since the early 1980s the OECD governments have attempted to create a new economic system based on the freemarket principles of privatization and deregulation.

Viewed from the conservative standpoint within the leading OECD countries, the world economy patterns which were emerging from the contractionary policies were seen as promising in their restructuring of a major change of power both nationally and internationally. The policies' side effects – the depression of international commodity prices, a high interest rate and the reduction of capital flows to the LDCs – have at the same time, as would be expected, very adversely weakened both the economic and political power of the LDCs.

Despite much discussion of the benefits of policy co-ordination among industrial countries, the central objective of the current preoccupation with policy cohesion is not to bring about an overall increase in world demand, but rather to redistribute the current level of demand among the leading countries in such a way as to reduce their own imbalances and to help them restore a degree of stability to the currency and financial markets. If these priorities are combined with an expected deceleration in demographic growth and structural shifts towards slow productivity service sectors (which are already occurring), the forseeable prospect for the OECD countries, and hence for the world economy must, at best, be one of continuing slow growth. In the absence of some kind of Keynesian policy on a global scale, the most realistic future for the LDCs in the coming years of relatively slow and fluctuating growth in the world economy is a worsened economic situation.

What kind of Keynesian policy and what kind of growth?

It is clear that the burden of the huge government deficits in the industrialized countries is making politicians nervous about more government spending. It is also clear that public awareness about environmental issues and resource preservation is making the traditional drive for growth less desirable. There remain, however, serious economic imbalances. Too many people in both the industrialized countries and LDCs are unemployed. The income disparity between classes and between nations is widening again. East–West *détente* is providing a strong incentive for the long-term dismantling of the military industry which will exacerbate further the general slowdown in economic activity and employment. World population continues to grow at a rate much faster than world production. An important event which is slowly having an impact on world economic order is the recent collapse of the planned economies in Eastern Europe. The failure of communism and the disappearance of that challenge is now making the Western market economies more relaxed and less pressured to counterbalance leftist ideas with government programmes, such as welfare, medicare, education and social assistance.

It is clear that the world of the 1990s is drastically different from that of the period of high prosperity. Many structural adjustments are slowly taking place. Given the new situation, an economic solution in the context of the new globalization must emerge. What kind of solution that is to be, will depend on how all the new forces coalesce to establish a new momentum.

It is possible, for example, that with concerted and thorough fiscal incentives, the governments in the leading industrialized economies can exercise influence, whether domestically or internationally, in directing capital flows towards economic sectors that can generate both wealth and employment. By the same token they can make their efforts compatible with environmental concerns and the efficient use of resources. Some such steps, for example, garbage disposal, recycling, fuel efficiency and nutritive efficiency, have already been fostered and are slowly affecting industry. Sooner or later the LDCs will follow the lead. As for market share, the LDCs need not engage themselves internationally in directly competitive sectors where the market is already saturated or difficult to enter, but should instead, with some co-operation, become engaged in those markets where their industries have a comparative cost advantage. A feasible policy which would be beneficial to both debtors and creditors could, for example, be devised whereby a significant part of the international loans to LDCs would be conditional, for specific projects, with some joint venture strings attached and based on both international market viability and domestic need. Although the LDCs' export earnings are in many cases vital, for fairness their urgent domestic needs cannot totally be overlooked either. Most LDCs are required to expand at a rate of 8 to 10 per cent per annum to have any reasonable chance of providing employment for their populations (which are increasing at 3 to 4 per cent per annum) and of meeting the minimum needs for feeding their people. It should be noted that whether the LDCs' loans are used to purchase equipment or food, most of them will end up back in the hands of the creditors as suppliers, and will therefore only increase demand for goods and services in the creditor countries.

In the new global context, the conventional 'inward' Keynesian policy of the leading industrialized economies, that of over-spending. ought to be replaced by a more realistic reallocative Keynesian fiscal policy which takes into consideration not only domestic economic concerns but also commitment to world economic stability. Such a framework will require a new economic and political configuration, with an international commitment to a very different pattern of development and social order, and to a particular growth rate in world trade, feasible and sustainable with low inflation and based on a new institutional and behavioural framework.

Domestically, there is a need for a more co-operative relationship, not only between the labour-force, management and government, but also within each group (for example, sheltered workers and non-sheltered workers, big corporations and small firms, different levels of government). That is to say there is a need for more flexible programmes of work-sharing and labour participation; incentives for productivity and innovation, and flexible mechanisms to adapt production to new economic realities and to new technologies. Finally, schemes whereby governments can be made more responsible in providing leadership, and not be allowed to content themselves only with short-term gain for electoral purposes, must at least be tried.

Internationally, a rather different system of regulation which will involve some orderly and fair movement of commodity prices is required, even though this is resisted by some members of the GATT. As is now the case with all the new federations of nations (for example, the EEC and the probable EIC), some stability in the exchange rate must be established. Excessive capital mobility, especially that which takes advantage of the weaknesses of the LDCs, can and ought to be moderated by some international fiscal control Facing the new giant economic blocs (North America. Europe and Asia), the LDCs should be encouraged to form their own federation of nations in order together to have a stronger voice and to be better able to take advantage of their own potential than each might individually. A dynamic and responsible union of LDCs could eventually alleviate the past economic and political abuses which are the sources of their inefficiency and misery. The world of the 1990s has developed both the structure and the institutional framework necessary for implementing the above policy. All these initiatives, however, call for firm resolve on the part of both the developed and developing countries.

Note

* I would like to thank Betsy Price, Lorie Tarshis and Ajit Singh for numerous discussions about ideas developed in the present paper.

Bibliography

Engel, C and Kletzer, K. (1986), 'International Borrowing to Finance Investment', NBER Working Paper Series, No. 1865, March.

Gersovitz, M. (1985), 'Banks' International Lending Decisions', in G. Smith and J. Cuddington (eds), *International Debt and the Developing Countries*, Washington, D.C.: IBRD, 61–78.

IMF, The World Debt Tables, 1990–91.

Kaldor N., 1960, *Essays on Stability and Growth*, Illinois: The Free Press of Glencoe.

McDonald, C.D. (1982), 'Debt Capacity and Developing Country Borrowing: A Survey of the Literature', IMF Staff Paper, **29**, 603–46.

Sachs, J. (1984), *Theoretical Issues in International Borrowing*, No. 54. Princeton: Princeton Studies in International Finance.

Tarshis, L. (1984), *World Economy in Crisis: Unemployment, Inflation and International Debt*, Toronto: Canadian Institute for Economic Policy.

World Bank (1990), World Development Report.

11 Structural changes in financial markets and financial flows to developing countries

J.A. Kregel

The role of capital flows in international economic development

One of the major functions of the international financial market is the allocation of investment resources, ensuring that they reach those uses which yield highest returns, irrespective of location. Historical experience suggests that there is a secular decline in expected rates of return as the level of development of an economy increases, so that returns in the more advanced industrialized economies have tended to decline relative to prospects in developing countries. International capital markets have thus traditionally allocated capital from the more advanced to the lesser developed countries.

The long-term capital outflows of the developed economies are reflected in the developing countries by deficits on current account. These are a result of the purchase of imported capital equipment and durable consumption goods output of the developed countries, as well as from the payment of interest and repayment of principal on their international borrowing. This deficit is balanced by the credits represented by the capital investments and loans received from developed economy investors.

These international loans and investments are expected to be repaid from the foreign currency proceeds of increased future exports of the developing countries, either of raw materials exploited as a result of the investments, or from the creation of an internal industrial base which eventually will be sufficiently competitive to sell manufactured goods in international markets. In this way development is spread throughout the international economy.

Changes in international capital flows

This traditional pattern of capital flows was interrupted by two World Wars, and when stable international conditions were re-established in the 1960s it did not reappear. Without any discernible change in the differentials between the relative expected rates of return between developing and advanced economies, the outflow of capital from the latter, and in particular from the United States, started to decline as American foreign lending and political and military expenditures came into conflict with the stability of the post-war Bretton Woods international monetary system based on a fixed dollar price for gold.

Stability would have required the US to cut back on its capital outflows and to increase its current account surplus in order to reduce outstanding dollar claims or to increase the demand for dollars. The former could have been achieved either by reducing domestic growth to cause a decline in imports, or by reducing capital outflows by increasing domestic interest rates. The US government, facing declining internal growth and falling profitability in manufacturing, found neither alternative politically acceptable and instead chose to introduce voluntary, and then obligatory, restrictions and regulations to reduce capital outflows. Capital outflows from the US have continued to decline since that time, and in the 1980s have been reversed. The US is now a capital importer with a substantial current account deficit; instead of providing funds for development, it now competes with developing countries for funds in international capital markets.

The planned economies of Eastern Europe and the Soviet Union remained separate from this international flow of investment funds, generally keeping their international trade and payments with each other and with the Western economies in rough balance. This position started to change in the 1970s and 1980s as private banks started to lend to the German Democratic Republic, and then to Poland and Hungary. With the recent decisions to transform these economies into market economies, they now also represent new development opportunities. They will compete for international investors' funds with the United States and the already heavily indebted developing economies of South America.

The structure of the US financial system and the change in capital flows
Thus, much of the reversal of the traditional international flow of capital is due to the change in the US position. One possible explanation of this change may be found in the changes in the US financial system which occurred during this period. As a result of the official policy to restrict capital flows during the 1960s and 1970s, US commercial banks found their ability to compete domestically and internationally reduced. Since the US banking system is unique with respect to both Britain and continental Europe, the response was also unique. This is because the process of consolidation which has produced a relatively small number of large, multi-functional commercial banks that are sufficiently large to compete against each other and against foreign competitors has been slowed in the US by regulations limiting the growth of commercial banks, such as restrictions on branching and on price competition. With bank operations limited to a small geographical area, growth in absolute size is limited. In addition, limitations on the proportion of bank capital committed to a single borrower often mean that a bank cannot supply all the banking needs of a single client if the client is growing more rapidly than the bank.

Regulation Q, introduced in the banking legislation of 1933, gave the Federal Reserve powers to set limits on interest rates on deposits; these limits were set at zero for demand deposits and at low, fixed and relatively rigid rates on other deposit liabilities. This eliminated competition among banks, and between banks and other financial institutions, for deposit liabilities via price.

With limited potential for growth via domestic expansion, US banks looked to international markets. The regulations on capital outflows introduced in the 1960s threatened them with a loss of business to international competitors. In order to retain their international lending activities, United States banks expanded into offshore markets and the Euromarkets. From 1965–70, the number of Federal Reserve System member banks operating foreign branches grew from 13 to 79; by 1973 the number had reached 125. Gross assets grew from $9.1 billion in 1965 to $118 billion in 1973. The total number of foreign branches grew from 211 in 1965 to 694 in 1973.

At the same time banks sought to reduce the impact of lending regulations on their domestic profitability via a series of 'financial innovations'. The first of these responses was the introduction in the early 1960's of the negotiable Certificate of Deposit, which brought escape from Regulation Q. As commercial banks found ways to compete for deposits, they attracted funds from thrift institutions who sought to defend their deposit base by offering customers transactions accounts called 'negotiable order of withdrawals' (1972), a form of checking account which side-stepped regulations which forbade them from offering such services. The competition for depositors' funds became sharper with the introduction in 1973 of money market deposit accounts (which offered limited transactions services but paid market rates of interest); finally in 1980 brokerage houses introduced 'cash management accounts'. The common denominator of all these innovations was that they all bypassed the Regulation Q controls on interest rates and restored the interest rate competition for deposits which the New Deal legislation was supposed to eliminate.

Having opened the competition, the commercial banks found strong competition for deposits from both the savings and loans banks, and large stockbroker–investment banks which were normally precluded from offering such services. There was also competition for lending, as large corporations started to bypass banks as their basic source of short-term funding in favour of short-term commercial paper underwritten by large brokers and investment banks. This combination of increased competition for deposits and the loss of traditional corporate borrowers to brokerage houses finally forced commercial banks to seek elimination of the Glass 1933 legislation which reserved underwriting to non-bank financial institutions and prevented them from offering similar services to their commercial clients.

The increasing presence of US banks in the Euromarkets and the increased use of financial innovations, coupled with calls for 'deregulation', may thus be seen as part of the result of attempts of US banks to isolate themselves from the decline in the position of the United States in international finance which was initiated by the attempt to control foreign lending in the US. To preserve growth prospects, US banks sought to escape domestic regulations by moving their operations outside the US and to create new financial products which were exempt from control. They also sought the elimination of prudential or historical regulations on their domestic activities.

Implications of financial innovation and deregulation for the stability of financial flows
Thus the 1979 decision by the Federal Reserve to shift its policy from interest rate targeting to control of monetary aggregates occurred in conditions in which the combined effects of financial innovation and deregulation were freeing interest rates from controls and allowing financial institutions to use interest rates to compete for deposits and other borrowed (or managed) funds. The combined result of the decision of the Federal Reserve and the relaxation of regulations via innovations was increasing variability in interest rates (and, as a result, an increase in the variability of exchange rates). Since interest rates are simply an alternative expression for asset prices, the new environment was one in which asset price variability also increased.

This variability was increased by the 1980 Monetary Control Act which eliminated state usury law ceilings on interest rates and made possible the introduction of adjustable interest rate financial instruments, such as had already found widespread use in the Euromarkets. Variable interest rates payable on assets effectively eliminate the impact of changes in interest rates on the price of the asset. This means that there is no risk of capital loss due to a change in market interest rates. By issuing adjustable rate assets, financial institutions could escape the increased risks to the value of the assets on their balance sheets which was associated with the new variable interest rate environment.

This removal of restrictions on prices of assets, the apparent reduction in risks due to the lenders' belief that risks of variable rates could be sold, and the failure of borrowers to evaluate the real magnitude of the burdens they were undertaking (and lenders to recognize the increased credit risks), led to a rapid increase in the creation of financial assets via an overall increase in indebtedness of both households and businesses in the US economy.

Efficiency of capital markets and capital flows to developing economies
If the results of the regulatory changes in the structure of the US banking system, now extending to Japan and other European economies, has been to

increase the variability of asset prices and, as a consequence to increase the variability of financial flows, it appears that the increased efficiency claimed for an unregulated financial system has been achieved only at the expense of increased instability. Yet the traditional definition of efficiency does not give any direct attention to the stability of capital flows as a factor in international development, nor does it appear to explain the recent increase in instability.

First, it is unclear whether there has been any substantial change in relative marginal productivity of capital with respect to the US and developing countries, as the major part of capital inflows to the US has been used to finance government deficit expenditures. Rather than financing real investment, these have primarily been transfers to families. Secondly, the variability in exchange rates which has accompanied the move to flexible asset prices has meant that the exchange rate is itself a variable asset price so that the variability in interest rates has a direct effect on the variability and evaluation of real rates of return. Indeed, in a system of flexible rates of exchange it is more difficult, if not impossible, to determine the relevant 'real rates' of return to which resources should be allocated on an international basis. This is because they will depart from the marginal physical productivity of capital because of the divergence of nominal and real rates, as well as because of the divergence of nominal exchange rates from their real equilibrium values. Indeed, over the recent past, exchange rates have often tended to move counter to underlying real factors for sustained periods of time. In 1989 for the G-7 countries (with the exception of France and Great Britain), nominal exchange rates movements tended to amplify cost and price differences, for example, the value of the yen depreciated by 5 per cent, while unit labour costs fell and profitability increased relative to other countries.

These difficulties suggest that the application of the conception of 'allocative efficiency' used to justify deregulation of the financial system may not be directly applicable to the problems of international capital flows, or even that efficiency in the domestic financial system may create inefficiency in the international capital markets. This may be of crucial importance in a period when international markets are being called upon to provide increased lending, not only to the traditional developing countries, but also to those economies in transition from a command to a market-based system. This is especially important because the traditional conception of efficiency, based on the idea of real loanable funds, leads to the conclusion that there will be a shortage of international capital to meet likely investment needs, while at the same time proposing changes in the system which appear to direct capital towards countries such as the US which do not seem to be using it more productively than the developing countries.

The reversal of capital flows and relative interest rates

Thus, a large number of the factors leading to deregulation have produced conditions of higher interest rates in both the money market and in the capital markets, leading to a reversal of relative interest rates. Short-term rates in the US are not only absolutely higher, but also relative to other financial markets, because of the elimination of controls over deposit rates and the increased use of interest rates to compete in order to increase size and market position. Although this increase in short-term rates need not have spilled over to an increase in long rates, a number of additional factors have led to this result.

First, increasing government deficits may place a burden on asset markets to the extent that they are issued merely to finance government transfer payments, which banks believe can find a place in portfolios only at lower prices because they have a lower income multiplier than the financing of government investments. This is the case of the current financing of German reunification.

On the other hand, the introduction of prudential capital ratios in conditions of increasing bad debts and depressed capital markets may lead banks to adjust their assets in order to increase those with low weights. Thus, throughout 1991 US banks increased their holding of US Treasury and Agency securities; in particular FHA and VA mortgages and GNMA mortgage backed securities, all of which have zero weighting. They also sharply reduced their lending to commercial and industrial borrowers and engaged in large-scale securitization of their consumer lending, for example, credit card lending. Further, the creation and growth of the junk bond market reduced bank lending to small and medium sized high-risk borrowers and substituted it with additional demands on long-term bond markets. All of these shifts meant that assets which would previously have been financed in the short-term loan market by banks through the money creation process were being shifted to capital markets. This shift in the stock of existing assets from the money market to capital markets exerts a similar pressure on the capital markets to a shift in asset preferences or to an increase in liquidity preference.

To the extent that the introduction of capital ratios leads banks to adjust assets or to increase their own borrowing in the capital markets to support the existing level of lending, capital market interest rates will tend to be higher. This factor is independent of any other demands which may be forthcoming for recovery from the current recession or for reconstruction in Eastern Europe. Although there is no reason for an increased demand for investment funding to increase long-term interest rates, the shift in funding from short-term bank financing to long-term capital market financing that has resulted from a decade of financial innovation and deregulation in the

1980s can lead to increased interest rates and lower asset prices. At the same time, the increase in variability of interest rates and asset prices increases the variability in capital flows, and thus decreases the overall efficiency of the financial system to satisfy the needs of developing country borrowers.

The increase in variability of rates and the shifting of risk to the ultimate borrower have tended to increase overall risk and to increase bankruptcies, leading to an increase in long rates. This is in addition to that caused by the shift of bank assets to capital market assets due to innovation and the application of prudential capital ratios. There has thus been a shift in the supply of long-term assets without any concomitant current investment, and which is thus unmatched by any change in saving. The result has been an overall increase in the rate structure; given conditions determining goods' prices, this has fed through to an increase in real rates of interest which cannot be traced to any shortage of real savings, but simply to the change in the institutional and regulatory environment.

Funding for new investment must compete with existing financial assets to find places in investors' portfolios. This means that the flows of new assets will tend to have a relatively small impact on prices, while shifts in investor preferences, in liquidity preferences and the efficiency of the financial system, will tend to have more dominant effects. Financial innovation has produced once-over shifts in the supplies of assets to capital markets which have had substantial impact on market conditions. With respect to international markets, the role of the variability of exchange rates adds an additional element to interest rate variability which separates the assessment of risk by the borrower and the lender, and increases the costs of intermediation and the long-term rate of interest.

Thus, one of the factors which may have been responsible for the reversal of international capital flows in the post-war period is the process of structural change which has occurred in the US financial system. Since this is a process which has yet to be completed, it is unlikely that the traditional flow of resources from the developed to the developing countries is likely to be restored in the near future. The development process in the coming decade will, then, have to depend on increased economic integration, rather than increased financial flows. This process may already be seen to be at work in the increased interest in the formation of trading areas such as the North American Free Trade Association of Canada, the US and Mexico.

12 Some scenarios for money and banking in the EC and their regional implications

Victoria Chick

Introduction

The pieces of the jigsaw puzzle we call the map of the world are shifting and recombining in largely unpredictable ways. With these changes come changes in monetary systems, which in modern times are closely bound to the nation-state. Indeed, those who oppose a common currency for Europe tend to fear a hidden or not so hidden agenda for political unification.

Whether a common currency comes about, and even its significance, is more a political than an economic problem. Nevertheless, there is room for discussion among economists – and goodness knows there has been a lot of discussion already. The debate about monetary arrangements in the EC has centred around currency and monetary policy: is the EC a DM zone? Will there be a common currency? How much independence of monetary policy is desirable? What policy priorities should there be? This paper will, instead, sketch the implications for the distribution of economic activity among member countries of some alternative monetary scenarios.

The basis for the present paper is an earlier paper co-authored with Sheila Dow (1988), which combined theories of regional development with a consideration of the historical development of banking systems. Regional theory is not strong on the monetary side, yet it is a monetary theory of regional activity which is needed for the analysis of possible developments within the EC. It is early for such a theory, and the present paper is a very preliminary excursion.

A central question addressed by Chick and Dow was the significance of trade and payments between regions with banking systems in different stages of development, and this is a problem within Europe. Indeed, it is a most serious problem within one EC country: united Germany. While the problem of German monetary unification is too specialized for this paper, there are general issues of EC monetary union among countries which, though their economies are more similar than the economies of East and West Germany, still have different styles and habits of banking. This paper will address some of these issues and their implications for the participants in the European adventure.

Monetary unification involves three separate issues which are not normally distinguished: whether or not there are fixed or flexible exchange rates or a common currency; whether there is a single monetary standard; and whether there is or will be a unified banking system. The next section will elaborate on these distinctions, giving examples of various combinations from different times and places. Section 3 will discuss possible scenarios from the point of view of regional analysis, and Section 4 concludes.

Scenarios for the European Monetary System
National currencies provide a kind of tariff wall with other countries which encourages the development of national banking systems with particular characteristics. The stateless or multinational Euromoney market, a recent phenomenon by historical standards, is an exception to the norm. Incursions into a country's banking system by banks based in other countries (also a recent phenomenon) are important, but in large measure these banks conform to the habits and styles of the host country except that their typical orientation is towards wholesale and overseas business. These exceptions are noted here in order later to concentrate without distraction on the more typical case of banking that is developing distinctively within national state/ currency boundaries and is confined within them.

The state is also typically the border of a common currency. We take this for granted today, though of course it was not always the case – as proponents of the idea of competing currencies are happy to remind us. We also take for granted the unity of the concept of a monetary standard and the existence of a common currency. But while the existence of a common currency throughout a region is a matter of fact, the character, or even the existence, of a monetary standard is debatable – witness the numerous comments on the nature of the Bretton Woods system: was it a gold exchange standard, a dollar exchange standard, or a dollar standard? All the while, there was little dispute that the dollar was the common currency of world trade outside the Eastern bloc, even though there were, of course, some transactions in other currencies.

The concept of a monetary standard is bound up with the maintenance of par value between different elements of a monetary system: that is, between notes and coins and between state money and bank deposits domestically, and between different currencies internationally. Internationally, maintenance of a monetary standard is a matter of convertibility into gold or currencies acceptable abroad. Domestically, where we seldom think about it in this way, the concept of a monetary standard embodies all the questions of maintenance of convertibility of deposits into cash (the liquidity of the banking system and the lender of last resort).

Fixed exchange rates are a case of a monetary standard without a common currency; there are domestic examples in monetary history and the combination is very familiar in the international context. It is very nearly the position in the EC at the moment. (The EC is now almost unanimously committed to fixed exchange rates within narrow bands, and 'peer group pressure' will probably bring Portugal and Greece into line. Thus, I take it for granted that flexible exchange rates are not part of the future shape of the EC – at any rate not the planned future.) It is also perfectly possible to have a common currency but not a monetary standard: this was the case in the United States during the period of wildcat banking, when the dollar was the common currency but bank notes exchanged at large and variable discounts.

The role of prudent banking in maintaining the monetary standard is perhaps more obvious in the case of the purely domestic standard, but as Kregel has pointed out (1990), the sterling exchange standard was also chiefly maintained by the banks and the market for foreign exchange bills. The notion that maintenance of international parities is the exclusive responsibility of central banks is a very modern concept; one could debate whether it began with Bretton Woods or with the struggle between London and New York for the centre position in the inter-war period, but one would be hard-pressed to justify going back any further.

Within the confines of a single currency area (a nation-state or the EC with a common currency) there is the further question of integration of the banking system. There are two elements in a unified banking system: its regional dispersion (by branching) and the universality of functions performed under a single management. Since regional issues are the chief focus of this paper, preponderant emphasis will be given to the first of these. Though the question of universality enters in, good communication between retail and wholesale, and commercial and merchant/industrial banking is assumed throughout. Therefore a unified banking system will be defined as a network of banks with branches widely distributed throughout all or part of a region/state/community, and with easy and rapid communication (for example, clearing facilities, inter-bank lending) between them. Whether a banking system conforms to this definition is a qualitative judgement: unification is a matter of degree.

It is doubtful that uniform coverage throughout a currency area is to be found anywhere. Nevertheless, one can say that despite the network of correspondent relationships and holding companies in the US, legal and institutional restrictions (including separate Federal Reserve districts) have resulted in a banking system which communicates very imperfectly, though it is now changing very rapidly. British retail banking, by contrast, despite the existence of regional banks, has achieved a wide spread of branches and strong inter-bank communication as regards both deposits and reserves. The

Table 12.1: Some present monetary systems and their possible futures

	Common currency	Monetary standard	Unified banking system
USA			
now	y	y	n
future	y	y	y?
International Trade/Payments	(y) $ dominant	n (flexible exchange rates)	y (a few key banks)
A European country, e.g. UK	y	y	y
EC			
now	n	(y) (in ERM) n (out of ERM)	n
future 1	n	(y) fixed exchange rates	n
future 2	n	(y) fixed exchange rates	y? (1992)
future 3	y	y	n
future 4	y	y	y

banking systems of individual member countries of the EC of course vary, but perhaps it can be said that they are closer to the British banking scene than to the American one. Post-unification Germany is an exception – such an extraordinary exception to the whole history of the evolution of monetary systems, that 'Germany' will be taken to mean the old Federal Republic; readers must make allowance for this drastic simplification themselves.

Scenarios for the future shape of money and banking in the EC, then, have three major elements: whether there will be a common currency or if unification will stop at fixed exchange rates; which mechanisms are put in place to ensure parities (which is an issue even with a common currency, as explained above); and whether a unified banking system emerges. It may be helpful to summarize the foregoing as in Table 12.1, on which some further comment will be made. In Table 12.1, yes is indicated by 'y' and a qualified yes by '(y)'. No is 'n'.

The US banking system is a prime example of the effects of legal impediments; as is well known, the system was prevented from unification at an early stage by restrictive legislation. Both the reasons for this legislation and the move now to remove obstacles to a united banking system are instructive in developing future scenarios for European banking. Two elements are directly pertinent: one is that the individual states were anxious to guard their independence from the federal government, the power to charter banks being one manifestation of that independence. State-chartered banks exist alongside nationally-chartered banks and operate under different rules (for example, nationally-chartered banks must be members of the Federal Reserve system and are subject to its regulation; state-chartered banks may choose to be members but more often opt for the less rigorous conditions of state control).

The second element is the fear that, with a unified banking system, savings collected up by the banks in one region, say the Midwest, would be used to finance development in the already prosperous East. The power over financial resources was, from early days, concentrated in the East, especially, of course, in New York. Thus barriers to the flow of funds were deliberately set up to thwart 'Eastern money-power' and to retain some considerable control over a region's savings, which were to be invested in the region's own development. There is a theory of regional development in this view to which we shall return later.

The federal nature of the American Federal Reserve system further emphasized the disunity of the banking system; indeed it was to cater for regional differences in a period of comparatively poor communications that the Federal Reserve was set up as it was. Even in the late 1950s, there were persistent interest rate differentials among regions. To some extent these still exist on retail deposits, for while it is perfectly possible to bank by mail or even modem across the country, geography still counts for something.

With the spate of bank failures in the US over the last few years, the monetary standard is showing marked signs of fragility. To strengthen the survival potential of individual banks it has been recommended that the interdiction on inter-state banking be removed to speed up the creation of a unified banking system. This raises the interesting question of the optimal size of a bank, which will also be a question for Europe.

The Canadian system (not shown in Table 12.1) offers an instructive contrast. Widespread branching was established very early, yet distinct banking regions remain, even in the absence of the legal restrictions which are sometimes offered as the sole explanation for the structure of her neighbour's banking system. Dow (1990) has argued convincingly for the application of dependency theory to the Canadian case, with urban Ontario and Quebec constituting the 'centre', where decisions are made that are not always to the benefit of the 'peripheral' regions.

The international monetary system, or rather non-system, is an illustration of the sort of arrangements which can arise when there is a lack of political will and the corresponding institutions needed to maintain par values. As a degenerate system it bears resemblance to the non-par-banking episode in US domestic banking, also a period when the monetary system was without a centre. This is not to say that central control (especially a lender of last resort) is *necessary* for the maintenance of a monetary standard: after all, the free banking period in Scotland had no more central control than that exercised by 'the market' through the clearing house. The standard was maintained by prudent banking, against the background of the restraint imposed by the gold standard.

The remainder of Table 12.1 has to do with Europe present and future. The 'futures' are arranged in order of increasing uniformity, from the present to a situation similar to that in a single EC country today. We assume that steps will be taken to ensure that whatever currency relationship is decided – fixed exchange rates or common currency – internal or external par values will be maintained. This may be a heroic assumption, but it allows us to concentrate on the central issue, which (here) is the dispersion of banking: will the banks remain national institutions or will a European banking network emerge?

It is Commission policy that a unified banking system should be encouraged. There are also natural forces tending towards concentration in banking. A large bank, particularly one which has a wide geographical purview, can most easily diversify its lending portfolio while retaining economies of scale in the administration of its lending business. On the deposit side, the larger a bank's share of the market, the lower its reserve losses as a consequence of expansion. On the other hand, there are impediments to concentration. In the context of the EC these include differences of currency, language, laws and regulations, and customs and practice, as well as the less tangible but very real matter of national and regional sentiment.

The immediate question is whether, after 1992, the Single Market will bring about a spate of take-overs and mergers among European banks, taking us towards Scenario 2. The admirable study by Molyneux (1989) assesses this possibility, based largely on profitability and relative share of domestic market. The important question of disparities of banking practice is not addressed. A less far-reaching proposal is that made by Kregel (1990), in which the banks are enjoined to hold assets of other EC countries in those countries' currencies, and thus take on, at the very least, joint responsibility with the central banks for the maintenance of fixed exchange rates. This (very sensible) proposal leaves national banking intact, however, and thus is a modification of Scenario 1.

A common currency would remove an important impediment to the establishment of a unified banking system, but since the existence of different currencies at present is not the only impediment to the evolution of such a system, there is no presumption that adoption of a common currency will lead to a unified banking system. Scenarios 3 and 4 are both possible. Indeed, the example of Canada suggests that banking regions will remain in an area as large as the EC, even if a common currency is adopted.

There remains the question of disparities in the evolution of banking practice. This has two important dimensions. One is the degree to which banks have 'innovated their way out' of dependence on either their depositors or the central bank as sources of reserves, and the related matter of the progressive reduction of bank liquidity by 'efficient' banks. The other is the degree of universality of banking. Consider the latter point first.

Zysman (1983) has treated the question of national differences in the financing of industry in an evolutionary way. He distinguishes bank-based finance, of which Germany and Japan are the typical examples, from market-based finance, in which debenture and share capital play the major role as, say, in Britain. The polar cases of the roles of British and German banks in industrial finance have often been noted (though more usually in connection with attempts to explain Britain's poor economic performance). Even Molyneux does not discuss the reorientation of British banking which might occur if the weaker British banks are taken over, as he predicts, by the major German banks, and there has been little discussion of the complementary role played by the market for financial assets. Most economists seem to feel that universal banking is desirable, but the scenario in which EC-wide universal banking is accomplished needs a good deal of fleshing out.

The other question which requires further consideration regards disparities in what has elsewhere (Chick, 1986; Chick and Dow, 1988) been called 'stages of evolution' of banking systems. The evolutionary process is one of gradually increasing the extent to which banks can expand lending independently first of depositors and then of external sources of reserves. The early stage of being confined to 'lending on' deposits has long since passed in EC countries, with the widespread adoption of bank deposits as means of payment. But after this stage the banks are constrained by reserves. Interbank lending of reserves ensures their efficient distribution, but only for the system as a whole; reserves are ultimately available only from the suppliers of high-powered money.

Until the banks developed liability management they were largely dependent on central bank policy. Liability management, where it persuades holders of government debt to hold deposits instead, forces monetization and the supply of reserves. This can always be 'undone', of course, but the initiative no longer lies with the central bank. Both the degree of development of liability management and the scope for causing discomfort to the Treasury and/or central bank surely differ among EC countries.

At a much simpler level, the whole role of reserves in maintaining central bank control is viewed differently in various EC countries. In the UK, formal reserve requirements have been given up, though informal ones remain. In Germany and Italy, and perhaps elsewhere, they are still thought of as key instruments of monetary control. Liability management and the more recent trend towards securitization again involve the role of financial asset markets, for neither innovation is successful without broad and deep markets for both government and private debt instruments. All these disparities in financial market development and in banking custom, practice and mode of control, are at issue when the likelihood of a unified banking system is under consideration. The next section questions whether such a system is desirable.

Banking structure and regional development
A move from a commitment to fixed exchange rates to a common currency would relieve members of the EC of exchange conversion costs and the threat, here considered remote, of exchange rate realignments. Contrary to popular opinion there is, as we know, no relief from balance-of-payments problems; these problems just show up, initially, as monetary drains from deficit regions and influxes to surplus regions. If, in addition to a common currency, there is an EC-wide interest rate policy, there is no opportunity to adjust these monetary flows with differential interest rates. A unified banking system would, in these days of rapid communications, have a similar effect (but see the comment on differential interest rates in the US, above).

This leaves the scenario of adjustment through changes in output and employment, which will result in regional variations in economic activity.

Whether one believes that the benefits of a common currency and a unified banking system outweigh the costs, or *vice versa*, depends on the theory of regional adjustment to which one subscribes. As an extreme position, neoclassical theory denies the possibility of persistent differences in regional development. In neoclassical theory, funds systematically flow to those projects with the highest perceived rate of return, wherever they may be. 'Disequilibrium', in the form of different rates of growth between regions, is assumed to be the result of an inequality of saving and investment in each region. If exports from one region are low relatively to imports, there will be insufficient saving to finance investment locally. The resulting excess demand for funds will be met by an inflow of funds from regions with high exports and thus excess saving. Insofar as financial markets are considered separately, integrated national financial markets are assumed to contribute substantially to equalizing rates of regional development.

Yet casual observation of common-currency, unified-banking-system countries provides plenty of examples of regions that are permanently depressed. By contrast to neoclassical theory, Keynesian theories provide explanations for uneven development between regions. They are based (often implicitly) on the credit–finance rather than saving–finance view of investment. They thus conform to modern banking, which has progressed beyond mere on-lending, and do not give weight to crowding out.

Regional multiplier theory applies the familiar idea of induced expenditure to the question of uneven regional growth and employment: those regions which get investment expenditure will be further favoured by the multiplier. Economic success is thus to some extent self-reinforcing: investment in a region improves the level of activity in that region and attracts further investment. Depressed regions become unattractive to potential investors, lose income and become more depressed. If workers respond by moving to more prosperous regions, it deprives the depressed region of their unemployment benefit. These effects, it need hardly be said, are precisely the opposite of the evening-out of growth rates predicted by mainstream theory.

The theory of cumulative causation includes a dynamic interplay between investment and productivity growth to reinforce regional differences. Competitive advantages are enjoyed by those regions which are already most developed. Growth itself generates dynamic economies of scale by embodying new technology, expanding markets and the like. The faster-growing regions have faster productivity growth, making it progressively harder for the slower regions to compete. These negative effects are compensated to some extent by the positive effects which spread from the faster-growing regions; for example, the transfer of new technology from the advanced regions, and improvement in the market for the products of the lagging regions resulting from growth in the advanced regions.

Dependency theory shares with the Keynesian theories the capacity to explain persistent regional variation. Dependency theory describes the world in terms of a controlling centre and a somewhat helpless periphery. The periphery produces output with a value to the centre which is continually greater than its value to the periphery. As a corollary, a continued, if at times erratic, flow of funds is directed by the centre to investment in those products. That funds should flow to investments with an expected high rate of return is not surprising. From the point of view of neoclassical theory, what needs to be explained is the failure of the marginal efficiency of these investments to fall. In terms of dependency theory's traditional concern with underdeveloped countries as the periphery, this failure is explained by the roles of technological advance and economies of scale in the centre, which continually maintain the value to the centre of periphery food and raw materials.

The roots of dependency would seem to lie in the nature of the region's resources, so it is not a theory with obvious application to the EC, with its relatively similar economies – at least not where 'regions' are defined as countries. (One can easily think of regions *within* individual EC countries which are 'peripheral'.) But 'real' dependency is reinforced by the financial power of the centre, and that aspect may be relevant. At the present time, financial power, while it has a centre in each EC country, is dispersed around the EC as a whole. A unified banking system, however, is likely to downgrade some national centres. Let us assume for purposes of the argument that a single centre of the unified banking system develops in, say, Frankfurt. This would tend to create a financial, if not a real, periphery, distinguished from the centre by the ease or difficulty of obtaining and evaluating information about the prospects of businesses in different parts of the Community. The more centralized banking decisions are, the more likely it is that funds will flow to enterprises with head offices in the centre.

In the circumstances just outlined, the continued existence of separate national banks and/or currencies might be to the advantage of those countries in danger of finding themselves on the periphery. This was, in effect, the rationale for imposing by law a separation of banks by state boundaries in the United States. If separation were maintained, managers would have an incentive to consider 'local' (that is, national) marketability of their bank's services and thus to evaluate potential projects according to their value locally rather than their value to the centre. Second, 'local' banks are more likely to retain the deposits of periphery residents if centre banks do not compete in the periphery. The case is even more compelling when one is dealing (as would be the case in the EC) with several peripheral regions; there is no guarantee that money drained away from one such region to the centre would find its way back as investment to the same peripheral region.

Concluding remarks

The economic consequences of a common currency and unified banking system for the EC are complex, and one's stance as an economist, on the question of whether to embrace these particular forms of 'progress', depends crucially on one's theory of regional growth and development. Living in Britain is likely to make one slightly schizophrenic on this issue, as the UK is likely to be at least a contender for the financial centre but is almost certain to be on the real periphery. Those who believe a common currency and a unified banking system to be an unalloyed blessing are likely to be subscribers to a neoclassical theory of regional economics.

References

Chick, V. (1986), 'The Evolution of the Banking System and the Theory of Saving, Investment and Interest', *Economies et Sociétés*, Série MP no. 3. Reprinted in V. Chick (1992), *On Money, Method and Keynes: Selected Essays*, edited by P. Arestis and S.C. Dow, London: Macmillan.

Chick, V. and Dow, S.C. (1988), 'A Post-Keynesian Perspective on the Relation between Banking and Regional Development', *Thames Papers in Political Economy*, Spring. Reprinted in P. Arestis (ed.), *Post Keynesian Monetary Economics*, Aldershot: Edward Elgar.

Dow, S.C. (1990), *Financial Markets and Regional Economic Development*, Aldershot: Gower.

Kregel, J.A. (1990), 'The EMS, the Dollar and the World Economy', in P. Ferri (ed.), *Prospects for a European Monetary System*, London: Macmillan.

Molyneux, P. (1989), '1992 and Its Impact on Local and Regional Banking Markets', *Regional Studies*, **23**, (6), 523–33.

Zysman, J. (1983), *Governments, Markets and Growth: Financial Systems and the Politics of Industrial Growth*, Oxford: Martin Robertson.

13 A post-Keynesian perspective of European integration

*Philip Arestis**

Introduction

This paper argues that the theoretical ingredients of a political economy model appropriate to the realities of an integrated European Community (EC) are engrained in Myrdal's (1957) 'circular and cumulative causation' and the related views of Kaldor (1970, 1972) and Perroux (1955). They are also embedded in the development which has come to be known as the Fordist model. This is the polar opposite of a more recent contribution, the post-Fordist model, and I comment upon this, too, in so far as it impinges upon EC developments.

European economic integration entails the following assumptions: there are no 'artificial' barriers between the member states of Europe, and there is free flow of goods and services, capital and labour within the EC. There is a European Central Bank responsible for issuing a single currency and for the conduct of monetary policy. Similarly, I assume that there is fiscal harmonization so that transfers can be initiated from the federal to the state system. There is, thus, full co-ordination of both monetary and fiscal policies, a situation, I argue, which is not entirely unproblematic.

The paper also argues that the postulated theoretical framework implies certain economic policies. Traditional fiscal and monetary policies may, in principle, push the economy towards a full-employment situation. The accompanying 'circular and cumulative' effects, though, clearly imply that rich regions become even richer, and poor regions even poorer. I suggest that regional and industrial economic policies which aim at controlling and directing investment along with 'planning of incomes' are of paramount importance. These economic policies, however, should recognize local needs. Consequently, a certain degree of decentralization is inevitable.

Main theoretical constructs

My analysis concerns itself with the capitalist mode of production. Markets distribute income according to relative power (Nell, 1980, p. 26). In this power relationship, capital's objectives are in conflict with labour's objectives so that 'class conflict' is at the heart of analysis.

'Class conflict' is highlighted in the wage determination theory where bargaining in the labour market is the kernel of this analysis. Unionized or non-unionized workers have drives and aspirations, as well as economic and political power, which are described in terms of a target relative real wage. Deviations of actual real wages from the desired level affect the level of money wage demands, thereby causing an upward pressure on money wages if the desired level is greater than the actual. Similarly, there would be a downward pressure on money wages when the real wage falls short of the target relative real wage. Expectations of price inflation and of profits over the contract period, the rate of change of unemployment (seen as a proxy of the speed of expansion or contraction of 'the reserve army of unemployed'), and the workers' position in income distribution relative to certain reference groups are further variables that are thought to be important determinants of nominal wages (Arestis and Skott, 1991). Clearly, this consideration is particularly relevant to the EC context. The rate of wage inflation relative to productivity, along with that of prices of imports and raw materials, is taken to be the most vital determinant of price inflation. Inflation, then, belongs squarely in the 'conflict theory' framework, reflecting the struggle of labour for its income share.

Pricing behaviour is, of course, important in the process just outlined. Modern advanced industrial economies are characterized by the duality of the 'small competitive' and the 'oligopolistic' sectors. The 'small competitive' sector portrays the type of behaviour that is more suitable to the neoclassical firm, where demand and supply determine price, so that firms are price-takers. In the dominant 'oligopolistic' sector it is the megacorp that has become the representative form of enterprise (Eichner, 1987). The pricing behaviour of the megacorps is simply to add a certain percentage mark-up on their unit cost of production. The mark-up is determined by the need of the megacorps to finance their investment plans (Eichner, 1976), so that pricing decisions are inextricably linked to capital accumulation.[1]

Capital accumulation in the political economy tradition is determined by expected profitability. But whilst *expected* profitability induces capital accumulation, *realized* investment creates the profitability which makes investment possible, partly through internally generated funds. Expected profitability is essentially influenced by the marginal efficiency of investment and by the expected growth of sales. Expectations, however, under uncertainty are pervasive. So much so that entrepreneurs' 'animal spirits' are held responsible for the structural breaks and crises that are an inherent aspect of capitalism. The pace of technical change, viewed as endogenous rather than exogenous (Sawyer, 1989), is another influence on investment. But whilst technical change stimulates *net* investment, the implementation of technical change requires gross investment to facilitate the application of new technology. Consequently, faster technical change is closely associated with a higher rate of investment in this two-way relationship.

Investment, in its turn, is the most important variable in distribution theory. The assumption that the marginal propensities to consume out of wages and profits differ is alluded to, from which the very well-known proposition follows that on a steady-state growth path the shares of profits and wages are related to the marginal propensities to consume but, most importantly, to the ratio of investment to income. Pasinetti (1974, p. 113) has shown, in fact, that control over the rate of investment implies control over distribution and the rate of profit.

Distribution and investment, now, are the fundamental determinants of growth dynamics and business cycles. It is recognized that trend and cycle are, in fact, interdependent, with the study of the two comprising what Eichner (1987) referred to as 'the economy's macrodynamic behaviour'. Secular and cyclical developments are at the heart of the political economy approach; features which emanate from its concern with an economic system that is expanding over time in the context of history. Harrod's (1939, 1948) well-known ratio of the average propensity to save to the capital/output ratio is modified whereby the propensities to save out of profits and wages are hypothesized to differ, so that redistribution of income affects growth.

In terms of the cyclical behaviour aspect of the model, it is argued that business cycles are endogenous phenomena, caused by the normal functioning of the capitalist economic system (Kaldor, 1940; Kalecki, 1971, ch. 11; Goodwin, 1967). Exogenous shocks, for example, technological innovations, oil price changes and so on, can spark cyclical fluctuations, but they simply accentuate an underlying endogenously embedded instability. This instability arises from the motive of producers and financial investors alike to accumulate wealth for its own sake.

Money in this model is completely integrated within production and exchange. As such, money is viewed as endogenous in a money credit economy. Credit is emphasized in enabling spending units to bridge any gap between their desired level of spending and current rate of cash flows. Money is the result of credit creation, and its behaviour is governed by the portfolio needs of firms, persons, governments and financial institutions. Any attempts to curtail the required flow of money will produce severe cut-backs in production. The European Central Bank should aim to create financial stability, which is so important in discouraging funds to be devoted to speculation rather than to productive activity. However, when speculation causes liquidity to increase excessively, direct credit controls should be used to curb it. It is, thus, the case that the European Central Bank should be in a position to regulate the financial system considerably.

The European Central Bank controls the European discount rate (and thus national discount rates), changes of which influence directly changes in market interest rates via a mark-up. Clearly, Kalecki's (1971) theory of mark-up pricing as applied to interest rate determination is alluded to in this regard, so that the rate of interest is viewed as being the control variable in this approach. Furthermore, the discount rate affects the exchange rate. This link brings into the fore the foreign sector aspects of the integrated EC. These aspects are incorporated into the analysis through the current and capital accounts of the balance of payments, where the exchange rate influences, and is influenced by, the state of both accounts. A novel feature of the imports element of the current account is the hypothesis that the marginal propensities to import out of workers' income and out of the income of capitalists differ (Arestis and Driver, 1987). This is, of course, an extension of the idea referred to above in terms of distinguishing income classes in consumption.

These theoretical positions are based on the premise that effective demand, and investment in particular, is the prime mover of the capitalist system. Such a system is marred with inequalities which market forces cannot and do not reduce. By contrast, market forces tend to exacerbate the disparities that are evident in such a system. The capitalist system is inherently cyclical and unstable. Left to itself it would not achieve, let alone maintain, the full use of existing resources nor their equitable distribution. These features of the capitalist system are due mainly to the behaviour of private investment, which is attributed to volatile expectations and business confidence.

Further theoretical considerations

The theoretical propositions discussed above are consistent with, and reinforced by, the 'circular and cumulative causation' thesis of Myrdal (1957) and Kaldor (1970, 1972). This is essentially based on the dynamic interplay between investment and productivity growth which reinforces inequalities and, from the point of view of this paper, regional disparities.[2] Consequently, the unequal impact of industrial development is explained by endogenous factors in the process of historical development rather than by the exogenous 'resource endowment' (Kaldor, 1970, p. 343). Regions which are already developed enjoy competitive advantages so that the growth that takes place generates 'dynamic increasing returns' to scale (Kaldor, 1972), by attracting more skilled labour (especially young) and capital, which embody new technology by taking advantage of expanding markets and so on. All these forces cause higher productivity and rate of profit in the faster-growing regions, which makes it progressively harder for the slower regions to compete. This inflow of capital and skilled labour allows still further expansion of production, and the reaping of further economies of scale, higher productivity and rate of profit.

These 'backwash' effects are thought to be modified, however, by certain advantages accruing to the slower regions. These are the 'spread' effects, which can accrue, for example, from expanded markets and the transfer of new technology from the advanced regions, and so on. These advantages, however, can never be strong enough to outweigh the negative effects emanating from 'cumulative causation'. Even if by chance the 'spread' and 'backwash' effects are in balance, this would not be a stable equilibrium, for any change in the balance of the two forces would be followed by cumulative movements.

It follows from this analysis that the freeing, as well as widening, of markets within the EC confers advantages to already established and successful centres of expansion. The free movement of capital and labour exacerbates regional disparities. Consequently, the market mechanism reinforces regional disparities and imbalances rather than eliminating them. In the case of the EC, the implication of the model is that there is a north/south divide, the north being the economic heartland (Paris, London, Ruhr, Frankfurt and North Italy), and the south comprising Southern Italy and the other Mediterannean countries as well as the Republic of Ireland. There is, further, the idea that 'cumulative causation' in economic terms generates inequalities in non-economic terms, such as political power, cultural domination and so on. It is thus expected that those regions which are relatively rich dominate, not just in the economic power sense, but also in terms of their ability to exert political superiority. In this way they are in a position to impose their policies and culture over the less powerful regions. In this scenario, democratic institutions are under severe threat. Cowling (1985) has actually extended these ideas to the political level to suggest that transnationalism and centripetal economic developments are two tendencies which can cause a vicious circle of relative decline, with the inevitable result that whole communities can lose control over their affairs and thus their democracy. The policy implications of such a model are crystal clear: comprehensive intervention at a regional level becomes paramount to reinforce the 'spread' effects and, indeed, to counterbalance the impact of the market forces.

There are two further views in this context which are worth considering. There is the growth-pole model (Perroux, 1955), which assumes that there are certain 'poles' in the system which, like magnets, attract factors of production at the expense of depressed areas. A new industrial unit could have a very significant effect in a depressed area through the creation of demand-induced growth. Such a 'pole' can create a healthy environment for other firms in the region; it can be the engine of economic growth via its secondary effects in the manufacturing and service sectors. It can, however, have devastating effects on firms outside the region, which may find that labour and capital are absorbed by the 'pole'. The available evidence suggests that, in view of the need for satisfactory infrastructure, skilled labour and a suitable environment for management, the tendency is that new industrial units locate their production in areas which are already prosperous, thus accentuating regional disparities. This view is closely related to the centre/periphery argument (for example, Baran, 1957; Frank, 1969) whereby uneven development is the result of the subordination of the needs of the periphery to those of the centre. The financial power of the centre reinforces the relative dependency of the periphery. At the policy level, governments should encourage regional development by establishing 'counter–poles'. Essentially, this can be promoted through assistance given to companies to locate production in depressed areas and, also, through financial centres in the form of regional central banking (Chick and Dow, 1988).

The second view is that which has come to be known as Fordist, with its polar opposite, the post-Fordist model (Aglietta, 1979, 1982; Piore and Sabel, 1984). The Fordist model suggests that mass production and consumption were the result of the needs of economic agents during the post-war period. It was a regime of monopolistic accumulation, whereby capital concentrated into large multi-plant enterprises taking advantage of economies of scale provided by big markets. The manufacturing sectors were, in this view, the prosperous/'pole' centres. This concentration was relevant both in terms of industrial production and employment, and was thought to be remarkable because of its size and consistency in many countries, especially in the EC (Keeble *et al.*, 1983). A historical compromise manifested itself in the relationship between capital and labour. Productivity gains produced steady improvements in workers' real incomes, institutionalized as an 'inflation plus' norm for wage deals. The Keynesian welfare state at the same time expanded the social wage along with the private wage.

Fordism was, then, a period of high profits, high growth and rising wages. It depended on a balanced distribution between wages and profits which kept mass production and mass consumption growing in tandem. It also depended on the inevitable capital intensity being prevented from causing the rate of profit to fall. Wages had to move in harmony with increasing returns to scale, the propensity to consume and the relationship between investment and demand. Oligopolistic pricing that finances investment is, therefore, most appropriate in a Fordist regime: monopolistic competition does play a key role in accumulation (in this sense, Eichner's theory (1976) is most appropriate). Also, wages are required to be tied to productivity. For if they are not, problems will arise: if wages are too high, profits and investment will fall. If wages are too low relative to productivity, mass consumption will fall short of mass production. Clearly, the institutions of collective bargaining, the relationship between banks and industry, and the role of the state are central issues in Fordism. Monetary and fiscal policies become central in economic management. Their aim is to keep the balance between mass consumption and mass production.

But this Fordist era, it is argued, came to an end in the late 1960s, thus giving rise to what has come to be known as post-Fordism. The problems of inflation, overaccumulation and declining rates of profit, the enhanced bargaining power and political weight of the trade unions, the development of the affluent consumer who rejected standardized, mass produced commodities and so on, caused capital to develop new strategies. Traditional industries were forced to restructure or close down, thus deserting whole areas, while new 'high-tech' industries and service activities mushroomed in other regions. From about the early 1970s onwards there has been a dramatic change in terms of organization of production, including the manufacturing sector, and the development of the service sector. Bade (1986) has argued that this is definitely the case for production-oriented services (accountancy, legal services, communication services, and so on). The Fordist process reversed itself as a result, and thus produced the post-Fordist era.

Post-Fordism is precisely the polar opposite to mass production. It contends that in response to market changes and technology, more flexible units producing customized products of different types (Piore and Sabel, 1984), rather than the inflexible Fordist production unit, have become the dominant engine of growth. The standardized products of Fordism are replaced by customized products of post-Fordism. The production of the latter is made increasingly cheaper, essentially because of their reliance on microprocessor-based technologies. Examples offered to highlight the distinction between Fordism and post-Fordism include mini steel mills, chemicals and machine tools. The car industry is, however, the most notable case, in that the strategy for a world car has been replaced by a greater emphasis on model selection. Unlike Fordism, which depends on inflexible, unskilled or semi-skilled labour, subordinated to machines, post-Fordism is very much based on flexible, skilled workers who are prepared to learn new skills and move between jobs according to the wishes of the market. Thus, a new polarization of service workers has emerged: the high-skilled and the low-skilled sectors.

It is contended that these structural changes have produced massive deindustrialization and regional restructuring which have hit the old manufacturing sector in particular, thereby causing it to suffer a huge reduction in employment. The growth of the service sector tended to compensate to some degree the loss of jobs in the manufacturing sector, but it was never sufficient to match it completely.[3] Further general characteristics of post-Fordism are the attempt to counteract trade union resistance, the dismantling of the welfare state, and the search for new forms of production based essentially on the neo-liberal accumulation strategy of flexible acceleration. One important implication of this shift in production is that the degree of economies of scale is thought to be weakened, whilst the cost of producing a range of differentiated products is seen as reduced. Consequently, economic policies within this new economic climate should aim at providing the necessary training to meet the demands of the newly established service sector, at assisting small firms, and at rejuvenating the urban environment. Conflict between capital and labour is recognized still to be there, but it is expected that labour makes concessions so that the work-force can bargain flexibly with management. Macro-regulation is, thus, not so crucial, but regional policies are necessary. These should aim to boost small firms, the heart of the post-Fordist era.

Post-Fordism, however, has not escaped criticism. There is the contention that the power of the transnational corporations, both financial and industrial, does not appear to be declining – if anything, it is growing. Economies of scale do not appear to be waning, and the markets for consumer durables adhere to Fordism rather than to post-Fordist characteristics (for evidence of the failure of the post-Fordist model in the cases of 'Third Italy' and London, see O'Donnell and Nolan, 1989). It is also questioned whether post-Fordism is actually 'a core development in the economy or merely a highly touted epiphenomenon' (Luria, 1990, p. 129). For example, it is argued that the current extent and efficiency of the small unit of production is very unlikely to replace to a considerable degree a substantial share of the big mass production units. It is further argued that it is very difficult to identify clearly and indisputably cases of industrial structures which are characterized by either mass production or flexible accumulation features. In any case, flexibility at one stage of production may be associated with inflexibility at another stage; a situation which may have always prevailed. As Williams *et al.* (1987, p. 415) rightly note, there are three characteristics – dedicated equipment, product differentiation and length of production run – according to which Fordism and post-Fordism are at extreme opposites to each other.[4] It makes it absolutely impossible for all three characteristics to identify each case of firm or industry as belonging to a specific pole. The inevitable conclusion must surely be that mass production and flexible specialization cannot be identified even at firm or industry level. The argument of post-Fordism is, in any case, based essentially on the notion that Fordism reached a stage of crisis. But then, crises are not unusual in mass production economic processes. These are regulation crises, however, concerning institutions that are vital to the production and consumption relationship. They are not, thus, crises of the type suggested by post-Fordism which have more to do with technological advances that imply 'flexible' specialization and the end of mass production.

Leborgne and Lipietz (1990) argue that Europe may grow in a way that can produce destabilizing developments. Spots of success may very well take place in a background of post-Fordism. But large and increasing wage disparities may be hard to sustain in regions where strong historical solidaristic tendencies exist. Disparities of this nature can pose insurmountable difficulties in implementing appropriate macroeconomic policies. The views I have portrayed above clearly corroborate this thesis: that not only are regional inequalities expected to prevail, they may very well vary. There is not just north/south, or centre/periphery, or Fordist/post-Fordist, but different kinds of centres, multiple forms of periphery, and regions in between. Regional inequalities exist as a result of a dynamic process, with a cyclical and evolutionary perspective. Regional inequality is, therefore, a multivariate phenomenon. Regional disparities cannot be subscribed by one single indicator but by a combination of factors. This is especially so within the EC, where there are so many regional differences in terms of economic development, politics, history, tradition, culture and customs.

These theoretical positions indicate that important constraints in the development of an integrated Europe are regional dimension and regional disparities. In an attempt to throw some light on these issues, Table 13.1 provides relevant data for all the EC member countries over the last ten years or so. The disparities suggested by the theoretical framework considered in this study are very much in evidence. More concretely, Table 13.1 cites GDP per capita in three years (1980, 1984, and 1988) for the 12 members of the EC. Whenever possible, for each country the lowest and the highest GDP statistics in the regions are reported for each country. The data clearly show that regional differences are very significant, not just within countries but, more importantly, across countries. For example, the lowest GDP per head in Germany is considerably higher than the richest region in any of the peripheral countries (Spain, Greece, Portugal and Ireland) and for the three years that data are reported in Table 13.1. Comparing intercountry differences for the three years, it is disturbing to note that during the 1980s there has been no improvement in the disparities. If anything, there has been a deterioration both within regions and countries. Indeed, when we look at the ratio of the lowest to the highest regional GDP per head in each country during the 1980s, it is clear that in all countries, with the exception of the Netherlands, the ratio has either remained the same (Spain, Greece) or has deteriorated (Belgium, Germany, France, Italy and the UK). In the case of the Netherlands there was a distinct deterioration from 1980 to 1984, but the ratio had improved by 1988.[5] Data for the percentage rate of unemployment, shown in Table 13.2 for 1987, tell a similar story. Disparities within and across countries in terms of unemployment are apparent. But the cases of West Germany, Italy, Portugal and the UK are particularly noticeable when

Table 13.1:   Range of GDP per capita in EC countries

GDP (per capita)

Country	1980				1984				1988			
	Highest (H)	Lowest (L)	Average	L/H	Highest (H)	Lowest (L)	Average	L/H	Highest (H)	Lowest (L)	average	L/H
B (Belgium)	159	87	104	55	157	85	103	55	155	84	101	54
DK (Denmark)			108				114				109	
D (W. Germany)	179	99	114	55	188	97	114	52	182	94	113	52
E (Spain)	88	59	73	67	86	56	72	65	88	59	75	67
GR (Greece)			58		60	50	57	83	58	48	54	83
F (France)	161	93	112	57	166	93	112	56	164	90	108	54
IRL (Ireland)			64				65				65	
I (Italy)			103		133	68	103	51	138	67	104	49
NL (Netherlands)	140	96	111	68	143	87	107	60	122	85	103	70
L (Luxembourg)			119				121				121	
P (Portugal)			55				52				54	
UK (United Kingdom)	119	77	101	65	122	79	103	65	130	80	107	62

Note:
The indices are calculated on the basis that EUR 12 (all twelve countries in Europe) = 100 in each year.

Source: Eurostat, Rapid Reports: Regions, 1990(2).

Table 13.2: Unemployment rate 1987

Country	Total (%)	Highest (H) (%)	Lowest (L) (%)	L/H
B (Belgium)	11.3	14.4	9.4	0.65
DK (Denmark)	6.1	—	—	—
D (West Germany)	6.3	11.6	3.6	0.31
E (Spain)	20.8	29.9	15.5	0.52
GR (Greece)	7.4	8.3	4.6	0.55
F (France)	10.4	14.0	8.6	0.61
IRL (Ireland)	18.1	—	—	—
I (Italy)	10.6	21.2	6.1	0.29
NL (Netherlands)	9.7	11.6	9.3	0.80
L (Luxembourg)	2.7	—	—	—
P (Portugal)	7.1	10.2	4.2	0.41
UK (United Kingdom)	11.1	18.9	8.1	0.43
EUR 12	10.6	—	—	—

Sources: As in Table 13.1

compared with the rest of the EC member countries. Their L/H ratios are conspicuously lower than the other countries' ratios. We may also note that the ratio of the highest unemployment rate to the lowest is just under a factor of eight. This is worse than corresponding figures reported for the 1970s, for which a factor of less than seven was identified (Nicol and Yuill, 1982).

Further disparities worth mentioning are expenditures on R&D and on venture capital. There is a considerable technology gap between the weaker and the more developed regions. In the case of Greece, Ireland, Portugal, Southern Italy and Spain, technology can be lagging behind by as much as a hundred times than elsewhere in the EC. In addition, these 'poorer 'countries have almost zero R&D capacity; it is estimated that 7 billion ECU in the form of annual investment in R&D would be required to bring them to the EC average (Mair, 1991). Similarly, the availability of venture capital is unevenly distributed. The 'poorer' countries just mentioned muster only something like 10 per cent of the total EC venture capital (at any rate in 1985 as mentioned in Mair, 1991).

Containing inequalities and achieving full employment
The analysis so far clearly indicates that an integrated Europe is very un-likely to achieve full employment and to contain the inequalities identified above. These problems are even more awkward to tackle in an EC set-up,

given the institutional, cultural, historical and economic diversities of the member states. It is also the case that traditional fiscal and monetary policies, by boosting aggregate demand, could potentially set the economy on a full-employment path. But there are still very real problems in this regard. Traditional fiscal and monetary policies would soon run into difficulties created by inequalities. For example, the achievement of full employment in certain regions may very well be accompanied by considerable unemployment elsewhere. Furthermore, it will be some time before there is a community budget of sufficient size to provide any significant leverage over the EC economy. Fiscal policy at the state level becomes increasingly circumscribed, and fiscal policy at the community level needs to be strengthened substantially. Similar problems exist in the area of monetary policy, where it is conceivable that a strong European Central Bank might alleviate difficulties of this nature.

There are further 'European' problems in that co-ordination of economic policies has been marred by different perceptions among the member states as to the operation of economic policies and their impact. Monetary policy is one obvious example: witness the difference of opinions on the EMS/EMU. Also, in terms of fiscal policy, and as Boltho (1990) has argued, divergent views are held within the Community on how these policies are expected to operate and, indeed, affect the economy. The same study shows that the leading EC countries are, in any case, hostile to any form of discretionary policy co-ordination. There are also worries that the major partners are very much in favour of diminishing the role of the state, especially that of the welfare state, and of giving more credence to the power of market forces. There are still other worries which emanate from the experience of other countries. In North America, for example, where currency union and economic integration took place across a more linguistically and culturally homogeneous area and with much more labour mobility than the EC, persistent regional differences in terms of both per capita income and unemployment have been predominant. An integrated Europe, so very different from North America in this respect, should expect economic divergences on a much larger scale.

In addition, the problems Kalecki (1943) was so concerned with in terms of the difficulties of achieving and maintaining full employment (the dislike by big business of full employment, the unfounded argument of crowding-out and the need to balance the budget and so on), are very pertinent and, probably, more relevant in the case of an integrated Europe than at the national level. There is also the possibility of workers 'getting out of hand': a situation which the 'captains of industry' would not be prepared to tolerate. Rentiers, too, would not tolerate this situation since they would be disadvantaged by the inflationary pressures which are inevitable at full employment.

These, and no doubt other problems, notwithstanding, federal government intervention is necessary in principle to achieve and maintain full employment. It is interesting to note at this stage that even the EC Commission recognizes and, indeed, offers evidence to suggest that rapid and wide growth within the Community is a necessary precondition if convergence of the economies within the EC is to be achieved (Commission of the European Communities, 1990, p. 212). However, the forces of 'cumulative causation' and the associated question of regional disparities, point to the need for two types of policy. One such type is a strong regional policy; another is industrial policy.

At the level of the individual country, in addition to any formal regional policy, there is some quasi-automatic regional policy in that taxation is lower and public expenditure higher in depressed regions than in prosperous ones. At the Community level both quasi-automatic and formal regional policy require transfer of resources from the very few rich countries, notably Germany, to the less prosperous, such as Greece and Portugal. The expectation surely must be that the very few rich will not readily agree to the required loss of resources on their part.

The Treaty of Rome (Article 2) refers to regional problems and suggests that it is important to ensure 'harmonious development, by reducing both the existing differences between the various regions and the backwardness of the less favoured regions'. But the Treaty did not specify policies whereby intervention might take place. It is also the case that the regional dimension has not received the attention it deserves in the discussions to create the Single Market (see, for example, Cecchini, 1988; Commission of the European Communities, 1988). The only exception is the Delors report on economic and monetary union (Delors, 1989), which assigns regional policy a more prominent role. It is argued in the report that a more balanced economic structure within the EC is necessary if full economic and monetary union is to succeed; consequently: 'particular attention would have to be paid to an effective Community policy aimed at narrowing regional and structural disparities and promoting a balanced development throughout the Community' (Delors, 1989, para. 29).

Some form of regional policy was, nonetheless, inaugurated in 1975. Under the European Regional Development Fund (ERDF),[6] policies were designed to provide financial assistance and incentives to member countries in the form of quotas determined by the severity of the regional problems of the EC members. But the EC regional policies do not appear to have been successful in terms of mitigating regional disparities. Table 13.1 suggests

Table 13.3:   Growth differential rates for convergence[1]

	GR	E	IRL	P	EUR 4[2]
Historical record					
1961–73	3.1	2.1	–0.2	2.9	2.3
1974–79	0.6	–0.9	1.0	–0.5	–0.6
1980–87	–1.0	0.0	0.0	0.0	–0.1
1988–92[3]	–1.0	1.4	0.3	0.7	1.0
Growth differential required for reducing the prosperity gap to 90%[4]					
1992	10.6	3.9	7.1	10.8	5.6
1997	5.2	1.9	3.5	5.3	2.8
2002	3.4	1.3	2.3	3.5	1.8
2007	2.5	1.0	1.7	2.6	1.4

1: Measured as percentage point difference with EUR 12 of annual growth of GDP per capita.
2: EUR 4: GR, E, IRL, P.
3: Based on medium-term projections 1988–92, October 1988.
4: In order to obtain some orders of magnitude of the differential required, the real convergence objective is fixed at 90 per cent of the average of EUR 12. This perspective is only put forward as a numerical example and is in no case to be considered as a policy standard.

Source: Commission services (as reported in Grahl and Teague, 1990).

that 'cumulative causation' effects have been strengthened rather than mitigated by these policies.

Table 13.3 reinforces this argument. It cites the growth differential rates required for the poor countries (Greece, Spain, Ireland and Portugal) to catch up with the richer countries. Two sets of data are provided: the historical record for the period 1961–1992 and projections for the period 1992–2007. It clearly is the case that the reduction of regional disparities in the EC will be a horrendous task. Furthermore, with European integration there is the real danger that the situation might be even more bleak, since 'cumulative causation' is expected to exacerbate regional inequalities. The balance of opinion is actually that the likely effects of European economic integration will lead to increased regional disparities (see, for example, Mair, 1991).

Clearly, enhancing regional investment would have to be the prime objective of any policy that hopes to have any impact at the regional level. Considerable extra investment would have to be directed to the poorer regions, both in infrastructure and in local firms as a means of creating new permanent jobs. But in this process it is very important to consider needs and problems at the local-regional level. The 'indigenous potentials', that is infrastructure, training and the educational level of the work-force, demographic characteristics, natural resources, industrial patterns and tradition, specific regional activity and so on, would have to be looked at carefully, and regional problems tackled in the process. Decentralization of key activities in order to improve regional integration becomes of paramount importance.[7] Regional capital markets are another dimension in this analysis. There is the real danger at the moment that an unhelpful system may very well emerge whereby capital markets serve the requirements of the multinational companies with the smaller regional companies not being able to satisfy their less sophisticated needs. The decentralized banking system advocated by Chick and Dow (1988) is, once again, particularly apt in this context.

The other type of policy referred to above is industrial policy. It has been argued that this policy assumes a renewed role within an integrated EC (Sawyer, 1991). A coherent European industrial policy can be very problematic, given the experience with this type of policy among the EC members, especially between the UK and continental Europe. In the UK industrial policies have been based on the notion that they are needed to cure 'market failures', as, for example, in the case of monopolistic tendencies. The role of the state in this context is one of control and regulation, but of no direct involvement in industry. In the rest of the EC, by contrast, industrial policies have been predicated upon a different role for industrial policies: the state should aid development and promote new opportunities, from which it obviously follows that the state becomes a lot more involved in industrial affairs. Interestingly enough, the Treaty of Rome and the Single European Act support, surprisingly, the UK approach to industrial policy (Sawyer, 1991). It is to be noted, nonetheless, that the more successful European economies have relied upon comprehensive involvement of the state in industry. The position taken in this paper clearly and strongly supports the latter approach. Such policy, however, requires substantial co-operation between industry and the state, which may be more efficient and effective at a regional level than at the European level, although a certain degree of co-ordination is inevitable to avoid any remaining cumulative causation problems. An interventionist and supportive industrial policy with a regional focus stands a better chance of success.

Regional and/or industrial policies, however, would have to be accompanied by other interventionist policies. The control of investment suggested above by itself may not be effective if co-operation from the trade union movement is not forthcoming. But trade unions would be willing to co-operate if they were to be involved in the decision-making mechanism. The type of investment control envisaged here is socialization of investment, which would actually involve the trade unions in the process. This form of socialization of investment, therefore, gives active roles not just to governments but also to the trade unions. In this way there is direct involvement of the trade union movement in the process of capital formation.[8]

Socialization of investment of the type I am suggesting would also remove the obstacles to achieving full employment that Kalecki was so worried about, especially as the dislike of the socio-political change normally associated with attempts to sustain full employment disappears altogether. Changes of this nature would be welcomed by the trade unions since they could strengthen the position of their members by enhancing their industrial muscle. In this environment, trade unions would be more willing to engage in permanent 'incomes planning' (another important feature of the political economy menu of economic policies), which would contain to a considerable extent the inflationary pressures that emanate from the 'conflict' nature of inflation.[9] These types of policies, however, would have to be accompanied by active labour market and manpower policies to encourage labour mobility and thus facilitate labour market adjustments for the unemployed. Tackling unemployment should be top priority for this set of policies; for if these policies are not pursued with a firm commitment to full employment, their chances of success would be seriously threatened.

These economic policies require a degree of consensus and the existence of relevant institutional arrangements (for example, fairly centralized trade unions and employers' organizations). These conditions do not exist, and will not exist for many years, in the European Community, despite the fact that in some member countries the rudiments of these institutions exist. Thus, the constraints on achieving and maintaining full employment and other policy objectives which political economists identify, will be much more severe under the Single Market than in national economies. In one sense, the exception may be the foreign trade constraint, but that is transformed into a 'regional' problem. Genuine 'European' institutions of the type suggested in this paper are desperately needed if progress is to be made towards a prosperous but fair integrated Europe.

Concluding remarks

This paper has offered a theoretical framework, appropriate I have argued, to the realities of an integrated Europe. There are certain economic policies which follow from it. It is interesting to ask what the chances of success are of the combination of economic policies I have suggested above.

It must surely be the case that the answer is negative. For in addition to the constraints recognized in the text, there are a number of problems involved. First of all, harmonization of fiscal and monetary policies *per se* could not save 'cumulative causation' effects from materializing. This means that a certain degree of autonomy is required to tackle regional problems. 'Planning of incomes' and 'labour and manpower' policies require mobility of labour and capital. The latter might be possible, but the case of labour may very well be insurmountable given the existence of serious language, cultural, historical, sociological and political differences among the member states. Similarly, the 'socialization of investment' type of policy may be acceptable to certain member states but not to others.

We may, therefore, conclude that whilst analysis points to certain important economic policies, their implementation may be rather problematic. In this sense I would like to suggest that the future of European integration does not look as bright as its proponents argue it to be.

Notes

*   I am extremely grateful to Malcolm Sawyer, Eleni Paliginis and Keith Bain for very useful comments. Eleni very kindly let me draw on her data bank (my Tables 13.1 and 13.2), for which I thank her. I would also like to thank the participants to the conference on 'Global Macroeconomic Perspectives' held in Rome, May 29/30 1991, for their constructive comments.

1.   It can be argued that small firms operating in networks may be seen as the industrial structure of the post-Fordist era, while Eichner (1976) portrayed the Fordist industrial structure.

2.   Kaldor (1970) defines regional disparities as consisting of unequal rates of growth of regions.

3.   The growth in the service sector was based entirely in the private sector, unlike previous cases where it was the public sector that provided the platform for increases of this nature. The development of the service sector, however, entailed an important and interesting dimension which reflected directly women's opportunities in the market-place. There has been a conspicuous increase in the involvement of women in the labour market.

4.   Clearly, Fordism is characterized by low product differentiation, high dedicated equipment and a long length of production run. By contrast, post-Fordism is a regime with high product differentiation, low dedicated equipment and a short length of production run (Williams et al., 1987, p. 415).

5.   It would be interesting to compare regional disparities in the EC with those of the US. Kowalski (1989, especially fn 2) suggests that regional disparities are twice as high in the case of incomes, and three times as high as in the case of unemployment, in the EC than in the US.

6.   Other agencies were also created for regional policy purposes. The most important are: the European Investment Bank, the European Coal and Steel Community, the European Social Fund and the European Agricultural and Guidance Fund. However, the ERDF was by far the most important.

7.   The policies suggested in the text are similar to what follows from the analysis pursued by Albrechts and Swyngedouw (1989), which they label as 'a top-down and bottom-up' approach.

8.   Socialization of investment was one of Keynes's (1936, 1980) policy prescriptions. But Keynes's notion of socialization lacks trade union involvement which is the *sine qua non* of its success (Arestis, 1990).

9.   It should be noted that the differences in living standards, union traditions and spread of unionization seem to make any form of European incomes policies a very long way off. Within the EC there is the additional disparity that some countries are much less prone to inflation than others, yet the single currency requires equal rates of inflation.

Bibliography

Aglietta, M. (1979), *A Theory of Capitalist Regulation: The US Experience*, London: Verso.

Aglietta, M. (1982), 'World Capitalism in the Eighties', *New Left Review*, November/December, No. 136, 5–41.

Albrechts, L. and Swyngedouw, E. (1989), 'The Challenges for Regional Policy Under A Flexible Regime of Accumulation', in Albrechts *et al.* (1989).

Albrechts, L., Moulaert, F., Roberts, P. and Swyngedouw, E. (1989), *Regional Policy at the Crossroads: European Perspectives*, London: Jessica Kingsley Publishers Ltd.

Arestis, P. (1990), 'Post-Keynesianism: A New Approach to Economics', *Review of Social Economy*, Autumn, **XLVIII**, (3), 222–46.

Arestis, P. and Driver, C. (1987), 'The Effects of Income Distribution on Consumer Imports', *Journal of Macroeconomics*, Winter, **9**, (1), 83–94.

Arestis, P. and Skott, P. (1991), 'Conflict, Wage Relativities and Hysteresis in UK Wage Determination', *Journal of Post Keynesian Economics* (forthcoming).

Bade, F. (1986), 'The De-industrialisation of the Federal Republic of Germany and its Spatial Implications', in P. Nijkamp (ed.), *Technological Change, Employment and Spatial Dynamics*, Berlin: Springer.

Baran, P. (1957), *The Political Economy of Growth*, New York: Monthly Review.

Boltho, A. (1990), 'Why Has Europe Not Co-ordinated its Fiscal Policies?', *International Review of Applied Economics*, June, **4**, (2), 166–81.

Cecchini, P. (1988), *1992 : The European Challenge*, Aldershot: Wildwood House.

Chick, V. and Dow, S.C. (1988), 'A Post-Keynesian Perspective on the Relation Between Banking and Regional Development', in P. Arestis (ed.), *Post-Keynesian Monetary Economics: New Approaches to Financial Modelling*, Aldershot: Edward Elgar Publishing Limited.

Commission of the European Communities (1988), 'The Economics of 1992', *European Economy*, December, No. 35.

Commission of the European Communities (1990), 'One Market, One Money', *European Economy*, October, No. 44.

Cowling, K. (1985), 'Economic Obstacles to Democracy', in R.C.O. Matthews (ed.), *Economy and Democracy*, London: Macmillan.

Delors, J. (1989), *Report on Economic and Monetary Union in the European Community*, Luxembourg: Office for Official Publications of the EC.

Eichner, A. S. (1976), *The Megacorp and Oligopoly: Micro Foundations of Macro Dynamics*, Cambridge: Cambridge University Press.

Eichner, A.S. (1987), *The Macrodynamics of Advanced Market Economies*, Armonk: M.E. Sharp.

Frank, A.G. (1969), *Capitalism and Underdevelopment in Latin America*, New York: Modern Reader Paperbacks.

Goodwin, R.M. (1967), 'A Growth Cycle', in C.H. Feinstein (ed.), *Socialism, Capitalism and Economic Growth*, Cambridge: Cambridge University Press.

Grahl, J. and Teague, P. (1990), *1992 – The Big Market: The Future of the European Community*, London: Lawrence and Wishart.

Harrod, R. (1939), 'An Essay in Economic Theory', *Economic Journal*, March, **49**, (1), 14–33.

Harrod, R. (1948), *Towards a Dynamic Economics*, London: Macmillan.

Kaldor, N. (1940), 'A Model of the Trade Cycle', *Economic Journal*, March, **50**, (1), 78–92.

Kaldor, N. (1970), 'The Case for Regional Policies', *Scottish Journal of Political Economy*, November, **17**, (4), 337–48.

Kaldor, N. (1972), 'The Irrelevance of Equilibrium Economics', *The Economic Journal*, December, **82**, (4), 1237–55.

Kalecki, M. (1943), 'Political Aspects of Full Employment', *Political Quarterly*, October/December, **14**, (4), 322–31.

Kalecki, M. (1971), *Selected Essays on the Dynamics of the Capitalist Economy, 1933–1970*, Cambridge: Cambridge University Press.

Keeble, D., Owens, P. and Thompson, C. (1983), 'The Urban–Rural Manufacturing Shift in the European Community', *Urban Studies*, **20**, (4), 405–18.

Keynes, J.M. (1936), *The General Theory of Employment, Interest and Money*, London: Macmillan.

Keynes, J.M. (1980), *Activities, 1940–46: Shaping the Post-War World: Employment*, Collected Writings, Vol. XIV, London: Macmillan.

Kowalski, L. (1989), 'Major Current and Future Regional Issues in the Enlarged Community', in Albrechts *et al.* (1989).

Leborgne, D. and Lipietz, A. (1990), 'How to Avoid a Two-tier Europe', *Labour and Society*, **15**, (2), 1–15.

Luria, D. (1990), 'Automation, Markets and Scale: Can Flexible Niching Modernize US Manufacturing?', *International Review of Applied Economics*, June, **4**, (2), 127–65.

Mair, D. (1991), 'Regional Policy Initiatives from Brussels', *The Royal Bank of Scotland*, March, No. 169, 33–43.

Myrdal, G. (1957), *Economic Theory and Underdeveloped Regions*, London: Duckworth.

Nell, E.J. (1980), 'The Revival of Political Economy', in E.J. Nell (ed.), *Growth, Profits and Property*, Cambridge: Cambridge University Press.

Nicol, W. and Yuill, D. (1982), 'Regional Problems and Policy', in A. Boltho (ed.), *The European Economy: Growth and Crisis*, Oxford: Oxford University Press.

O'Donnell, K. and Nolan, P. (1989), 'Flexible Specialisation and the Cyprus Industrial Strategy', *Cyprus Journal of Economics*, December, **2**, (2), 1–20.

Pasinetti, L.L. (1974), *Growth and Income Distribution: Essays in Economic Theory*, Cambridge: Cambridge University Press.

Perroux, F. (1955), 'Note on the Concept of Growth Poles', *Economie Appliquee*, (Nos 1 and 2). Reprinted in I. Livingstone, *Economic Policy for Development*, London: Penguin, 1971.

Piore, M. and Sabel, C. (1984), *The Second Industrial Divide: Possibilities for Prosperity*, New York: Basic Books.

Sawyer, M.C. (1989), *The Challenge of Radical Political Economy: An Introduction to the Alternatives to Neo-Classical Economics*, Hertfordshire: Harvester Wheatsheaf.

Sawyer, M.C. (1991) 'Reflections on the Nature and Role of Industrial Policy', *Metroeconomica*, **43**, (2), 1–20.

Williams, K., Cutler, T., Williams, J. and Haslam, C. (1987), 'The End of Mass Production?', *Economy and Society*, August, **16**, (3), 404–38.

14 Monetary economics after financial restructuring

John Smithin

Introduction

During the current era of rapid evolutionary change in financial markets which began in the late 1970s, a popular and controversial topic for discussion has been the relevance of traditional monetary economics in the context of radically innovated and deregulated financial markets. In particular, the adherents of what Cowen and Kroszner (1987) have called the 'new monetary economics' (NME) have collectively presented a vision of a system in which numerous competing media of exchange exist side by side in a *laissez-faire* financial environment in which many of the precepts of traditional monetary theory lose their relevance. There would be separation between the media of exchange and the unit of account, no well-defined concept of the 'money supply', no role for institutions resembling contemporary central banks, and no need for 'monetary policy'.

Alternative versions of NME are sometimes presented as extrapolations from current trends in financial systems and sometimes as normative reform proposals, but in all cases are claimed to have desirable stability properties when compared to existing monetary systems. The approach clearly represents a challenge to much of the rest of the monetary theory literature across the entire spectrum, from Friedman's (1987; 1989) revival of the quantity theory, through Lucas's (1981) 'monetary misperceptions' theory of the business cycle, to the Post Keynesian 'endogenous money' theories of Kaldor (1970, 1982) and Moore (1988). The point is that all of these theories take for granted the existence of a central bank-type institution at the centre of the system, while differing on such issues as whether the bank controls the monetary base or short-term interest rates, whether the bank or some other force in the system is responsible for inflation, and whether monetary policy is neutral or non-neutral with respect to output and employment.

On the specific issue of the role of the central bank, the analysis of this paper (which updates the discussion in Smithin (1984) and draws on joint work reported in Dow and Smithin (1991)), would tend to support the traditional theorists rather than the NME approach. It will be argued that the technological, institutional and regulatory changes[1] currently taking place will likely have less impact on the *fundamentals* of monetary theory than it may appear at first sight. Such a conclusion, however, is obviously highly dependent on what the fundamentals are conceived to be. It will be suggested that, because of the crucial co-ordinating role of monetary exchange in market-based economic systems, there is always a tendency towards a concentration of financial power, even in the absence of government intervention and more or less independently of the level of technological sophistication in the financial services sector. If, therefore, a fundamental assumption of standard theory is that there will always exist some relatively powerful financial institutions (at either the national or global level) which are capable of manipulating certain monetary or financial variables, then that theory is on fairly safe ground. This conclusion, however, may still not be adequate for the purposes of orthodox monetarism, which would require, in addition, a relatively unchanging institutional structure and a well-defined concept of the money supply (Smithin, forthcoming). Observed changes in financial markets may well therefore tip the balance in favour of those who argue that the rate of interest is the ultimate monetary control variable. Nonetheless, if the requirements of the monetary payments system continue to give rise to concentrations of economic power in the shape of central bank-like institutions, economists will have to continue to grapple with some of the familiar and awkward issues of monetary policy.

Financial systems without money

Among the most widely cited contributors to the NME literature are Black (1970), Fama (1980, 1983), Hall (1982a, 1982b), Greenfield and Yeager (1983, 1989) and Cowen and Kroszner (1987, 1989). A distinction is sometimes made between work in this tradition and that of the so-called 'legal restrictions' theorists (LRT), whose leading figure is Wallace (1983, 1988). More commonly, however, the similarities between the two groups are stressed. This point is explicitly made by Cowen and Kroszner (1989), for example, who treat both the NME and LRT contributors as presenting a united front against other approaches to monetary economics. Although it nonetheless inevitably does a disservice to individual contributors, who all have their own distinctive points of view, certain common themes can certainly be distinguished.

These authors have all considered the feasibility of one version or another of a completely deregulated competitive payments system which is 'cashless' (in the sense of lacking an outside or base money) and in which the media of exchange in circulation are separated from the unit of account. The latter is defined in terms of some composite commodity bundle, chosen such that prices quoted in it can be expected to be relatively stable, and plays a role in the financial world analogous to weights and measures rather than that of units of some reserve asset into which promises to pay are ultimately redeemable. The only role of government in the system would be to define this unit of account and possibly conduct its own transactions in terms of it. The exchange media themselves need not be restricted to the fixed-nominal-value deposit liabilities of institutions similar to banks, but could also include, for example, transferable claims to shares of an equity-based portfolio analogous to contemporary money-market mutual funds. There would be a completely deregulated *laissez-faire* financial environment, in which there are numerous competing media of exchange whose unit of account value may vary with market conditions. There would be no well-defined concept of the money supply, all the potential exchange media would pay competively determined yields, and the preconditions for the conduct of conventional monetary policy (such as open market operations) would not exist.

It is recognized, as in Greenfield and Yeager (1989), that for claims against diverse financial institutions to be acceptable, there must exist some general redemption medium. This is not, however, the composite commodity defining the unit of account, because of the assumed inconveniences of transporting and storing the commodities involved. The redemption medium is, rather, some more generally acceptable asset which itself varies in unit of account value. It is argued that price level stability is then assured by a system of 'indirect convertibility'. An exchange medium with a value of (say) a hundred units of account is supposedly always exchangeable for a quantity of the redemption medium equivalent to literally a hundred units of the actual composite commodity at current market ratios.

It is apparent, therefore, that the adherents of NME have put forward what Trautwein (1991) aptly calls 'theories of finance without money'. These describe what are essentially 'sophisticated barter system(s)' (Fama, 1980; Cowen and Kroszner, 1987) in which the characteristic problems of a monetary economy do not arise. The questions which this poses for other monetary economists are whether such a result is a feasible outcome of the evolution of actual market processes, and whether the system would persist if somehow imposed by fiat. In other words, is it possible to imagine the market mechanism operating without the existence of money and the standard problems that the management of money entails?

Money and the co-ordination of economic activity

White (1984, 1987) in his critique of the NME–LRT approach argues that this literature tends to consider the various monetary assets primarily in their 'store of value' role, rather than as performing the traditional monetary function of facilitating transactions. This seems to be a valid point, in spite of the numerous references to 'exchange media', given the final emergence in these models of what is essentially a state of barter. The neglect of the transactions facilitating role of money is shown up particularly in the assertions in the LRT literature that the coexistence of non-interest-bearing monetary assets with interest-bearing assets of similar risk characteristics (more generally the phenomenon of monetary assets bearing a lower yield than market conditions otherwise seem to warrant), is a conundrum which can only be explained by legal restrictions (White, 1987; Goodhart, 1986). If there is something distinctive about the transaction services performed by 'money', however, which only 'monetary' assets can perform, the discount is readily explained as the price of transaction services. The apparent absence of such considerations from the literature under discussion therefore seems to indicate the continuing influence of Walrasian ideas according to which the co-ordination of market exchange activities presents no problems.

It has been recognized by a number of authors, including Hahn (1983), Rogers (1989) and Laidler (1990a, 1990b), that models based explicitly or implicitly on Walrasian microfoundations have no real role for money to play, and that the various devices employed to incorporate monetary elements into such models have only succeeded in doing so in a superficial fashion.[2] The Walrasian auctioneer provides a (fictitious) method of co-ordinating activities in a market economy without the need for monetary exchange. Hence, it is not surprising that models which easily solve problems of information and co-ordination via the auctioneer can find no role for money. Laidler (1990a), though with explicit reference to 'new classical' economics rather than NME, has recently argued strongly that such constructs are of little relevance to the real world. In this view, monetary exchange is the real-world substitute for Walrasian markets which are non-existent in practice, and for this reason it is a mistake to base monetary theory on Walrasian foundations. It is suggested here that similar sentiments apply equally to the NME–LRT approach, as the implicit model of the economy in that literature (even though presented less formally) is little different from that underlying the more mathematically precise new classical approach. It is not really surprising, therefore, that the contributors to the NME–LRT literature find it relatively easy to develop theories of finance without money in the hypothetical, completely deregulated environment of the future.

The logic of Walrasian models pushes the researcher into considering money as just one of many assets which can be held (with no special properties), and eventually into a completely non-monetary explanation of economic phenomena. It is therefore inevitable that the 'new monetary economics' would dissolve into nothing more than standard theories of finance.

Properties of a monetary exchange economy

One contemporary group of advocates of *laissez-faire* in the financial services industry takes a somewhat different view from that of the NME–LRT literature. This group might be termed the 'modern free banking' (MFB) school, represented by the work of White (1984, 1987, 1989), Selgin and White (1987) and Selgin (1988), and finding inspiration in the earlier work of Hayek (1976; 1978) and Smith (1936; 1990). The MFB school has stressed that earlier theories of money, particularly those in the so-called 'Austrian' tradition, did in fact lay great emphasis on the medium of exchange function in facilitating the transactions process. White (1984, 1989) and Selgin and White (1987), for example, make explicit reference to the theory of Menger (1892) and assert its relevance even in the present day. The Mengerian theory is able to explain the convergence of a market system on a common monetary standard purely in terms of the self-interest of traders in the system, and without the need to invoke any form of legal restrictions. An 'invisible hand' argument is used to suggest that the trader's interest in reducing transactions costs will prompt eventual convergence on a single commodity as the standard. This will be the commodity which is the most generally acceptable or 'saleable' to others, a property which is self-reinforcing once a particular choice begins to emerge.

For obvious historical reasons Menger's account was couched in terms of a metallic commodity money such as gold. In the view of the MFB school, however, a similar process would be equally likely to occur in some completely deregulated system of the future. It is not suggested that the metallic commodity representing the standard would be the only actual medium of exchange; as in the other *laissez-faire* scenarios, there would be numerous competing media of exchange, in this case consisting primarily of the (brand name) note and deposit liabilities of institutions resembling contemporary banks. In a 'mature' system (Selgin and White, 1987) the commodity standard may not even need actually to be in circulation. All the circulating exchange media, however, would be denominated in terms of the standard, and their acceptability to the public at large would depend ultimately on a pledge of convertibility at the last resort.

Transaction costs arguments, and the historical record, are used to suggest that the unit of account function is likely to be inextricably bound up with that of the medium of exchange (White, 1984). The separation of the two functions, as suggested in the NME literature, is believed to be unlikely to occur spontaneously due to efforts to minimize calculation and negotiation costs. In this view, the separation of unit of account and medium of exchange functions could not occur (and be maintained) except by legislative intervention.

It should be pointed out, of course, that not all contemporary advocates of free banking accept the scenario laid out here, and some have concerns about the definition of an external unit of account similar to those which arise in the NME literature.[3] However, the works cited here are particularly notable in setting out what is essentially a different approach to monetary *theory* than in the NME literature, in spite of a similar commitment to *laissez-faire* and a free market in financial services. This theory concentrates on the unique role of money in the transactions process in the absence of a Walrasian auctioneer, as opposed to 'money' as a heterogeneous collection of financial assets, all of which are more or less amenable to barter for other goods and services.

Centralizing tendencies in monetary systems
Clearly, of the alternative views discussed above, the 'Mengerian' approach takes more seriously the specific role of money in the market economy and the need to provide a coherent explanation of the development of monetary institutions, than do the various theories of undifferentiated finance. However, if the purpose of the exercise is to develop a framework in which the impact of contemporary innovations can be understood (as opposed to accounting for the emergence of historical systems based on precious metals), then it can be argued that this line of argument also requires further development.

There are two main points to be made. First, if it is established that the functioning of market economies does require some ultimate repository of purchasing power, to which all of the actual circulating media must be related, this immediately raises issues of centralization, power and control which tend to be elided in discussions of free banking. These issues surely arise even in the simplest commodity-based system, as there are clearly cogent reasons to believe that pressures for the concentration and 'pyramiding' of reserves will arise even in the absence of government legislation favouring a particular institution (Goodhart, 1988).[4]

Secondly, the idea that the ultimate reserve asset of the system must indeed be one of the precious metals (or any physical commodity) seems anachronistic in the late 20th century, after eight decades of experience with fiat money systems, abstract units of account, and the notion that 'the payment of a debt is an exchange of debts' (Hicks, 1982). As Laidler (1990c) and Hicks (1982) have recently pointed out, Wicksell's ancient (and originally fanciful) notion of the 'pure credit economy' has become a more and more realistic description of actual monetary systems as the years have passed. In many ways, therefore, the culmination of that process is perhaps a more plausible conjecture about how a deregulated system might evolve than a reversion to something approximating the 19th-century gold standard.

The virtue of evolutionary-type theories of the development of monetary institutions is precisely that they emphasize the point that the ultimate determinants of what qualifies as 'money' are the demand-side factors of trust and confidence, and that these qualities are self-reinforcing. The reason that a precious metal becomes the most 'saleable' commodity in Menger's theory is simply that the transactors will always be prepared to accept this commodity because they have confidence that others will later do the same. It was always recognized that the actual 'use values' of the precious metals concerned were rather limited. But the point is that the reason why precious metals were elevated to supreme position in the past was obviously a product of concrete historical circumstances which may or may not be repeated in the evolution of some completely deregulated and innovated financial system emerging out of current conditions.

Although (obviously) if demand-side factors predominate, the analyst is not entitled to rule out any particular candidate for the role of the monetary base, if the hypothesized system is thought of as evolving from contemporary conditions (as opposed to emerging *de novo* with no previous history), it nonetheless seems more plausible that the ultimate repository of purchasing power will come to be a uniquely trustworthy financial asset, such as the 'liabilities' of some long-established and commercially successful financial institution. As with the liabilities of contemporary central banks, these may originally have been 'promises to pay' in terms of some pre-existing final redemption medium, but eventually they come to be acceptable in and of themselves as representing ultimate payment. They will, of course, be 'backed' by the institution's asset portfolio (which, by hypothesis, is regarded as particularly solid), but a point is reached at which there is no danger of any creditor actually requiring payment in (say) some subset of the bundle of physical assets underlying the portfolio.

On these terms, a 'pure credit economy' would seem to be as viable a monetary system as ancient commodity money standards or contemporary fiat money systems, all of which rest on no firmer foundation than a convention (sometimes reinforced with legal restrictions) as to what shall represent the ultimate means of payment.

In the credit economy (see Hicks, 1982), the only method of discharging the payments function is by an exchange of debts. When a retailer accepts from a consumer a cheque drawn on a financial intermediary, the retailer is simply exchanging the debt of the consumer for the debt of the financial intermediary. From the point of view of the retailer this is a workable system as long as there is a third party who will, in turn, be prepared to accept those promises to pay in exchange for goods and services. But promises to pay are inevitably of different quality in the eyes of those who have to accept them, and hence there will be a tendency towards 'pyramiding' of reserves, just as in the commodity-based system. The retailer will regard the promises to pay of some established financial intermediary as more reliable than those of an isolated individual, but may only accept claims against some peripheral institution if 'backed' by claims against a more reputable concern, and so on down the line.

At the centre of the system will be a single institution (or perhaps a small group of institutions) whose promises to pay have come to be regarded as more reliable and more widely acceptable than those of the others. At a certain stage they are no longer, in practice, redeemable into anything else, and will have come to be regarded as effectively the 'base money' of the system. Monetary 'policy' will then boil down to the setting of interest rates by the central institution (Hicks, 1982; Moore, 1988), which will provide the incentive or otherwise for the other agents in the economy to take credit denominated in terms of that institution's liabilities.

Presumably, again, if the system is thought of as evolving from current conditions, an abstract unit of account, such as the dollar or yen, would continue to be in use, and the value of the abstract unit would be influenced by the portfolio choices of the institution which had come to occupy the central position (in much the same way as the choices of contemporary central banks influence the exchange value of the unit of account today). The arguments of the MFB school would continue to bear on the issues of whether a system characterized by monetary separation would be likely to arise (in the absence of deliberate policy design), and whether the bulk of the exchange media would be fixed nominal value debt-based liabilities (once it is established what nominal values mean in the system) or otherwise. The key issue would be what is acceptable in practice on the part of individual agents on the demand side (as opposed to systems which are theoretically conceivable and have desirable macroeconomic stability properties from the point of view of a social planner).

As mentioned above, even in the case of the definition of some external unit of account by the authorities, as in the NME scenarios, it seems to be admitted on all sides that the system must generate for itself some ultimate means of payment or redemption medium. If the unit of account is defined separately, the redemption medium itself is supposed to be variable in unit of account value. However, the redemption medium (and not the bundle of goods implicit in the unit of account) is by definition the most 'saleable' or acceptable asset. Hence, in the absence of more comprehensive legislation than simply defining the unit of account, there seems to be nothing to prevent the redemption medium itself from evolving into a true base money and, driven by the minimization of calculation and negotiating costs, also usurping the unit of account role. This point has already been made; for example, by Meltzer (1989) in his comment on the work of Greenfield and Yeager.

Conclusions

If it is accepted that functioning market economies, as opposed to theoretical Walrasian systems, will always need to generate some ultimate repository of purchasing power to which circulating exchange media must be related (for example, by redemption pledges), then a case can be made that monetary economics after financial restructuring must continue to deal with a number of traditional themes. In particular, it would seem that the emergence of powerful institutions similar to contemporary central banks is a likely outcome of the process, even in the absence of government intervention and special legislative privileges for particular institutions. Power would simply accrue to the most commercially successful enterprises, whose promises to pay inspire most confidence, rather than to those who inspire confidence because they are backed by the state. The conclusion that the emergence of central banks is a 'natural' development is in line with arguments recently put forward by Hicks (1982, 1989), Goodhart (1988) and Dow and Smithin (1991).

Our conclusions must be qualified in two respects, however. First, a rapid pace of financial innovation, whether classified as technological, institutional or regulatory, obviously does make it more difficult to sustain monetarist-type arguments that credit money economies can be made to behave 'as if' they were commodity money economies by appeals to stable money multiplier relationships between an exogenous fiat base money and the proximate exchange media (Rogers, 1989; Smithin, forthcoming). In the 'credit economy', the ultimate asset will clearly not be in fixed supply, but will be demand-determined, with changes in interest rates regulating its rate of growth.[5] As Hicks (1982, 1986, 1989) and some Keynesian and Post Keynesian economists (Dow and Saville, 1988, 1990; Kaldor, 1970, 1982; Moore, 1988) have argued, the rate of interest charged by the central institution then becomes the ultimate monetary control variable. The nature of the appropriate monetary control variable has, however, been one of the traditional debating points, so in this sense at least familiar themes will continue.

Secondly, in practice, even with complete deregulation and *laissez-faire* in the financial services industry in most respects, it must be expected that the existing central banks will continue to occupy the commanding heights in national monetary systems, unless they are abolished outright and such legislation as legal tender laws repealed. Similarly, the central bank (or banks) of the most commercially successful nations will dominate the world stage, with the relative positions of the players changing with the evolution of their international creditor or debtor status. However, there would be little point in calling for abolition of state central banks, as do members of all the *laissez-faire* schools discussed above if, in any event, the market is likely to throw up similarly powerful private sector institutions which would then be responsible *de facto* for the monetary policy of the system. These institutions would presumably either have to 'socialize themselves', as Keynes (1926; 1972) claimed was the case with the Bank of England historically, or else be subjected to government regulation in the public interest.

Notes

1. This classification is due to Tobin (1983). See also Smithin (1984).
2. The reference is to such analytical devices as 'cash in advance', 'overlapping generations' and 'money in the utility function' and so on. It is not suggested that these methods have contributed no additional insights, and the present author has recently collaborated in work employing cash in advance constraints, for example. However, it is generally accepted, even by the most skilful practitioners, that these techniques do not really get to the bottom of the role of money in the market economy.
3. See Dow and Smithin (1991) for further discussion and references.
4. Dow and Smithin (1991) provide a more detailed discussion of this issue.
5. Clearly, it is possible to envisage a situation in which an inappropriate interest rate policy is pursued, growth is too rapid, confidence is lost, and the identity of the central asset changes.

Bibliography

Black, F. (1970), 'Banking and Interest Rates in a World Without Money', *Journal of Bank Research*, **1**, 9–20.

Chick, V. (1986), 'The Evolution of the Banking System and the Theory of Saving, Investment and Interest', *Economies et Societes*, **20**, 111–26.

Cowen, T. and Kroszner, R. (1987), 'The Development of the New Monetary Economics', *Journal of Political Economy*, **95**, 576–90.

Cowen, T. and Kroszner, R. (1989), 'Scottish Banking Before 1845: A Model for Laissez-faire?', *Journal of Money, Credit, and Banking*, **21**, 221–31.

Dow, J.C.R. and Saville, I.D. (1988; 1990), *A Critique of Monetary Policy: Theory and British Experience*, Oxford: Clarendon Press.

Dow, S.C. and Smithin, J.N. (1991), 'Change in Financial Markets and the "First Principles" of Monetary Economics', University of Stirling, mimeo.

Fama, E.F (1980), 'Banking in the Theory of Finance', *Journal of Monetary Economics*, **6**, 39–57.

Fama, E.F. (1983), 'Financial Intermediation and Price Level Control', *Journal of Monetary Economics*, **12**, 7–28.

Friedman, M. (1987; 1989), 'Quantity Theory of Money', in J. Eatwell, M. Milgate and P. Newman (eds), *The New Palgrave: Money*, London: Macmillan, 1–40.

Goodhart, C.A.E. (1986), 'How Can Non-Interest-Bearing Assets Co-Exist with Safe Interest-Bearing Assets?', *British Review of Economic Issues*, **8**, 1–12.

Goodhart, C.A.E. (1987), 'Why Do Banks Need a Central Bank?', *Oxford Economic Papers*, **39**, 75–89.

Goodhart, C.A.E. (1988), *The Evolution of Central Banks*, Cambridge, Mass.: MIT Press.

Greenfield, R.L. and Yeager, L.B. (1983), 'A Laissez-Faire Approach to Monetary Stability', *Journal of Money, Credit, and Banking*, **15**, 302–15.

Greenfield, R.L. and Yeager, L.B. (1989), 'Can Monetary Disequilibrium be Eliminated?', *Cato Journal*, **9**, 405–21.

Hahn, F. (1983), *Money and Inflation*, Cambridge, Mass.: MIT Press.

Hall, R.E. (1982a), 'Explorations in the Gold Standard and Related Policies for Stabilizing the Dollar', in *Inflation: Causes and Effects*, Chicago: University of Chicago Press.

Hall, R.E. (1982b), 'Monetary Trends in the United States and the United Kingdom: A Review from the Perspective of New Development in Monetary Economics', *Journal of Economic Literature*, **20**, 1552–6.

Hayek, F.A. (1976; 1978), *Denationalization of Money – The Argument Refined*, London: IEA.

Hicks, J.R. (1982), 'The Credit Economy', in *Money, Interest and Wages: Collected Essays on Economic Theory*, Vol. 2, Oxford: Basil Blackwell, 266–75.

Hicks, J.R. (1986), 'Managing Without Money', in *Chung-Hua Series of Lectures by Invited Eminent Economists*, **11**, 19–29, Tapei: Academia Sinica.

Hicks, J.R. (1989), *A Market Theory of Money*, Oxford: Oxford University Press.

Kaldor, N. (1970), 'The New Monetarism', *Lloyds Bank Review*, July, 1–18.

Kaldor, N. (1982), *The Scourge of Monetarism*, Oxford: Oxford University Press.

Keynes, J.M. (1926; 1972), 'The End of Laissez-Faire', reprinted in *Collected Writings*, Vol. IX, *Essays in Persuasion*, London: Macmillan.

Laidler, D.E.W. (1990a), *Taking Money Seriously and Other Essays*, London: Philip Allan.

Laidler, D.E.W. (1990b), 'Hicks and the Classics: A Review Essay', *Journal of Monetary Economics*, **25**, 481–9.

Laidler, D.E.W. (1990c), 'Was Wicksell a Quantity Theorist?', presented at a conference in honour of Don Patinkin, Jerusalem, May.

Lucas, R.E., Jr. (1981), *Studies in Business-Cycle Theory*, Cambridge, Mass.: MIT Press.

Meltzer, A.H. (1989), 'Eliminating Monetary Disturbances', *Cato Journal*, **9**, 423–8.

Menger, C. (1892), 'On the Origin of Money', *Economic Journal*, **2**, 239–55.

Moore, B.J. (1988), *Horizontalists and Verticalists: The Macroeconomics of Credit Money*, Cambridge: Cambridge University Press.

Rogers, C. (1989), *Money, Interest and Capital: A Study in the Foundations of Monetary Theory*, Cambridge: Cambridge University Press.

Selgin, G.A. (1988), *The Theory of Free Banking*, Totowa, N.J.: Rowman & Littlefield.

Selgin, G.A. and White, L.H. (1987), 'The Evolution of a Free Banking System', *Economic Inquiry*, **25**, 439–58, reprinted in White, *Competition and Currency*, 218–42.

Smith, V.C. (1936; 1990), *The Rationale of Central Banking and the Free Banking Alternative*, Indianapolis: Liberty Press.

Smithin, J.N. (1984), 'Financial Innovation and Monetary Theory', *Three Banks Review*, **144**, 26–38.

Smithin, J.N. (1989), 'Hicksian Monetary Economics and Contemporary Financial Innovation', *Review of Political Economy*, **1**, 192–207.

Smithin, J.N. (forthcoming), 'Milton Friedman's Monetary Thought and its Relation to Recent Developments in Monetary Economics', in French translation. In M. Lavoie and M. Secareccia (eds), *Milton Friedman et son Ouvre*, Paris: Dunod.

Tobin, J. (1983), 'Monetary Policy: Rules, Targets, and Shocks', *Journal of Money, Credit and Banking*, **15**, 506–18.

Trautwein, H.-M. (1991), 'A Fundamental Controversy about Money: Post-Keynesian and New Monetary Economics' in G. Mongiovi and C. Ruhl (eds), *Macroeconomic Theory: Diversity and Convergence*, Aldershot: Edward Elgar.

Wallace, N. (1983), 'A Legal Restrictions Theory of the Demand for Money and the Role of Monetary Policy', *Federal Reserve Bank of Minneapolis Quarterly Review*, Winter, 1–7.

Wallace, N. (1988), 'A Suggestion for Oversimplifying the Theory of Money', *Economic Journal*, Supplement, **98**, 25–36.

White, L.H. (1984), 'Competitive Payments Systems and the Unit of Account', *American Economic Review*, **74**, 699–712, reprinted in White, *Competition and Currency*, 169–94.

White, L.H. (1987), 'Accounting for Non-Interest-Bearing Currency: A Critique of the Legal Restrictions Theory of Money', *Journal of Money, Credit, and Banking*, **19**, 448–56, reprinted in White, *Competition and Currency*, 243–54.

White, L.H. (1989), *Competition and Currency: Essays on Free Banking and Money*, New York: New York University Press.

Index

Abegglen, James C. 165
Abernathy, William 168
absolute advantage theory 31
absorption, domestic
international trade and 28, 29, 36, 38
acceleration principle 19
Acocella, N. 123, 131, 133
Adler, Paul 168
Aglietta, M. 206
agricultural sector
Common Agricultural Policy 157
and diffusion of new organizational
principles 169
foreign direct investment in, in Spain
153
international trade in 78–9, 80, 84,
88, 89
Akhtar, M.A. 102
Albrechts, L. 217
Alesina, A. 24
Alexander, Sidney S. 44
America see United States
Andres, Ascension Calatrava 157
Aoki, M. 168
Arestis, Philip 11, 202, 204, 217
Aronowitz, Stanley 163
Ashoff, Guido 156
Asian trade bloc 81, 83, 89, 136, 180
assembly trade
Spain 151
asset prices 186–7, 189
automobile industry
Japan 165
manufacturing strategies in 165
Spain 150, 151
average propensity to save 203

Bailey, Martin J. 102
Bailey, Martin Neil 102
Baker plan 176, 177
balance of payments
exchange rates and 84, 91, 92, 93
LDCs (current account) Ch. 10, 183
balance of trade

EEC 85, 86
as excess of income over expenditure
42, 43–9
exchange rates and 6, 47
as measure of gains from trade 42,
49–58, 59, 63
mercantilism and 4–5, Ch. 2, Ch. 3
Spain, with EEC 8, 137
and standard of living 4–5, 42, 56,
59–61, 62–3
terms of trade and 62, 73, 86
trade restrictions and 34
United States 85, 86, 87
Balassa, B. 113
Baldwin, R. 106, 108
Balogh, Thomas 48, 63
bank-based finance 196
banking and credit systems
Britain 192, 194, 196
Canada 195, 196
Germany 22, 190, 194, 196
integration of, in EEC 2, 11–12, 190–
97 passim
and regional development 197–
200, 206, 215
Japan 196
stages of evolution of 190, 196, 197
United States 4, 22–3, 192, 193, 194–
5, 199
and capital flows to LDCs 10,
183–9
Bank of England 33
Baran, P. 206
Barbon, Nicholas 73
barriers to entry 106–7, 116–17, 162
Barro, R. 24
Belgium
gross domestic product (GDP) 209,
210
unemployment rates 211
Beveridge, Sir William 34
Bhagwati, Jagdish 37, 68, 82
bilateral trade
agreements 81, 82

see also trade blocs
exchange rates and 6, 96–7
Spain, with EEC 8, Ch. 8
Bini Smaghi, L. 105, 112
Black, F. 221
Blinder, Alan 102
Branson, W. 113
Bretton Woods Agreement 5, 6, 27, 36,
    91, 95, 101, 183, 191, 192
Britain
    banking and credit system 192, 194,
        196
    international trade 5, 29, 31–6, 37, 38
        with East India 45, 52–8, 72
    see also United Kingdom
British Merchant 30
Brunner, K. 15
Buchanan, J. 13
Buckley, P.J. 113
Buigues, P. 110
bullion 30, 41–9 *passim*, 53–8 *passim*,
    72–3
    terms of trade and 32–4, 38
business cycle *see* trade cycle
Business Week 168

Cairnes, J.E. 73
Canada
    banking and credit system 195, 196
    exchange rates 6, 94, 95, 96, 97, 98,
        101
    exports 6, 96, 97
    and North American Free Trade
        Association 81, 83, 87, 88, 89,
        136, 180, 189
    productivity growth 98, 99, 100
    wages 100, 101
Cannan, Edwin 72–3
Cantwell, J. 113, 126, 159
capital
    accumulation *see* investment
    ignored by mercantilists 44–5, 49, 72
    marginal efficiency of 16, 187
    markets
        efficiency of 186–7, 215
    mobility
        exchange rates and 93, 102
        flows to/from US 183–9
        flows to Eastern Europe 184, 188
        flows to LDCs *see* LDCs

and intra-industry specialization
    108–10
    and regional disparities 204–5
capital/labour ratio 108
capital/output ratio 164, 203
Cassel, G. 18, 20
Caves, R.E. 112
Cecchini, P. 100, 213
central banks
    and monetary policy 2, 4, 11–12, 17,
        19–20, 21–4, 33, 185, 186, 192,
        195, 196, 197, 201, 203–4, 212,
        220–21, 227, 228–9
    and provision of public goods 2
    rationality of 4, 22–3
    *see also under names of individual
        central banks*, e.g. European
        Central Bank
centre/periphery argument *see* depend-
    ency theory
Chakrabarti, Alok K. 102
Chandler, Alfred Jr 162, 169
Chandler, L. 22
change, management of 167–8, 170
Chick, Victoria 10, 190, 197, 206, 215
Child, *Sir* Josiah 72
Chipman, John S. 5, 41, 53, 66
circular and cumulative causation *see*
    cumulative causation theory
Clapham, F.G.H. 34
class conflict 201–2, 208, 216
Colander, D. 13
collective bargaining 163, 202, 206–7
Cominotti, R. 131
Commission of the European Commu-
    nities (CEC) 110, 112, 213
commodity prices
    regulation of 180
Common Agricultural Policy 157
common currency
    EEC 2, 27, 84, 190–98 *passim*, 200,
        201, 217
    United States 193
Community of Independent States
    (*formerly* Soviet Union) 2
comparative advantage
    classical theory of 5, 27, 28, 31, 37,
        81–2
    in EEC92 sensitive sectors 111, 146–
        7

exchange rates and 7, 105, 107, 110, 112
industrial policies and 81–2, 111
of LDCs 180
see also comparative disadvantage
comparative disadvantage 107, 109, 111
see also comparative advantage
compensating variation 5, 42, 53, 54, 59, 60, 61, 62
consumer prices
EEC 85, 86, 89
Japan 89
United States 85, 86, 87, 89
Contractor, F. 120, 123, 128
Cooper, Richard N. 91, 93
Corn Laws 5, 31–2, 34, 37, 38
Cowen, T, 220, 221, 222
Cowling, K. 205
credit economies 225–7, 228–9
crowding out 198, 212
Crowther, Geoffrey 48
Cukierman, A. 13
cumulative causation theory
and regional disparities in EEC 198–9, 201, 204–5, 213, 214, 216

Daly, A. 161
Davenant, Charles
on gains from trade 42, 52–8
debt, international, of LDCs 9–10, Ch. 10
current state of 173–7
alternative (globalization) attitude to 176–7
conservative (self-discipline) attitude to 173, 175–6, 178
IMF policies and 173, 175
OECD policies and 176, 177–8
solution to 177–8
in context of globalization 178–80
trade restrictions of developed countries and 9–10, 173
De Cecco, M. 112
decision-making
in joint ventures abroad 121
Delgado, Josè Hernandez 157
Delors, J. 104, 213
demonstration effect 49
Denmark
gross domestic product (GDP) 210

specialized training in 9, 161
unemployment rates 211
dependency theory 195, 199–200, 206
Deubner, Christian 156
developing countries *see* LDCs
Dixit, A. 112
dollar shortage 27, 36, 48, 62, 63, 64
Dornbush, Rudiger 38
double factoral terms of trade 32
Dow, S.C. 190, 195, 197, 206, 215, 220, 228, 229
Doz, Y.L. 122
Driver, C. 204
Dubois, A. 72
dumping 78, 80
Dunning, J.H. 113, 126, 170
DUP activities 13

Eastern Europe *see* Europe, Eastern
East India
British trade with 45, 52–8, 72
economic growth *see* growth, economic
economies of scale
cumulative causation theory and 198, 204
industrial globalization and 160
in integrated EEC 108, 109, 110, 111, 113, 156
post-Fordist model and 208
Economist 22, 23, 168
EEC *see* European Economic Community (EEC)
Eichengreen, B. 112
Eichner, A.S. 202, 203, 206, 217
employment
exchange rates and 93
flexible labour contracts, in Spain 154
see also unemployment rates
energy and mining sector
foreign direct investment in, in Spain 153
England *see* Britain
environmental problems 3, 180
equilibrium analysis
and mercantilist model 30
and regional development 198
and trade cycle 14, 18, 20–21
equity participation
limits on, to foreign firms 123, 128, 129, 132, 154

equivalent variation 42, 54, 60, 61, 62, 63
escape clause protectionism 6
European Central Bank
    and monetary policy within EEC 2,
        11, 12, 201, 203–4, 212
    and provision of public goods 2
European Economic community (EEC)
    agricultural support programmes in
        78, 79
    balance of trade 85, 86
    bilateral trade with Spain *see* Spain
    consumer prices 85, 86, 89
    cumulative causation theory in
        and regional disparities 198–9,
            201, 204–5, 213, 214, 216
    estimates of effects of full integration
        on EEC 85–6, Ch. 6
            sectoral impact 110–11, 146–7,
                156
            on United States 85–7, 89
    exchange rates 85, 91
        and international specialization Ch.
            6
        monetary union and 191–7 *passim*,
            204
    exports
        growth of, to Spain 139, 144–5, 146
        to Spain by SITC group 148–50,
            151–2
    fiscal policy in 201, 212
        and regional disparities 201, 212,
            216
    Fordist model and 201, 206–7, 208,
        217
    foreign direct investments 108–10,
        112–13
    gross domestic product (GDP) 85,
        86, 209, 210
    imports
        Japan's share in EEC total 146,
            156
        predicted impact on imports of
            relaxing quotas 139, 140–41
        Spain's import share in EEC
            consumption 139, 142–3, 146,
            156
        Spain's share in EEC total 146,
            147, 156
    interest rates 85, 86, 197
    membership of 2, 8, 136

monetary union in 2, 11–12, 27, 84,
    85, 86, 91, 104, 154, 201, 203–4
    and regional disparities 10, 11, 17,
        Ch. 12, 201, 212, 216
    see also banking and credit
        systems; common currency;
        exchange rates; monetary
        standard
    need for regional and industrial
        policies in 201, 205, 206, 208,
        213–16
    post-Fordist model and 201, 207–8,
        217
    research and development expendi-
        ture 211
    socialization of investment in 214,
        215–16, 217
    trade policies 27, 156
    trade restrictions by 78, 79, 86–7,
        88–9, 137, 140–41
        removal of 1–2, 8, 81, 110–11,
            136, 137, 139, 140–41, 146,
            156
    unemployment rates 209, 211
    venture capital 211
European Regional Development Fund
    (ERDF) 213, 217
Europe, Eastern
    capital flows to 184, 188
    liberalization of 179
Eurostat 210
Eussner, Ansgar 156
exchange, media of 220, 221, 222, 224,
    227, 228
exchange rates
    Canada 6, 94, 95, 96, 97, 98, 101
    EEC
        and international specialization 7,
            Ch. 6
        monetary union and 154, 191–7
            passim, 204
        *see also under names of
            individual EEC countries*,
            e.g. Italy
    effect of revaluation
        on exports 113–15
            given different price elasticities
                115–16
            under oligopoly with barriers to
                entry 116–17

on imports 113–14
  given different price elasticities
    117–18
fixed v. flexible
  and balance of payments 84, 91,
    92, 93
  and balance of trade 6, 47
  and cost of foreign trade 92
  and destabilization of domestic
    economy 93, 95
  and economic growth 7, 95, 96, 97,
    101
  and employment 93
  and export growth 6, 95–7, 101, 102
  in G-7 countries 6–7, 94–102, 187
    see also under names of
      individual G-7 countries,
      e.g. United States
  and income distribution 93, 95,
    99–102
  and policy implications 101–2
  and productivity growth 92, 93, 95,
    97–9, 101
  and real rates of return 187
  and speculation 92, 93
  theoretical arguments for 91–3
  and uncertainty 93, 102
  and wages 93, 95, 99–102
France 94, 95, 101
Germany 94, 101, 107
and international debt problems of
  LDCs 180
Italy 6, 94, 95, 96, 98, 101, 104–5,
  107, 109
Japan 6, 94, 95, 96, 97, 98, 101, 107,
  110
United Kingdom 94, 95, 97, 101
United States 85, 86, 87, 94, 95, 101
export restraints *see* trade restrictions
exports
  Canada 6, 96, 97
  deficits/surpluses *see* balance of trade
  EEC
    exports to Spain by SITC group
      148–50, 151–2
    growth of exports to Spain 139,
      144–5, 146
  exchange rate revaluation and 113–15
    given different price elasticities
      115–16

  under oligopoly with barriers to
    entry 116–17
  exchange rate volatility and growth
    of 6, 95–7, 101, 102
  Italy 6, 96
  Japan 6, 96
  LDCs 175, 179, 183
  share of, in national income 42, 68–9,
    71–2
  Spain
    exports to EEC by SITC group
      148–50, 151–2
    five most important exporting
      industries 137, 138
    growth of exports to EEC 139,
      142–3, 146–7

Fama, E.F. 221, 222
Federal Reserve Bank 4, 22, 23, 185,
  186, 194
Ferreira, Antonio Da Silva 156
flexible manufacturing 167, 207
Fomby, T.B. 132, 133
Fordist model
  and industrial globalization 9, 162–4,
    169, 170
  and integrated EEC 201, 206–7, 208,
    217
  see also post-Fordist model
foreign direct investments
  EEC 108–10, 112–13
  and industrial globalization 168, 169
  Italian joint ventures abroad 7, Ch. 7
  Spain 152–4, 157
  United States 113
foreign paid incomes argument 30–31
France
  exchange rates 94, 95, 101
  gross domestic product (GDP) 209,
    210
  productivity growth 99, 100
  unemployment rates 211
  wages 100, 101
Frank, A.G. 206
Friedman, M. 15, 17, 22, 91, 102, 220
Frisch, R. 15
full employment
  achievement of, in integrated EEC
    211–16

gains from trade
   balance of trade as measure of 42,
      59–58, 59, 63
   money measure of 42, 58–64
   terms of trade and 42, 51–2, 54, 58–
      9, 73
Galbraith, J. 21, 22
General Agreement on Tariffs and Trade
   (GATT) 1, 27, 77–9, 81, 83–4, 87,
   89, 175, 180
*General theory of employment, interest
   and money* (Keynes) 13, 15, 19,
   22, 35, 46, 93
Germany
   banking and credit system 22, 190,
      194, 196
   exchange rates 94, 101
      and international specialization
         107
   gross domestic product (GDP) 209,
      210
   productivity growth 99, 100
Ghoshal, Sumantra 160
Giavazzi, F. 112
Giovannini, A. 112
globalization
   and international debt trap *see* debt,
      international, of LDCs
   and new forms of industrial organiza-
      tion *see* industrial globalization
gold *see* bullion; gold standard
gold standard 6, 33, 35, 37, 91, 191,
   224, 225, 226
   see also bullion
Gomes-Casseres, B. 121, 122, 123, 124,
   130, 131, 132, 134
Goodhart, C.A.E. 223, 225, 228
Goodwin, R.M. 203
Gordon, D. 24
government securities 177, 188, 197
Graham, E.M. 113
Grahl, J. 214
Grampp, William 30
Granell, Fancesc 157
Greece
   gross domestic product (GDP) 209,
      210
   growth differential rates required for
      convergence 214
   unemployment rates 211

Greenfield, R.L. 221, 222, 227
Greenspan, Alan 22
Greenwald, B. 14
Gros, D. 112
gross domestic product (GDP)
   EEC 85, 86, 209, 210
      *see also under names of individual
         EEC countries*, e.g. Germany
   United States 85, 86, 87
growth, economic
   exchange rates and 7, 95, 96, 97, 101
   Greece 214
   income distribution and 203
   Ireland 214
   Japan 97
   LDCs 9, 179
   Portugal 214
   restoration of, in industrialized
      countries 1
   and international debt problems of
      LDCs 117, 177–8, 180
   Spain 214
   United Kingdom 97
growth-pole model 205–6
G-7 countries 2, 23, 24
   macroeconomic impact of exchange
      rate volatility on 6–7, 94–102,
      187
   see also exchange rates; *and under
      names of individual G-7
      countries*, e.g. United States
Guerrieri, P. 112
Gunn, Thomas G. 168

Haberler, G.
   on central banks 22
   on international trade 36, 48, 92
   on trade cycle 14, 16, 17, 18, 19
Hahn, F. 223
Hall, R.E. 221
harassment thesis 6
Harrigan, K.R. 121, 122
Harrod, R.
   on international trade 48
   on trade cycle 19–20, 23, 24, 203
Hatsopoulos, George N. 48, 63
Hawtrey, R.
   on central banks 22
   on trade cycle 14, 16–17, 20
Hayashi, Fumio 36

Hayek, F.A. von
  on monetary theory 224
  on trade cycle 14, 17–18, 20
Hayes, Robert 167
Heckscher, Eli F. 41, 62
Heckscher–Ohlin theory 136
Hennart, J.F. 120, 124, 133
Hicks, J.R.
  on international trade 42, 53, 59–62
    passim, 64
  on monetary theory 225, 226, 227,
    228
  on trade cycle 13, 14, 15, 17–18
high-tech industries
  joint ventures abroad and 121–2, 123,
    126
  subsidies to 80, 87–8
Hill, R.C. 132, 133
Hilton, R. Spence 102
Hine, Robert C. 147, 156
Hladik, K.J. 121, 133
Houthakker, Hendrik 102
Hume, David 42, 57
hysteresis effects 105, 112, 113

Ilzkovitz, F. 110
Imai, Ken-ichi 166
imports
  Britain 34
  capital goods 44–5
  deficits/surpluses *see* balance of trade
  EEC
    Japan's share in EEC total 146, 156
    predicted impact of relaxing quotas
      139, 140–41
    Spain's import share in EEC
      consumption 139, 142–3, 146,
      156
    Spain's share in EEC total 146,
      147, 156
  elasticity of demand for 66–72
  exchange rate revaluation and 113–14
    given different price elasticities
      117–18
  LDCs 176
  marginal propensity to import 204
  Spain
    EEC import share in Spain's
      consumption 139, 144–5, 146,
      156

  five most important importing
    industries 137, 138
  imports from EEC by SITC group
    148–50, 151–2
  predicted impact of relaxing quotas
    139, 140–41
impulse-propagation distinction
  and trade cycle 15–16, 17–18, 20–21
income distribution
  and economic growth 203
  exchange rates and 93, 95, 99–102
  international trade and 56–8
  investment and 203
  and trade cycle 203
incomes policies 216–17
industrial globalization
  defined 160
  organizational principles and 159,
    160–61
    Fordist model 9, 162–4, 169, 170
    post-Fordist model 164–70
  process of 160–61
  technical progress and 159, 160–61,
    165, 166, 167, 169–70
industry-specific resources 106–7, 112,
    160–61, 162, 169, 170
inflation
  determinants of 202
instrumental analysis 4, 12
interest groups 170
interest rates
  in credit economies 221, 227, 228,
    229
  EEC 85, 86, 197
  mark-up pricing and 204
  OECD countries 176, 178
  Spain 154
  United States 10, 85, 86, 87, 185, 186
    relative 188–9
inter-firm linkages
  and industrial globalization 165, 166,
    167
INTERLINK model (OECD) 157
International Monetary Fund
  policies of, and international debt
    problems of LDCs 173, 175
  and provision of public goods 2
  statistics by 94
International Monetary System 193,
    195

International Standard Industrial
Classification (ISIC)
industrial categories 137, 138,
140–41, 142–3, 148–50, 151,
157–8
international trade
in agriculture 78–9, 80, 84, 88, 89
alternative systems 79–82
classical theory of 31–2
and income distribution 56–8
mercantilism and 4–5, Ch. 2, Ch. 3
model of 29–31
present system 77–9
profitability of 28–9, 31–2, 33, 36,
37, 38
in services 78, 79, 84, 89
trade policies and future of 82–4, 87–
90
see also exchange rates; trade
restrictions; *and under names of
individual countries*, e.g. Japan
investment
of bullion 45–7, 72
foreign direct 7, 108–10, 112–13, Ch.
7, 152–4, 157, 168, 169
and income distribution 203
marginal efficiency of 202
and productivity growth 198–9, 204–
5
profitability and 11, 202–3
savings and 30, 32, 42, 46, 189, 198
socialization of, in integrated EEC
214, 215–16, 217
technical progress and 202–3
and trade cycle *see* overinvestment
theories of trade cycle
Ireland
gross domestic product (GDP) 209,
210
growth differential rates required for
convergence 214
unemployment rates 211
Italy
exchange rates 6, 94, 95, 96, 98, 101
and international specialization
104–5, 107, 109
exports 6, 96
gross domestic product (GDP) 209, 210
joint ventures abroad 7, Ch. 7

see also joint ventures abroad,
Italian
productivity growth 98, 99, 100
specialized training in 8, 160–61
textile industry 160–61
unemployment rates 209, 211
wages 100, 101

Japan
agricultural support programmes in
78, 79, 80
and Asian trade bloc 81, 83, 89, 136,
180
automobile industry 165
banking and credit system 196
consumer prices 89
economic growth 97
exchange rates 6, 94, 95, 96, 97, 98,
101
and international specialization
107, 110
exports 6, 96
international trade 36–7
restrictions on 78, 79, 80, 87, 88–9
removal of 81
with United States 83, 87, 88
productivity growth 98, 99, 100
robotics industry 9, 161
share in EEC total imports 146, 156
specialized training in 9
wages 100, 101
see also J-firm
J-firm
organization of 9, 168, 170
Jaikumar, Ramchandran 167, 168
job classifications 163
Johanson, I. 122
Johnson, E.A. 30
Johnson, Harry G. 62, 64, 92
Johnson, S.R. 132, 133
joint ventures abroad, Italian 7, Ch. 7
changing pattern of, over time 128,
129, 130, 132, 133
costs and benefits 120–22
defined 123
and exchange of complementary
resources 122
financial constraints and 122, 127–8,
129, 132

host country abilities and 126, 129,
131, 133
host government restrictive policies
and 122–3, 128, 129, 132–3
international experience and 122,
127, 129, 131–2, 133, 134
intra-firm coordination and 121, 125,
129, 130, 133
and risk reduction 122, 128, 129,
132, 133
Sanna-Randaccio's study of
conclusion 132–3
data 123
estimation procedure 123–4, 133
hypothesis 125–8, 130
results 129, 130–32, 133
size of firm and 7, 122, 126–7, 129,
130, 131, 132, 133, 134
spider's web 122
and structural evolution of market
122
and technical knowledge
access to 121, 125–6, 129, 130,
131, 132
costs of sharing 121, 130
transfer of 125, 129, 130

Kahn, R.F. 36
Kaldor, N. 201, 203, 204, 217, 220, 228
Kalecki, M. 203, 204, 212, 216
Kamiga, Shotoro 165
Keeble, D. 206
Keynes, J.M.
*General theory of employment,
interest and money* 13, 15, 19,
22, 35, 46, 93
on international trade 28, 30, 31, 34,
35, 91
on marginal efficiency of capital 16
on monetary policy 229
on socialization of investment 217
on uncertainty 93
Kindleberger, Charles P. 3, 36, 48
Kobrin, S.J. 121, 130
Kogut, B. 121, 159
Korea, South
debt problems of 175
Kowalski, L. 217
Kravis, I.B. 113
Kregel, J.A. 10, 192, 196

Kroszner, R. 220, 221, 222
Krugman, Paul R. 48, 63, 82, 93, 106,
108, 111, 112, 113
Kydland, F. 15, 16, 19, 24

labour mobility
and regional disparities 204–5, 216–17
Laidler, D.E.W. 223, 225
Laspeyres trade variation 54, 60
Laursen, Svend 42, 62–3
Lawrence, P. 164
LDCs
capital flows to 176–7, 178, 180, Ch.
11
changes in, from US 10, 183–4
efficiciency of capital markets
and capital flows 186–7
implications of financial
innovation and deregulation
for stability of capital flows
186
reversal of capital flows and
relative interest rates 188–9
structure of US financial system
and 184–6
role of, in international economic
development 183
debt problem *see* debt, international,
of LDCs
economic growth 9, 180
export growth 175, 179, 183
import reductions 175
population 9, 179
Leborgne, D. 209
legal restrictions theorists (LRT) 221,
222, 223
Leijonhufvud, A.
on central banks 22
on trade cycle 15–16, 19, 20–21
liability management 196, 197
Linder, S.B. 112
Lipietz, A. 209
Lipsey, R. 113
liquidity trap 19
Locke, John 44, 57, 63
Lopez-Claros, Augusto 156
Lorange, P. 120, 128
Lowe, Adolph 12
Lucas, R. 15, 18, 20–21, 220
Luria, D. 208

Luxembourg
  gross domestic product (GDP) 210
  unemployment rates 211
luxury goods
  international trade in 45, 55–6

Maastricht Treaty 2
MacDougall, Donald 63
MacDuffie, J.D. 170
Maddison, A. 169
Mair, D. 211
Malthus, Thomas 32, 38
Malynes, Gerrard de 47, 49–50, 73
manufacturing, flexible 167, 207
manufacturing sector
  foreign direct investment in, in Spain
    153
manufacturing strategies
  and industrial globalization 165–6
marginal efficiency of capital 16, 187
marginal propensity to consume 203
marginal propensity to import 204
Mariotti, S. 131
market-based finance 196
mark-up pricing 11, 202, 206
  and interest rates 204
Marshall-Lerner condition 66
mass production
  in Fordist model 9, 162, 163, 164,
    206–7, 208
McKibbin–Sachs Global Model 85–7,
  89
megacorps 11, 202
Meltzer, A. 13, 15, 227
Menger, C. 224, 225, 226
mercantilism
  and international trade 4–5, Ch. 2,
    Ch. 3
    model of 29–31
  see also balance of trade; gains from
    trade; terms of trade
mergers and acquisitions
  in EEC 109, 112
  banks 196
Metzler, Lloyd A. 42, 62–3
Mexico
  debt problems of 177
  and North American Free Trade
    Association 82, 83, 87, 88, 89,
    136, 180, 189

Micossi, S. 112
Mill, John Stuart 33, 38
Miller, M. 112
Ministry of International Trade and
  Industry (MITI) (Japan) 36–7
Mishel, Lawrence 101
Misselden, Edward 44, 47, 48, 50, 63,
  73
Mitchell, W. 13
'modern free banking' school 224–5,
  227
Molyneux, P. 196
monetary policy
  central banks and 2, 4, 11–12, 19–20,
    21–4, 33, 185, 186, 192, 195,
    196, 197, 201, 203–4, 212, 220–
    21, 227, 228–9
  EEC 2, 11–12, 27, 84, 85, 86, 91,
    104, 154, 201, 203–4
  and regional disparities 10, 11, 17,
    Ch. 12, 201, 212, 216
  Germany 190
  Spain 154
  United States 193, 195
  see also banking and credit systems;
    common currency; exchange
    rates; monetary standard; money
monetary rule 17
monetary standard
  EEC 191–5 *passim*
  International Monetary System and
    193, 195
  Mengerian theory and 224, 225, 226
  United States 193, 195
  see also gold standard
monetary theory of trade cycle
  (Hawtrey) 16–17, 70
  see also overinvestment theories of
    trade cycle
money
  centralizing tendencies in monetary
    systems 225–7
    see also central banks
  and coordination of economic
    activity 222–3, 229
  financial systems without 221–2
  and media of exchange 220, 221,
    222, 224, 227, 228
  new monetary economics (NME) and
    Ch. 14

properties of a monetary exchange
economy 223–5
supply of 220, 222
and units of account 220, 221–2, 224,
225, 227, 228
see also banking and credit systems;
monetary policy; monetary
standard
Moore, B.J. 220, 227, 228
Morales, Antonio Carrascosa 152–3,
157
Morgan, Gareth 168
Morgan Guaranty Trust Company 113,
177
Morgenstern, O. 14
Mowery, D. 122
multinational firms 109, 111, 112, 162–
3
Italian, and joint ventures abroad 7,
Ch. 7
see also joint ventures abroad,
Italian
multiplier theory, regional 198
Mun, Thomas 28, 30, 35, 41–8 *passim*,
51, 72
Myrdal, G. 201, 204

nation-specific externalities 108, 112
Nell, E.J. 201
neo-mercantilism *see* mercantilism
Netherlands
gross domestic product (GDP) 209,
210
unemployment rates 211
network organization 166–7, 169–70,
217
Neven, D.J. 107
new classical monetarist (NCM)
economics 12, 21, 23, 24
new monetary economics (NME)
critique of Ch. 14
see also monetary policy; monetary
standard; money
Nichol, W. 211
Nolan, P. 208
non-price competition 104, 105
Nordhaus, W. 13
North American Free Trade Association
81, 83, 87, 88, 89, 136, 180, 189
Nurkse, Ragnar 48–9

Obstfeld, Maurice 62
O'Donnell, K. 208
oil prices 146, 177–8
Olson, M. 170
Oncken, August 72
Onida, Fabrizio 7, 131
organizational principles
and industrial globalization 159,
160–61
Fordist model 9, 162–4, 169, 170
post-Fordist model 164–70
and integrated EEC
Fordist model 201, 206–7, 208,
217
post-Fordist model 201, 207–8,
217
Organization for Economic Cooperation
and Development (OECD)
INTERLINK model 157
policies, and international debt
problems of LDCs 176, 177–8
statistics by 96
studies by 167, 170
Ouchi, W.G. 168, 170
overinvestment theories of trade cycle
derived demand-based (I.M. Clark
and Harrod) 19–20
monetary (Hayek, Robbins and
Hicks) 17–18, 20
non-monetary (Wicksell, Cassell,
Schumpeter and Spiethoff) 18,
20

Paasche trade variation 42, 53, 54, 58,
60–61
Padoan, P.C. 112
Padoa Schioppa, T. 112
Pagano, M. 112
Palinginis, E. 217
Pasinetti, L.L. 203
Patinkin, D. 13
Perroux, F. 201, 205
Peters, Tom 168
Petty, *Sir* William 44, 52
Phelps, E.S. 15
Pigou, A.C. 38
Piore, M.J. 162, 206, 207
political business cycle 13
political economy of trade cycles 13–
14, 34

Pollexfen, John 42, 44, 46–7, 48, 49, 50, 54–7
population
   LDCs 9, 179
Porter M.E. 112, 159, 160, 161
Portugal
   gross domestic product (GDP) 209, 210
   growth differential rates required for convergence 214
   unemployment rates 209, 211
post-Fordist model
   and industrial globalization 164–70
   and integrated EEC 201, 207–8, 217
   see also Fordist model
potential-welfare function 64–9
   with factor-augmenting technical progress 69–72
   with uniform technical progress 65–9
Power, Eileen 51
Prescott, E. 15, 16, 19, 24
Pressman, Steven 6
prices
   asset 186–7, 189
   commodity
      regulation of 180
   consumer
      EEC 85, 86, 89
      Japan 89
      United States 85, 86, 87, 89
   oil 146, 177–8
price takers 105, 107, 202
privatization
   in OECD countries 178
product differentiation
   exchange rates and 109, 110, 112, 113
   in post-Fordist model 164, 165, 168–9, 207, 208, 217
productivity growth
   Canada 98, 99, 100
   exchange rates and 92, 93, 95, 97–9, 101
   in Fordist model 164
   France 99, 100
   Germany 99, 100
   investment and 198–9, 204–5
   Italy 98, 99, 100
   Japan 98, 99, 100
   and trade cycle 16

United Kingdom 99, 100
United States 99, 100
   and wages 206–7
profitability
   of international trade 28–9, 31–2, 33, 36, 37, 38
   and investment 11, 202–3
   and joint ventures abroad 122, 127–8, 129, 132
property rights, intellectual 79, 169, 170
public goods 2, 3

quantity theory of money 220
quotas
   EEC 139, 140–41, 156
   Spain 139, 140–41, 156

rationality
   of central banks 4, 22–3
Razin, Assaf 62
reciprocity theorem (Samuelson) 69, 71
regional multiplier theory 198
Regulation Q 185
rent-seeking 13
research and development expenditure
   EEC 211
Ricardo, David 5, 28–9, 31–2, 33, 38, 73, 81
Rima, Ingrid H. 4–5
risk
   joint ventures abroad and reduction of 122, 128, 129, 132, 133
   to Spanish industry of accession with EEC 152–5
   variable interest rates and 186, 189
Robbins, L. 14, 17, 24
Robertson, D.H. 14
Robinson, Joan 35, 38
Rodger, Ian 157
Rogers, C. 223, 228
Rogoff, K. 13
Rolli, V. 130, 133
Roosa, Robert V. 92, 102
Roscher, Wilhelm 41, 72
Rybczynski theorem 71

Sabel, Charles F. 162, 206, 207
Sadamoto, Kuni 161
Salvatore, Dominick 6

Samuelson, Paul A.
  on comparative advantage 82
  reciprocity theorem 69, 71
  Stolper–Samuelson theorem 70, 108
Sanna-Randaccio, Francesca 7, 131
Sapir, A. 110, 111
Saville, I.D. 228
savings
  average propensity to save 203
  and investment 30, 32, 42, 46, 189,
    198
Sawyer, M.C. 202, 215
Schaefer, Jeffrey M. 101
Schiattarella, R. 131, 133
Schonberger, R. 168
Schumpeter, J.
  on international trade 72, 91
  on trade cycle 18, 20
Schwartz, A. 22
Scitovsky, T. 113
securities *see* government securities
Selgin, G.A. 224
Seligman, Edwin R.A. 72
Sengenberger, W. 161
service sector
  in EEC 207–8, 217
  foreign direct investment in, in Spain
    153
  international trade in 78, 79, 84, 89
  in OECD countries 178
Shimada, H. 170
silver *see* bullion
Singh, H. 121
size of firm
  and joint ventures abroad 7, 122,
    126–7, 129, 130, 131, 132, 133,
    134
Skinner, W. 164, 166, 167
Skott, P. 202
Smith, Adam 2, 31, 41, 45, 49
Smith, *Sir* Thomas 43
Smith, V.C. 224
Smithin, John 12, 220, 221, 228, 229
South Korea *see* Korea, South
Spain
  and accession with EEC 8, Ch. 8
    assembly trade 151
    assessing risks of accession 152–5
    automobile industry 150, 151
    bilateral trade balance 8, 137

EEC import share in Spain's
    consumption 139, 144–5, 146,
    156
  five most important exporting and
    importing industries 137, 138
  foreign direct investment 152–4,
    157
  gross domestic product (GDP) 209,
    210
  growth differential rates required
    for convergence 214
  growth of EEC exports to Spain
    139, 144–5, 146
  growth of exports to EEC 139,
    142–3, 146–7
  legal changes 153–4
  monetary policy 154
  need for increased efficiency 155
  pre-accession bilateral trade
    restrictions 137, 139, 140–41,
    146, 156
  predicted impact on imports of
    relaxing quotas 139, 140–41
  post-accession changes in bilateral
    trade 139, 142–52
  share in EEC total imports 146,
    147, 156
  SITC trade flows 148–50, 151–2
  Spain's import share in EEC
    consumption 139, 142–3, 145,
    156
  textile industry 139, 140, 142, 144,
    147, 156
  unemployment rates 211
  value added tax (VAT) 156, 157
  wages 147
Spaventa, L. 112
specialization, international
  exchange rates and, in EEC 7, Ch. 6
  *see also under names of individual
    EEC countries*, e.g. Italy
speculation
  in foreign exchange markets 92, 93
spider's web joint ventures 122
Spiethoff, A. 18
Stalk, George Jr 165
Standard International Trade Classification (SITC) commodity categories
  137, 138, 141, 143, 148–50, 151–
  2, 157–8

standard of living
    balance of trade and 4–5, 42, 56, 59–
        61, 62–3
    relative, of countries *see* welfare,
        relative, of countries
Steuart, *Sir* James 49
Stiglitz, J. 14
Stinchcombe, A. 21
Stolper, Wolfgag 63
    Stolper–Samuelson theorem 70, 108
Stopford, J.M. 121, 122, 123, 130, 131,
    134
Strongin, David G. 101
subsidies 6, 78–9, 80, 87–8
Summers, Lawrence H. 48, 63
sunk costs 106, 107, 112
suppliers, relationships with 166
Suviranta, Bruno 72, 73
Svensson, Lars 62
Swedish flag device 15, 16, 21
Swyngedouw, E. 217

Taiwan
    debt problems of 175
takeovers *see* mergers and acquisitions
tariffs
    EEC 137, 140–41
    GATT and 77–8, 81
    Spain 137, 140–41
    see also trade restrictions
Taussig, F.W. 32, 35
Tavlas, George S. 102
Tawney, R.H. 51
Taylorism *see* Fordist model
Teague, P. 214
technical knowledge
    and diffusion of new organizational
        principles 169–70
    joint ventures abroad and
        access to 121–2, 125–6, 129, 130,
            131, 132
    costs of sharing 121, 130
    transfer of 125, 129, 130
    see also technical progress
technical progress
    and countries' relative welfares 5, 42,
        64–5, 198–9, 205
    with factor-augmenting technical
        progress 69–72

    with uniform technical progress
        65–9
    and easing of resource constraints 3
    and Fordist production principles
        162, 164
    and industrial globalization 159,
        160–61, 165, 166, 167, 169–70
    and intra-industry specialization 108–
        10
    and investment 202–3
    see also technical knowledge
Teece, D.J. 159
Teixeira, Ruy A. 101
Temin, P. 14–15, 22
terms of trade 31
    and balance of trade 62, 73, 86
    and bullion movements 32–4, 38
    free trade and 34–6
    and gains from trade 42, 51–2, 54,
        58–9, 73
    technical progress and 5, 42, 64–72
textile industry
    Italy 160–61
    Spain 139, 140, 142, 144, 147, 156
Thornton, Henry 38
Thurow, L.A. 170
Thygesen, N. 112
Tobin, J. 229
trade blocs 6, 10, 81, 82, 83–4, 87, 88,
    89, 136, 180
    see also Asian trade bloc; European
        Economic Community (EEC);
        North American Free Trade
        Association
trade cycle
    central bank policy and 4, 21–4
    equilibrium analysis and 14, 18, 20–
        21
    impulse-propagation distinction and
        15–16, 17–18, 20–21
    income distribution and 203
    overinvestment theories of
        derived demand-based (I.M. Clark
            and Harrod) 19–20
        monetary (Hayek, Robbins and
            Hicks) 17–18, 20, 220
        non-monetary (Wicksell, Cassel,
            Schumpeter and Spiethoff) 18,
            20

political economy of 13–14, 24
purely monetary theory of (Hawtrey)
    16–17, 20
trade-indifference curves 52–4, 58–61
trade policies
    EEC 27, 156
    and future of international trading
        system 82–4
    United States 87–90
trade restrictions
    and diffusion of new organizational
        principles 169
    by EEC 78, 79, 86–7, 88–9, 137,
        140–41
        removal of 1–2, 8, 81, 110–11,
            136, 137, 139, 140–41, 146,
            156
    GATT and 1, 27, 77–9, 81, 82, 83–4,
        87, 89, 175, 180
    by Japan 78, 79, 80, 87, 88–9
    and LDC debt problem 9–10, 174
    non-tariff 6, 78, 79–82, 84, 86–7, 89,
        108, 110, 111, 123
    by Spain 137, 139, 140–41, 146, 156
    terms of trade and 34, 35, 36, 38
    by United States 1, 5, 6, 48, 78, 80,
        81, 88
        removal of 81
    see also trade blocs
trade unions 163, 177, 202, 207, 215–
    16, 217
trade–utility function, indirect 64, 67
training, specialized
    Denmark 8–9, 161
    Germany 9, 161
    Italy 8, 160–61
    Japan 9
Trautwein, H.-M. 222
Treaty of Rome 213, 215
Tsoukalis, Loukas 91
Tushman, M. 168

Ulan, Michael 102
uncertainty
    exchange rate volatility and 93, 102
unemployment rates
    EEC 209, 211
    see also under names of individual
        EEC countries, e.g. Germany
uneven development theory 198

United Kingdom
    economic growth 97
    exchange rates 94, 95, 97, 101
    exports 6, 97
    gross domestic product (GDP) 209,
        210
    productivity growth 99, 100
    unemployment rates 209, 211
    wages 100, 101
    see also Britain
United Nations
    Classification of commodities by
        industrial origin (links between
        the Standard International Trade
        Classification and the Interna-
        tional Standard Industrial
        Classification) 141, 157–8
    Trade Statistics 138, 143, 145, 150
United States
    balance of trade 85, 86, 87
    banking and credit system 4, 22–3,
        192, 193, 194–5, 199
        and capital flows to LDCs 10,
            183–9
    consumer prices 85, 86, 87, 89
    effect of EEC92 programme on 85–7,
        89
    exchange rates 85, 87, 94, 95, 101
    foreign direct investments 113
    gross domestic product (GDP) 85,
        86, 87
    interest rates 10, 85, 86, 87, 185, 186
        relative 188–9
    international trade 27, 36, 48
        policies 87–90
        restrictions on 1, 5, 6, 48, 78, 80,
            88
            removal of 81
        with Japan 83, 87, 88
    monetary policy 193, 195
        see also banking and credit
            systems
    and North American Free Trade
        Association 81, 83, 87, 88, 89,
        136, 180, 189
    productivity growth 99, 100
    standard of living 63
    wages 100, 101
United States International Trade
    Commission (USITC) 151, 157

units of account 220, 221–2, 224, 225, 227, 228
US Department of Labour
  statistics by 98, 99, 100

Vahlne, J.E. 122
value added tax (VAT)
  Spain 156, 157
venture capital
  EEC 211
Viesti, G. 131
Viner, J.
  on mercantilism 41, 42, 43, 45, 47, 51, 55, 58, 72, 73
  on US banking system 22–3
Volcker, Paul 22
volume of trade 72, 83
Vona, S. 105

wages
  Canada 100, 101
  exchange rates and 93, 95, 99–102
  France 100, 101
  Germany 100, 101, 147
  Italy 100, 101
  Japan 100, 101
  productivity growth and 206–7
  Spain 147
  theory of determination of 201
  United Kingdom 100, 101
  United States 100, 101
Wallace, N. 221
Walras, Leon 223
Walters, Roy 165

Walton, R. 194
Weiermair, Klaus 8–9
welfare, relative, of countries 63
  technical progress and 5, 42, 64–5, 198–9, 205
  factor-augmenting 69–72
  uniform 65–9
Wells, L.T. 121, 122, 123, 130, 131, 134
White, David 157
White, L.H. 222–3, 224
wholly owned subsidiaries 120, 123–4, 170
  see also joint ventures abroad, Italian
Wicksell, K. 18, 225
Williams, J.H. 36
Williams, K. 217
Williamson, John 27, 93
Williamson, O.E. 121
Wiseman, J. 13
Wolcott, Susan 8
Womack, J. 170
World Bank
  and provision of public goods 2

Yandle, B. 13
Yeager, L.B. 221, 222, 227
yen shortage 36–7
Yoshida, M. 170
Young, Warren
  on trade cycle 4, 13, 14, 15, 17, 19, 23
Yuill, D. 211

Zysman, J. 196